A MYSTERY OF MYSTERIES

ALSO BY MARK DAWIDZIAK

NONFICTION

The Barter Theatre Story: Love Made Visible

The Columbo Phile: A Casebook

Night Stalking: A 20th Anniversary Kolchak Companion

The Night Stalker Companion: A 25th Anniversary Tribute

Horton Foote's The Shape of the River: The Lost Teleplay About Mark Twain

Produced and Directed by Dan Curtis (with Jim Pierson and Herman Wouk)

The Bedside, Bathtub & Armchair Companion to Dracula

Jim Tully: American Writer, Irish Rover, Hollywood Brawler (with Paul J. Bauer)

Mark Twain in Ohio

Everything I Need to Know I Learned in the Twilight Zone

The Shawshank Redemption Revealed: How One Story Keeps Hope Alive

NOVEL

Grave Secrets

EDITOR

Mark My Words: Mark Twain on Writing

Richard Matheson's Kolchak Scripts

Bloodlines: Richard Matheson's Dracula, I Am Legend, *and Other Vampire Stories*

Beggars of Life by Jim Tully (with Paul J. Bauer)

Circus Parade by Jim Tully (with Paul J. Bauer)

Shanty Irish by Jim Tully (with Paul J. Bauer)

The Bruiser by Jim Tully (with Paul J. Bauer)

Richard Matheson's Censored and Unproduced I Am Legend *Screenplay*

Mark Twain's Guide to Diet, Exercise, Beauty, Fashion, Investment, Romance, Health and Happiness

Mark Twain for Cat Lovers: True and Imaginary Adventures with Feline Friends

Theodore Roosevelt for Nature Lovers: Adventures with America's Great Outdoorsman

A MYSTERY OF MYSTERIES

The Death and Life of Edgar Allan Poe

MARK DAWIDZIAK

ST. MARTIN'S GRIFFIN

NEW YORK

Published in the United States by St. Martin's Griffin, an imprint of
St. Martin's Publishing Group

www.stmartins.com

Designed by Omar Chapa

The Library of Congress has cataloged the hardcover edition as follows:

Names: Dawidziak, Mark, 1956– author.
Title: A mystery of mysteries : the death and life of Edgar Allan Poe /
    Mark Dawidziak.
Description: First edition. | New York : St. Martin's Press, 2023. |
    Includes bibliographical references and index.
Identifiers: LCCN 2022035450 | ISBN 9781250792495 (hardcover) |
    ISBN 9781250792501 (ebook)
Subjects: LCSH: Poe, Edgar Allan, 1809–1849. | Poe, Edgar Allan,
    1809–1849—Death and burial. | Authors, American—19th century—
    Biography. | LCGFT: Biographies.
Classification: LCC PS2631 .D37 2023 | DDC 818/.309 [B]—dc23/eng/20221024
LC record available at https://lccn.loc.gov/2022035450

ISBN 978-1-250-79251-8 (trade paperback)

Our books may be purchased in bulk for promotional, educational, or busi-
ness use. Please contact your local bookseller or the Macmillan Corporate and
Premium Sales Department at 1-800-221-7945, extension 5442, or by email at
MacmillanSpecialMarkets@macmillan.com.

First St. Martin's Griffin Edition: 2024

10   9   8   7   6   5   4   3   2   1

To Sara, with a love that is more than love,
and to our daughter, Becky, so gifted, loving, and brave ... much I marvel ...
To them both ... evermore

The breeze—the breath of God—is still—
And the mist upon the hill
Shadowy—shadowy—yet unbroken,
Is a symbol and a token—
How it hangs upon the trees,
A mystery of mysteries!

—FINAL STANZA OF "SPIRITS OF THE DEAD"
BY EDGAR ALLAN POE

CONTENTS

AUTHOR'S NOTE

Letters, magazine articles, newspaper pieces, and books from the nineteenth century, as well as Poe's stories, essays, and reviews, are quoted throughout this work. The original punctuation and spelling have been retained with no effort to make them conform with modern grammar and usage.

A MYSTERY OF MYSTERIES

A MATTER OF DEATH
AND LIFE

Then—in my childhood—in the dawn
Of a most stormy life—was drawn
From ev'ry depth of good and ill
The mystery that binds me still—

—FROM EDGAR ALLAN POE'S "ALONE"

Having completed just forty years of what was without question a most stormy life, Edgar Allan Poe took leave of this realm early Sunday morning, October 7, 1849. Nobody knows precisely why. Indeed, like so many aspects of his life, his death has been the topic of endless debate, conjecture, speculation, guessing, and second-guessing. Nobody can tell you with anything resembling certainty why, while traveling from Richmond to New York, he ended up in Baltimore. Nobody can tell you what happened to him during the missing days between his last sighting in Richmond on the evening of September 26 and his reappearance outside an Election Day polling place in Baltimore on the damp, chilly afternoon of October 3. Nobody has ever solved the identity of the person, Reynolds, for whom Poe supposedly called out for hours before he died at the Washington University Hospital of Baltimore. Nobody has ever produced conclusive evidence, or so much as a first cousin to it, regarding the cause of the delirium generally described as "congestion of the brain," "cerebral inflammation," or "brain fever." Even the melodramatic and rather pat last words attributed to him—"Lord help my poor soul!"—have been called into question. The source for that dying utterance is a shaky witness who trafficked in contradictory testimony, attending physician John J. Moran (who may or may not have been in attendance at the time of death). The one thing that can be said with absolute certainty is that Edgar Allan Poe died at the age of forty years, eight months, and change because he stopped drawing breath. Or, to put it somewhat more poetically, as he wrote in one of his poems, "For Annie":

> *The danger is past,*
> *And the lingering illness*
> *Is over at last—*
> *And the fever called "Living"*
> *Is conquered at last.*

Poe's death has become so much a part of his mystique that it is often the first topic broached by visitors to the major destination sites devoted to the writer: the Edgar Allan Poe House in Baltimore, where, in the early 1830s, he discovered both a family that accepted him and a gift for short fiction; the Edgar Allan Poe Museum in Richmond, the city where he did much of his growing up and where, in 1835, he launched his often-controversial career as an influential literary critic and magazine editor; the Edgar Allan Poe National Historic Site, the only one of his five Philadelphia residences from 1838–44 still standing; and the Edgar Allan Poe Cottage in the Bronx, his rented home from the spring of 1846 until his death. "I would be a millionaire if I had a dime for every time I've been asked how he died," said Steve Medeiros, a Poe scholar and former National Park Service ranger whose regular duties included greeting those who passed through the door of the Philadelphia house.

During an interview conducted for this book, Matthew Pearl, author of the acclaimed 2006 novel *The Poe Shadow*, observed, "His biography doesn't really start where most biographies traditionally start, with his birth; it starts with his death." Is there a hint here of Poe's observation that romance writers could learn from Chinese authors who had "sense enough *to begin their books at the end*"?

The ongoing fascination with his death is understandable. It is, after all, one of the great literary stage exits of all time—right up there with Molière, the actor-playwright who, suffering from pulmonary tuberculosis, overcame an onstage collapse and hemorrhage to finish a final performance before dying a few hours later in 1673, and Mark Twain, who correctly predicted that, having been born when Halley's Comet visited the Earth in 1835, he would die when it returned in 1910. Poe's death, however, takes on added significance because it is undeniably one of the major factors keeping him alive as one of the most instantly recognizable writers of all time and the most-read American author around the world. Here, too, Twain is in the running, but Poe probably is better read while Twain is more frequently quoted (although often inaccurately). Poe's death is not only a source of continuing fascination; it is also symbolic of what became his deeply entrenched literary identity. He died under haunting circumstances that reflect the two literary genres he took to new heights.

Poe might as well have been writing his own epitaph with the first line of his story "The Assignation": "Ill-fated and mysterious man!—bewildered in the brilliancy of thine own imagination, and fallen in the flames of thine own youth!" His death is a moment shrouded in horror. Poe died in a lingering, painful manner that would not have been out of place in one of his own incredibly influential terror tales. It is also a moment surrounded by mystery. It is, in fact, a double-barreled mystery. What was the cause of Poe's death, and what happened to him during those missing days before he was found "in great distress" on the streets of Baltimore, wearing ill-fitting clothes that were not his own? Why did he look so disheveled, his hair unkempt, his face unwashed, and his eyes "lusterless and vacant"? Pale and alternately described as both cold to the touch and burning up with fever, Poe in his delirium held conversations with what resident physician Moran said were "spectral and imaginary objects on the wall." Sound like the description of a character in one of his stories? It also sounds like a mystery worthy of Poe's master detective (and the model for so many super sleuths to follow), C. Auguste Dupin. Here, to be sure, is both mystery and horror aplenty. "The haunted writer and the father of the detective story leaves us with grim mysteries that have defeated every attempt to solve them," Medeiros said. "It's almost as if a publicist stepped in and said, 'Hey, you know, the best thing for you to do for the career is to die under mysterious circumstances at forty.'"

It has been suggested that one reason Poe was drawn to the horror genre was an attraction to the American nineteenth-century death culture, which resulted in increasingly elaborate mourning rituals, grander and more extensive cemeteries, and heartrending songs and poems dwelling on grief and loss. Death most assuredly was a constant companion throughout Poe's life. So perhaps it's fitting that something of a death culture has developed around him. An astonishing number of theories have been pursued but never proven examining both the missing days and the cause of death. The long list of candidates for what carried him off includes binge drinking, rabies, murder, a brain tumor, encephalitis brought on by exposure, syphilis, suicide, heart disease, carbon monoxide poisoning from illuminating coal gas, and dementia caused by normal pressure hydrocephalus. A new "answer" seems to pull into the speculation station every couple of years. Hang around that station for any length of time and you're pretty certain to run into someone claiming he or she has solved the mystery of Poe's death—unless, of course, that person is blocked out by someone claiming he or she just solved the identity of Jack the Ripper.

Does the investigation that follows settle on a favorite theory of how Poe died? Sure, absolutely. Can this or any other theory be conclusively proven using the most modern forensic tools and methods at our disposal? Well, let's put that question to a myriad of tests and see where the investigation takes us as we examine Poe's life through a lens fashioned from the mystery of his death. This is just the opening of the case file, and plenty of leading experts from several fields have been called in to consult. They include Poe scholars, museum curators, medical experts and historians, horror writers, forensic pathologists, best-selling true-crime authors, a specialist in forensic anthropology and archaeology, an actor beloved for his association with Poe, and a pioneering FBI agent. Each had something compelling to say about how Poe may have died but also, and ultimately more illuminatingly, about how he lived. Each had a piece of a challenging puzzle. The horror specialists, for instance, from Stephen King and Anne Rice to Ray Bradbury and Wes Craven, quickly moved beyond stereotype to dwell on the complete writer and complex individual who must have been behind those tales of terror and the macabre. Their ruminations helped bring the real Poe into focus, and that hasn't been easy, since our view of him has been terribly obscured by persistent efforts to keep it in the shadows. Poe might also have been in a prophetic mood when he penned these lines for "Shadow—A Parable": "Ye who read are still among the living; but I who write shall have long since gone my way into the region of shadows." So, yes, it starts with his death.

They buried Poe the day after he died, in Baltimore's small Westminster Presbyterian Cemetery. He was buried again the next day when editor and poet Rufus Griswold's notorious obituary appeared in the evening edition of the *New-York Tribune,* opening with the withering lines: "Edgar Allan Poe is dead. He died in Baltimore the day before yesterday. This announcement will startle many, but few will be grieved by it." It went downhill from there. Nursing grudges against Poe, Griswold used the scurrilous obituary to shovel all manner of dirt and mud on his memory, depicting him as immoral, arrogant, unbalanced, dishonest, envious, conceited, and dishonorable. Griswold built on this wildly inaccurate and grotesque picture of Poe, adding even more outrageous charges in later writings. Poe's drinking had already been acknowledged by his friends and exaggerated by his enemies. And there's no question that alcohol periodically played the role of Poe's personal "Imp of the Perverse." But if you want to start an academic dustup among Poe scholars, bring up the subject of alcohol. There is a lively and ongoing debate on how much he drank and how often. From his college days at the University of Virginia, there were many witnesses who said it took very little alcohol to throw Poe into a state of extreme inebriation. Regardless of how much he drank at one time, the result was the same. It invariably had a devastating effect on his system and his psyche, and recovery usually meant more than just suffering through a morning hangover. The more notorious reports of his public intoxication gave Griswold more than enough ammunition in an era that equated trouble with the bottle to a weakness of character.

Yet Griswold went further, adding the label of drug addict, which, although without foundation or justification, also became an enduring part of the caricature. As an influential anthologist and respected arbiter of literary tastes, as well as the designated editor of the first collected edition of Poe's works, he was believed by many. So, less than twenty-four hours after being laid to rest in Baltimore, Poe was interred under a noxious pile of distortions, malicious falsehoods, and lies. To Poe's ardent champion Charles Baudelaire, the French poet and critic, Griswold's ongoing campaign of character assassination was the crass and hateful work of "a pedagogic vampire." Casting Griswold in the role of miserable cur, Baudelaire famously asked, "Does there not exist in America an ordinance to keep dogs out of cemeteries?" Nevertheless, Griswold's brutal and often-despicable attacks on Poe created a false overall impression that, despite the best efforts of scholarly detectives to set the record straight, hasn't been completely dispelled to this day. "The damage this article did to Poe's reputation was incalculable," Arthur Hobson Quinn wrote in his landmark 1941 biography of Poe. Still, it is wise to keep in mind that, in a Poe story, nothing ever stays buried. "In death—No! even in the grave all is *not* lost," he had his narrator tell us in "The Pit and the Pendulum."

They actually did dig up Poe's body in 1875, reburying his remains in a northwest corner of the cemetery to make room for an impressive new monument. By that time there had been significant blowback to Griswold's bitter smear campaign, both by Poe's friends and his growing number of admirers in Europe. Among those leading the counterattack was Baudelaire, who, although passionate in his great admiration for Poe's work, contributed to the gradually entrenched stereotypes by arguing that Poe's characters were projections of his personality. It is yet another distortion that has held on as we moved from one century to another to another. Many a junior high school student reading "The Raven," "The Tell-Tale Heart," and "The Cask of Amontillado" has been encouraged to confuse Poe with his narrators caught in the grips of morbid obsessions, crippling grief over a lost love, a consuming thirst for revenge, or fixations that threaten to unhinge the mind.

"Poe certainly drew on his life and experiences for his stories and poems, as all writers do," said Scott Peeples, a College of Charleston professor and author of *The Man of the Crowd: Edgar Allan Poe and the City*. "But it's a fundamental misconception to confuse Poe with his narrators. Even with illustrations of 'The Raven,' the narrator often is drawn to look like Poe."

The twentieth and twenty-first centuries certainly had their way with Poe as well, burying him yet again, this time behind a shorthand kind of brand identification adored by Hollywood and the pop culture. He has become our original master of the macabre, the grandfather of all things Goth, the king of horror long before the world had heard of Stephen King. There's every good chance that the mention of his name conjures an image along those general lines for most Americans. Enduring fame, therefore, has turned into something of a double-edged sword for Poe. On the one hand, that small group of stories and poems has made his name and face instantly recognizable and marketable. You can walk into a bookstore and find entire shelves of Poe items aimed at a wide range of customers. Don't bother looking for the shelves devoted to Henry Wadsworth Longfellow, Ralph Waldo Emerson, or any of the other literary contemporaries whose fame was supposed to overshadow and outlast Poe's reputation. Commercialism may not be the best test of literary merit, but this kind of overwhelming presence can't be casually dismissed. Surely no author is as relentlessly merchandised as Poe. You'd probably recognize the mustached fellow whose gloomy, haunted face stares at you from T-shirts, coffee mugs, refrigerator magnets, blankets, wall clocks, scented candles, pendants, iPhone cases, earrings, lapel pins, flip-flops, socks, plush dolls, bobblehead dolls, wine stoppers, and even a surprisingly wide assortment of Christmas cards (because nothing quite says merry Christmas like replacing Santa bellowing ho-ho-ho with a raven croaking Poe-Poe-Poe). The e-commerce site Etsy lists more than ten thousand Poe-centric articles for sale. You know this Poe. He looks moody, perhaps doomed.

With the pop culture doing its part, Poe at the same time remains the renewable literary force being constantly reintroduced in public and private school curricula from the seventh grade onward. Teachers adore getting to those sections devoted to Poe, and even those students who find reading a chore tend to be delighted with an author who is dismembering corpses, walling up pompous jerks in crypts, slapping poor souls into torture chambers, and stuffing bodies up chimneys. What's not to love? Poe, the frightmeister, hits them at just the right impressionable age with visions potent enough to fire up the imagination.

"Students from the seventh grade on can intensely identify with Poe because he writes about characters who feel incredibly vulnerable or are haunted by things they've done or are stymied by oppressive figures or feel as if violence may come down upon them at any time," said J. Gerald Kennedy, author of *Poe, Death, and the Life of Writing* and the editor of *A Historical Guide to Poe*. "I did a workshop a couple of years ago in Dallas, and so many African American teachers told me that their students especially liked Poe because he talks about that vulnerability, and this really resonates with them. It helps to explain the powerful fascination that students develop with Poe."

Through it all, ever since Baudelaire and other admirers turned Poe into a tortured genius of an icon, Poe has remained, well, cool, demonstrating enormous street cred with generation after generation. He has an honored spot—top row center—on the cover of the Beatles' album *Sgt. Pepper's Lonely Hearts Club Band*. He's name-checked in John Lennon's "I Am the Walrus" ("Man, you should have seen them kicking Edgar

Allan Poe"), and one of his stories is referenced in Bob Dylan's "Just Like Tom Thumb's Blues" (with its advice about "When you're down on Rue Morgue Avenue"). His works have been given playful twists on *The Simpsons,* and his spirit has been summoned to help Goth and vampire kids on *South Park.* "The Tell-Tale Heart" got a Bikini Bottom makeover on *SpongeBob SquarePants,* and, on Halloween night in 2020, Jim Carrey opened *Saturday Night Live* as Joe Biden reading an Election Day retelling of "The Raven." Another of Poe's most famous poems, "Annabel Lee," has been turned into song versions recorded by such varied artists as Frankie Laine, Jim Reeves, Joan Baez, and Stevie Nicks. And, although hardly faithful to the writer's stories and poems (if, in fact, they bear any resemblance to them at all), Hollywood's Poe-"inspired" films, from Universal classics in the 1930s with Bela Lugosi and Boris Karloff to the Roger Corman delights of the 1960s with Vincent Price, have become iconic in their own right. In October 2021, Netflix announced *The Fall of the House of Usher,* a series based on multiple Poe works.

Yet our vision of Poe remains a blurry one, at best. And here's the other side of that whole double-edged fame sword. The Poe we know—or think we know—is a grotesque caricature. He's the sickly, pasty guy with the sunken eyes, huddled over a manuscript in an attic, a raven perched on his shoulder. A red-eyed black cat sits among the cobwebs at one hand, a bottle of cognac at the other. We've reduced him to this cartoonish image, letting a small part of his literary output completely frame that distorted perception. It's like getting a picture of Poe from the reflection in a funhouse mirror. Yes, the stereotype does have some basis in fact. The master of the macabre unquestionably is an essential part of who Poe was. There's a reason those few stories and poems continue to have such impact. There were platoons of writers trading in the same graveyard territory before and during Poe's literary prime, but none could approach his sublime skill for summoning feelings of dread, unease, fear, and terror.

"The Goth image of Poe can be limiting, but it sure is enduring because there's a lot of truth to it," Kennedy said. "From the very beginning of his career, he's obsessed with the problem of death."

Acknowledging this is key to understanding Poe, but letting it completely define him as a writer criminally sells him short as an artist and a person. We are seeing merely one part of this incredibly dedicated and deceptively versatile writer. It becomes just another way we've buried Poe—under a mountain of misconception, myth, misunderstanding, and, of course, mystery. Poe, the master of invention, has become an invention.

"There's almost no relationship between the myth and the man," said Harry Lee "Hal" Poe, a cousin whose published works include *Edgar Allan Poe: An Illustrated Companion to His Tell-Tale Stories* and *Evermore: Edgar Allan Poe and the Mystery of the Universe.* "Very little of what Poe wrote could be classified as horror, and just a part of that is supernatural. Poe had an absolute horror of being typecast. He thought it was important for a writer to display that diversity and show you could write in all sorts of different ways. But it has become the end of *The Man Who Shot Liberty Valance,* when the editor has heard the true story and taken down all of the facts, and then tears it all up, saying, 'When the legend becomes fact, print the legend.' That's Poe. He has become a legendary character, and people like the character. It's one reason people keep reading him, but the real Poe has been lost while the legend is uncritically accepted as fact."

The real Poe considered himself first and foremost a poet. The real Poe was best known in his lifetime as first a tremendously tough critic, second a poet, and third as the author of tales of mystery and horror. Our perception of Poe has reversed that order. But Poe also wrote a substantial number of satires, hoaxes, and humorous pieces, and, let's face it, nobody thinks of Edgar Allan Poe as a comedy writer. The man had quite a sense of humor, but that doesn't fit the myth. "The popular image of Poe is so far off the mark that it borders on the ludicrous," Poe and Twain scholar Dennis Eddings said. "Poe had a delicious sense of humor. He loved cats, a true test of character, as Mark Twain recognized. And he took his art seriously at the same time he made fun of it, surely a sign of a well-balanced mind."

Poe also wrote stories that would influence later science-fiction writers. There were essays and journalistic pieces. Many visitors to one of those Poe sites in Baltimore, Richmond, Philadelphia, or New York have crossed the threshold proclaiming, "I love Edgar Allan Poe. I've read everything he's written." They mean that they have one of those volumes of collected tales and poems, which they've read cover to cover. The charitably unspoken rejoinder is, "Really? You've read everything? Did you start with James A. Harrison's 1902 edition, which runs to seventeen volumes?"

"The madman howling at the moon was Griswold's invention, and, to this day, that invention keeps the real Poe hidden from us," Hal Poe said. "The real Poe was the life of the party—witty, clever, engaging. He would bring his flute, and he and his wife, Virginia, would perform duets. Poe loved humor, but he had no great love for the horror story, even though he excelled at it. He was courtly, and he had a lot of friends, despite what Griswold wrote."

We don't lose Poe the horror writer by disposing of the cartoon image of him and accepting that he had a lively sense of humor and an exacting work ethic. Indeed, by acknowledging the complete artist, we better understand why and how he could take horror to such sublime and terrifying heights.

"The image of Poe has been terribly exaggerated and distorted, but that tends to happen with almost anyone who becomes known for horror: writers, actors, directors," said Robert Bloch, the horror writer best known for his novel *Psycho*. "People create their own images of horror writers, and these images often crowd out realities. The problem is that no one looks beyond the gloomy, melancholy images of Poe and sees the guy playing leapfrog in the front yard and laughing himself silly. Nobody thinks of Edgar Allan Poe as a fellow whose mother-in-law called him Eddy. But you have to accept and understand and know that Poe before you can even begin to fully understand the fellow who wrote all of those wonderfully eerie tales that have haunted our imagination for a hundred and fifty years."

As a young man, Bloch was a pen pal with H. P. Lovecraft, who said of Poe, "To him we owe the modern horror story in its final and perfected state." Bloch became friends with most of the leading horror writers of the last half of the twentieth century, including Richard Matheson, Stephen

King, and Harlan Ellison, as well as horror actors Boris Karloff, Vincent Price, and Christopher Lee.

"You know what we all have in common and also have in common with Poe?" Bloch asked. "A great sense of humor. It's almost impossible to do this without a great sense of humor. It's an essential part of the basic equipment that you need to do this. So horror writers are almost always very funny people, and that always surprises people. A sense of humor is about the last thing people attribute to Poe, but if you know anything about writing horror, it's the first thing you would attribute to him. He wasn't funny despite writing great horror. He wrote great horror because he was funny and because he was a lot of other things. You must look past the relentlessly marketed image."

Humor is also a key component in horror fandom, said Enrica Jang, the executive director of Baltimore's Edgar Allan Poe House & Museum: "Go to a horror convention, and those are some of the happiest people you're ever going to meet. The laughter is constant." And Poe was expert at mixing the two: dropping horrific elements into humorous pieces and humorous interludes in the horror stories.

"Poe also enjoys the moment when someone is in on the joke and someone isn't. He's in control," said Paul Lewis, English professor at Boston College and past president of the Poe Studies Association. "He's in command. And you see this in the reviews, but you also see it in a story like 'The Cask of Amontillado.' Poe had every reason to be hyper alert to the incongruous, in order to see the opportunities for humor or horror. His sense of humor is deceptively complex."

Stephen King noted that, in addition to being surprisingly funny, horror writers also tend to be more down-to-earth and grounded than people expect. "One reason is that we work through our nightmares," he said. "Horror writing is cathartic. We process our fears. We put them down on paper and give them to you. It's your problem now."

Like King, Bloch, and Craven, many a fright merchant to follow Poe into the terror territory have articulated the reasons for his preeminence. One of these was Ray Bradbury, who fell under Poe's spell as a boy.

"Poe's call was irresistible," said the author of *The Martian Chronicles, The Illustrated Man,* and *Something Wicked This Way Comes.* "Poe was the master guide to the dark realms of the human heart and soul. And no matter how macabre the landscape got, he made those places not only frightening but fascinating and even thrilling. So Poe had an enormous impact on me. How could I not be drawn to Poe? He was one of my ancestors. He pioneered horror, mystery, and science fiction. He took all of these forms, worked his alchemy, and he made literature of them. Once you fall under Poe's influence, which I surely did at a young age, his work not only becomes an influence but a challenge, because he took these incredibly, often deceptively, difficult genres and showed us what could be done with them."

Bradbury specifically paid tribute to Poe in his stories "The Exiles," "Pillar of Fire," "Usher II," and "The Fruit at the Bottom of the Bowl" (reminiscent of "The Tell-Tale Heart," with a murderer undone by obsession).

"He was an exacting and remarkably careful writer who believed that each story and poem, and everything in then, should evoke a certain mood, emotion, feeling," Bradbury said. "Everything was minutely planned. No one before him or after could match his skill with psychological terror. He could hone in on one horror that resonated so hauntingly in your mind, your heart, your soul. So many people first read Poe when they're young, and that's a marvelous thing, because once Poe takes hold, he doesn't let go."

King cites Bradbury, Bloch, and Lovecraft as major influences on his writing. And since they all cited Poe as a major influence, Bradbury was correct when he stated that Poe's influence on horror can't be overstated. "I came along and read all those guys," King joked, "so you can say that we were all twisted by our evil grandfather."

Another of the many leading horror writers who proudly claimed Poe in her personal pantheon was Anne Rice. "I heard his voice and was drawn to it," she said. "I read his stories and poems. And my father, who owned one of those early model tape recorders, when not many people had one, made a recording of 'The Tell-Tale Heart' for me. He recorded his rendition for me. Isn't that wonderful? Poe, like Charles Dickens, had an enormous influence on me as a child. So if some people see the influence of Poe and Dickens in my writing, I wouldn't think that's at all surprising. There's so much to learn from Poe. With Poe, it was how much he packed into a story: the language, the mood, those settings, those characters, and always the threat of sudden, horrific violence."

In "The Exiles," Bradbury imagines a Mars where authors of the supernatural are dying as the last of their forbidden books are being burned on Earth. Poe seeks out Charles Dickens to ask for help in repelling the Earth travelers on their way to Mars. Dickens turns him down, saying he has been unfairly lumped in with Poe and other masters of the macabre because of his occasional ghost stories, including, of course, *A Christmas Carol*. The irony of this moment is that the objections voiced by Dickens would have been voiced by Poe, who would have thought himself completely and unfairly identified primarily as a horror writer. He might well have looked at his twenty-first-century popularity and protested that he couldn't escape the long shadow of the raven. Still, there would also be in this complaint a sense that the writer doth protest too much.

Poe gave definition and boundaries to the horror realm where he would be proclaimed king. He described the landscape in an 1844 poem, "Dream-Land." It's pretty much a roadmap for all who followed him in the fright field:

> By the lakes that thus outspread
> Their lone waters, lone and dead,—
> Their sad waters, sad and chilly
> With the snows of the lolling lily,—
> By the mountains—near the river
> Murmuring lowly, murmuring ever,—
> By the grey woods,—by the swamp
> Where the toad and the newt encamp—
> By the dismal tarns and pools
>   Where dwell the Ghouls,—

By each spot the most unholy—
In each nook most melancholy—
There the traveller meets aghast
Sheeted Memories of the Past—
Shrouded forms that start and sigh
As they pass the wanderer by—
White-robed forms of friends long given,
In agony, to the Earth—and Heaven.

For the heart whose woes are legion
'Tis a peaceful, soothing region—
For the spirit that walks in shadow
'Tis—oh, 'tis an Eldorado!

"Melancholy is the most legitimate of all the poetical tones," Poe proclaimed.

"He was drawn to macabre and melancholy subjects, and he even plays that up," said Poe scholar Edward G. Pettit, the manager of public programs at Philadelphia's Rosenbach Museum. "He adopts the Byronesque pose. He dresses in black. He cultivates the image of the tortured romantic genius. When 'The Raven' becomes a sensation, he loves being asked to read it all the time, loves being recognized as the Raven Man. It had to feel great, and that part of him would have been delighted that readers all around the world still are thrilling to 'The Tell-Tale Heart' and 'The Black Cat.' Yes, horror stories are only a fraction of his literary output, but nobody reads the criticism today. Much of his humor hasn't dated all that well. But the horror stories were great then, and they are great now."

Yes, but wouldn't he be even a little bit perturbed that people don't immediately think of him in the same way as his hero, Byron? Wouldn't Poe be upset that he wasn't known for his first love, poetry?

"He wanted to be Byron, but guess what?" Pettit said. "Nobody reads Byron anymore, unless you're studying him in college. But everybody reads Poe. He outlives Byron. He outpaces Byron. He outdoes Byron. He didn't get to be Byron, but he got to be something better. He got to be Edgar Allan Poe. He's going to be the best-read American writer in the world, and you wish he could have known that."

Poe's face is so familiar, twenty-first-century devotees might be fairly confident they would have recognized him if they had spotted him on a New York street corner. And maybe they would have if they had encountered Poe during the last three years of his life. There are eight known photographs of Poe—seven of them are daguerreotypes from those last three years, when Poe was wearing a mustache and the toll of a hard life was showing up on a face that looked increasingly puffy and unhealthy. That's the Poe we see on those buttons and T-shirts.

Would you, however, have recognized Poe if you passed him on the streets of Philadelphia in, say, 1841? This Poe would be slim and robust, sans mustache but with stylish sideburns. That's how he looked most of his adult life. That's how he looked when he was writing many of his best-known horror stories. And he would have introduced himself as Edgar Poe or Edgar A. Poe, rarely including the Allan in signatures or bylines. Again, these are realities that do not fit the myth. If one photograph existed that caught Poe laughing, how might it shatter the caricature? If Poe had lived in the late nineteenth century, when cameras were affordable, accessible, and easy to use for candid photography, he might have been caught not only enjoying the company of the friends denied by Griswold but also singing or playfully engaging in a leaping game, winning but bursting his gaiters (worn over the shoe and lower pants leg) in the process.

"There is an otherworldly quality to the later daguerreotypes," said Michael Deas, the painter and illustrator who has become our foremost expert on images of Poe. "And I think the photographs of Poe have contributed the most to the mystique that clings to him—that and his death. He looks like the tragic Byronic poet. But those pictures only represent how he looked for the last two or three years of his life. The pictures helped to create the myth around Poe, but, at the same time, they've done a disservice in representing him as he must have looked through much of his life. The pictures match up with the stereotype and embellish it, so they have gone a long way in creating our distorted picture of Poe."

The greatest disservice, perhaps, is the damage it has done to Poe as an extremely careful and exacting writer who constantly was revising his stories and poems, always pushing himself and the literature of his nation to higher standards. That's the undeniable reality behind the widely accepted fantasy vision of Poe.

"Poe was an incredibly prolific writer and hard worker," Pearl said. "The caricature is fun. It's fun to have a Poe plushy. The flip side of the fame is that he was in many ways the opposite of that caricature. He was trying to create a steady and stable home life and family life. He was trying, every way he could, to make his living as a professional writer."

In place of that reality, we have that fun-house mirror Poe, possibly mad, spinning out his tales under the influence of alcohol and drugs. Like Griswold's obituary, this view of Poe has done incalculable harm to the writer and the brilliance of his actual writing process.

"The favorite image of Poe is pasty-faced and cackling while he jots down spontaneous, perhaps drug-induced hallucinations," said Helen McKenna-Uff, the Poe scholar and former National Park Service ranger who was a regular presence at the Poe house in Philadelphia before her retirement in 2020. "People want Poe to be this mad genius, who somehow is not involved in a human process while he's writing. They actually want him to be crazy, twisted, and horrible. He was none of those things, yet nobody really likes the idea of Poe being a careful writer dedicated to art and craft. But he works, he toils, he chooses carefully. If you don't understand that Poe, you don't understand the writer behind the stories and poems you profess to love so much."

So, as we explore the mystery of Poe's death, expect regular debunking of the many misconceptions about how he lived. The deeper you dig, the more Poe comes alive and the more we restore the real writer, who seems to be completely recognized and appreciated only by the scholars who have so generously contributed their time and insights to this investigation. The structure of this investigation is one of parallel timelines—with chapters exploring the last three months before his death alternating with longer chapters detailing different periods of his abbreviated life. These two timelines meet in the concluding chapter that considers Poe's death and his literary afterlife. As irresistibly drawn as we are to how he died, it's far more crucial to understand how he lived.

Poe himself doesn't always make this easy. He did his own share of fabricating, embellishing, and falsifying when it came to his biography. Certainly not the first or last writer to have padded his résumé, he had a need to present himself as a more world-traveled and romantic adventurer than he was. The Poe scholars interviewed for this book have labored mightily to clarify the record, and it's an honor to recognize their vital work by including their voices throughout. Their books and articles that study specific aspects of Poe's work and personality form a kind of essential literary forensics, so they are called upon in this case as expert witnesses. This small group of academics and biographers has long acknowledged how skewed the legend of Edgar Allan Poe has become, but almost everyone else, even many an ardent Poe admirer, is surprised when told the prevailing impression of him is as misguided as it is unfair. That includes commonly cited "facts" about how he died. Chris Semtner, curator of the Edgar Allan Poe Museum in Richmond and author of *Edgar Allan Poe's Richmond: The Raven in the River City,* remembers encountering a visitor who informed him, "The only thing I know about Edgar Allan Poe is that he was a drug addict and he died drunk in the gutter." And while many touring the museum with him that day might have nodded in agreement, "no part of that sentence was true," Semtner said. "His death has been as mythologized as his life."

No matter how much the twisted record gets set straight, though, and no matter how many mysteries get solved, there will always be much about Poe that remains unknowable. We can never completely dispel the shadows that surround him. Rest assured, we will never lose the enigmatic Poe, and that's because the trail of evidence is positively littered with unreliable witnesses, contradictory statements, questionable memories, and missing time. Sifting through it all, you're reminded of the line from Poe's satirical story "The System of Doctor Tarr and Professor Fether": "Believe nothing you hear, and only half that you see." That's a bit extreme, and it must also be conceded that, sooner or later, any biographer writing about any subject must regularly cope with murky areas by falling back on such old reliable standards as *evidently, seemingly, presumably,* and *apparently.* But with Poe, these get an even more rigorous workout, and, while you're at it, you can toss in *supposedly, likely, possibly,* and *maybe.* This is not by any means a criticism. It is a simple acknowledgment of a necessity—a constant requirement—when dealing with aspects of Poe's life and death. "Around his name has accumulated a mass of rumor, conjecture, psycho-analysis, and interpretation based upon imagination rather than fact," Quinn wrote in his biography of Poe, setting the standard for decades of scholarship to follow. With Poe, it's often less a matter of what we know with absolute certainty and more a matter of settling for what we think we know.

"That's true of his death in spades, but it's also true of his life," said Jeffrey A. Savoye, the secretary and treasurer of the Edgar Allan Poe Society of Baltimore and the webmaster who oversees that organization's extensive and invaluable online archive of Poe material. "We accept a lot of information about Poe in absence of strong contradiction. And there's unquestionably a lot of information about Poe. But for a lot of it, we don't really have a way of verifying whether it's true or not."

You're continually reminded of this when grappling with the mysteries that have enveloped Edgar Allan Poe. You're also constantly reminded what a brief life he lived. Poe wrote so much of such high quality in so many different genres that he leaves the illusion of a complete literary life. The accomplishments are so impressive and influential, we might not give due consideration to the notion that he died at an age when many writers are just entering their prime—that forty-to-sixty sweet spot when maturity and experience can propel an artist to greater heights. "There is that arc of improvement with Poe," Peeples said. "It created the impression that he did what he was meant to do. There's such symmetry to it all, you don't tend to think of it as a career cut short."

Yet death is always there, a regular companion on Poe's trip to the grave in Baltimore. Death is always waiting for him, because, no matter where Poe happened to be in such a short span on this planet, he never was far from the end.

Things actually seemed to be looking up for Poe before fate and a steamer took him to Baltimore. While he was making plans to depart Richmond, he was holding on to many reasons for believing that the future would be a bit brighter. If not formally engaged to the love of his teen years, wealthy Richmond widow Elmira Royster Shelton, he certainly had reached an "understanding" with her. Poe's dream of having complete control of his own literary magazine also seemed within his grasp. One of the reasons he was traveling during the last months of his life was to raise money and solicit subscriptions for such a publication. Throughout his life, whenever he was at a point where some good fortune seemed imminent, things invariably fell apart because of bad luck, bad timing, or a self-destructive outburst. Without doubt, among his many other gifts, he had a positive genius for drinking or picking an ill-chosen fight at precisely the wrong moment. "There are so many instances where Poe is his own worst enemy," said Jeff Jerome, the former longtime curator of the Edgar Allan Poe House & Museum in Baltimore. "There are times when you just want to reach into the pages of the biography and slap him. You want to shake him and say, 'What are you thinking? What's the matter with you? Do you really think this was the right time to start arguing with this person who actually is going to help you?' You see this again and again with Poe."

Could he sense that the rug was about to be pulled out from under him one last time? Could he not stop himself from perversely pulling at the threads, contributing mightily to a final fall? There surely were many ill omens and troubling moments in the three months preceding his death. And there were the clear signs of the marked physical deterioration evident since the death of his beloved wife, Virginia, on January 30, 1847. The result of an undiagnosed illness, the drinking, years of battling poverty, the ravages of a grief that he described as taking him close to madness? He did not sound as if he suspected the end was so near when he took leave of his adoring mother-in-law and aunt Maria "Muddy" Clemm on June 29, 1849. They were still living in the modest Bronx cottage where Virginia died, and, although money was scarce, Poe hoped his journey would lead to an improvement in their fortunes. His destination was Richmond, the city where he had first made his name as a magazine editor and critic. Now he hoped his travels would yield financial support for a magazine of his own. Before he made it to Richmond, though, there would be a troubling stop in Philadelphia, another city where he had worked as an editor and critic. As Poe boarded a steamboat in New York that would take him to Perth Amboy, New Jersey, where he could make a train connection to Philadelphia, he told Muddy, "Do not fear for Eddy." He then assured her that he would "come back to love and comfort you." They were the last words she heard him speak.

"PALE AND HAGGARD"

LATE JUNE–EARLY JULY 1849

The last three months of Edgar Allan Poe's life can be viewed as something of a descent into a maelstrom, and the precipitous slide began in Philadelphia. One of the first and strongest witnesses to this unnerving decline was John Sartain, the artist, engraver, editor, and publisher who had known Poe since 1840. Yet the "pale and haggard" figure who dashed into the handsome, English-born Sartain's Philadelphia engraving studio in the early afternoon of July 2, 1849, displayed none of the courtliness and confidence of the Poe he had met in the very same city nine years before. This clearly troubled Poe was edgy and nervous, "with a wild expression in the eyes." Sartain would say that this final encounter with his friend was "under such peculiar and fearful conditions that it can never fade from my memory." Powerful words, but if his 1889 account of the bizarre episode is accurate, then, if anything, this characterization is an exercise in understatement.

Just three months older than Poe, the well-liked, well-regarded Sartain was born under a far luckier star. Immigrating to the United States at the age of twenty-two and settling in Philadelphia, he became known for reviving the mezzotint engraving process he had studied in England. Once he established himself in the City of Brotherly Love, employment opportunities, commissions, and requests rolled his way. Sartain and his wife, Susannah, had eight children, four of whom became artists. And Sartain hadn't even lived half of his extremely full life when the distressed Poe came calling in 1849. Sartain would die one day after his eighty-ninth birthday in 1897. Poe would be dead in fourteen weeks.

Yet when the fateful year had started, Poe sounded optimistic. His New Year's resolution had been to pull himself together and get his disordered life back on track. "I am about to bestir myself in the world of Letters rather more busily than I have done for three or four years past," he wrote to John Reuben Thompson, editor of the *Southern Literary Messenger,* on January 13, 1849. He had good reason to feel hopeful about writing. He was in the midst of a literary renewal that resulted in an impressive last burst of creativity especially notable for a dazzling return to his first love, poetry. Just eleven days after Poe's letter to Thompson, the California Gold Rush was sparked by the discovery of the precious metal at Sutter's Mill. Poe looked on with amusement as the get-rich-quick madness spread faster than the plague he had conjured in "The Masque of the Red Death." Approximately three hundred thousand people raced to California in search of riches. If anything, the money fever consuming the nation served to emphasize his love of the written word. "Literature is the most noble of professions," he wrote to a friend, the poet and novelist Frederick W. Thomas, on February 14. "In fact, it is the only one fit for a man. For my own part, there is no seducing me from the path. I shall be a *literrateur,* at least, all my life, nor would I abandon the hopes which still lead me on for all the gold in California." Certain he was addressing a like mind, Poe grew even more passionate:

Talking of gold, and of the temptations at present held out to "poor-devil authors", did it ever strike you that all which is really valuable to a man of letters—to a poet in especial—is absolutely unpurchaseable? Love, fame, the dominion of intellect, the consciousness of power, the thrilling sense of beauty, the free air of

Heaven, exercise of mind & body, with the physical and moral
health which result—these and such as these are really all that
a poet cares for:—then answer me this—*why* should he go to
California?

Which is not to say that Poe maintained an unflaggingly upbeat
demeanor for the first half of 1849. Far from it. He was often subject to
drastic mood swings, which you can sense in the letters he wrote during
those months. With Thomas, he is positively buoyant, writing, "You will
be pleased to hear that I am in better health than I ever knew myself to
be—full of energy and bent on success." But in early May, he wrote to
another friend, "I am full of dark forebodings. *Nothing* cheers or comforts
me. My life seems wasted—the future looks a dreary blank." That spring,
he also suffered a bout of illness so serious his adoring mother-in-law believed he might die. Still, the disease and existential gloom that threatened
to overwhelm him failed to do so. Providing a further boost to his spirits
was the possibility that he might finally launch his own magazine. He had
been corresponding with a young investor in Oquawka, Illinois, Edward
Howard Norton Patterson, an admirer who had read about Poe's plans for
The Stylus, "a monthly literary journal of literature proper, the fine arts
and the drama." In addition to financial backing, Patterson was promising
him complete editorial control. Brooklyn attorney Sylvanus D. Lewis, who
dined with Poe right before he left for Richmond in late June, described
his mood as hopeful. He was, after all, on his way to bolster prospects for
The Stylus by soliciting subscriptions he believed would be plentiful. He
left New York on a Friday. He showed up at Sartain's door on Monday. In
between, the sense of hopefulness collapsed. Poe had been derailed by a
familiar problem, alcohol, but Sartain was unaware of this as he contemplated the agitated Poe before him. "He had rushed in on me in terror for
his life, in fear that he might be killed," Sartain recalled. Not wishing to
further upset his visitor, Sartain decided it would be best not to mention
the obvious: "I did not let him see that I noticed it, and, shaking his hand
warmly, invited him to be seated."

"I have come to you for protection and a refuge," the frantic Poe told him. "It will be difficult for you to believe what I have to tell,—that such things could be in this nineteenth century. It is necessary that I remain concealed for a time. Can I stay here with you?"

"Certainly," Sartain assured him, "as long as you like: you will be perfectly safe here."

Poe then related a bizarre account of what happened to him after he had left Brooklyn three days before. He said he was on a train, and, because "his sense of hearing was so wonderfully acute," he overheard some men a few seats away planning his murder. They were going to kill him and toss his body from the platform of the train car. He managed to give them the slip at Bordentown, keeping hidden at the station until the train was on its way. He then made his way to Philadelphia and the shelter he knew Sartain would provide.

The artist had little doubt that Poe's wild tale was a hallucination, and he tried convincing him "that the whole thing was the creation of his fancy." Why would anyone want to kill him?

"It was for revenge," Poe said.

"Revenge for what?"

"Well, a woman trouble."

How reliable is Sartain as a witness? He left behind at least three accounts of an experience that must have been as disturbing as it was surreal. The most-quoted of these was for *Lippincott's Monthly Magazine,* published forty years after the events he described. A few Poe scholars have seized on the differences among these accounts, calling into question the accuracy of Sartain's memory, especially after the lapse of so many years. In addition, the line about "woman trouble" has been tantalizing fodder for those who believe Poe was the victim of foul play. Sartain also says that Poe was traveling home to New York, not Richmond, when he made his way to Philadelphia and the engraving studio. Could this be true? If so, as John Evangelist Walsh contended in *Midnight Dreary: The Mysterious Death of Edgar Allan Poe* (1998), then he sought out Sartain after he left Richmond on September 27. Walsh proposed that this could explain some of the missing days before he was found in such bad shape in Baltimore. Poe, after all, did plan to stop in Philadelphia on his way to New York, having agreed to edit a volume by the wife of piano manufacturer John Loud. And "woman trouble"? Here, Walsh declared, "is the sudden bright glare of reality." After the tragic death of his young wife, Virginia, in 1847, Poe proposed marriage to two women, both widows, Sarah Helen Power Whitman of Providence, Rhode Island, and Sarah Elmira Royster of Richmond. And he dreamed of marriage to a third, Annie Richmond of Lowell, Massachusetts, who was married (to a husband who encouraged her platonic friendship with Poe). It was Walsh's theory that Poe's fears were not the product of hallucination. He was not drunk. He actually had overheard men planning to kill him.

Walsh proposed that Poe was being followed by Elmira's three brothers, George, James, and Alexander, who were determined to prevent the marriage by brute force. In the dime-novel scenario put forward by Walsh, the Royster brothers followed Poe to Philadelphia, threatening him in a hotel room. He made a break for it and bolted to the safety of Sartain's studio, but the Roysters tailed him back to Baltimore, caught up with him at his hotel, beat him, and forced whiskey down his throat. The idea was that Poe, who had recently taken the pledge and joined the Sons of Temperance in Richmond on August 27, would be discovered in a debauched state on the streets of Baltimore. Word would get back to Elmira, who, realizing his promises to reform were hollow, would end the engagement. Although Walsh attempted to prove unintentional murder most foul, he lacked any proof to back up his sensational and fanciful speculation. No description of Poe's condition at the Baltimore polling place or Washington Medical College mentions any bruising, defensive wounds, or signs of a beating. There's no evidence that the brothers violently opposed his engagement to Elmira. And there's certainly no evidence that George, James, and Alexander made such an outlandish plan or pursued Poe when he left Richmond.

Walsh's strained attempt to pin a murder rap on the Roysters has been largely and sensibly dismissed by most Poe scholars and biographers, as well as forensic pathologists who have weighed the evidence that

actually does exist. Sartain's testimony, on the other hand, has been accepted as generally reliable, even allowing for the occasional discrepancy.
Indeed, when there are instances where he can't remember exactly what
Poe said, he tells the reader, "I was profoundly impressed, but I cannot
recall the words in my memory now. It's forty years since." The accepted
view is that he simply was mistaken about Poe being on his way to New
York. Or perhaps Poe, in his agitated state, wasn't clear about having just
left New York and when he hoped to return. The preponderance of likelihoods and logic place Poe in Philadelphia and Sartain's studio in late
June and early July. As Sartain's recollections continue, we also see why
the great train murder plot was most likely hallucinatory. Poe was reeling from another devastating bout with alcohol. Having made his friend
comfortable, Sartain continued with his work, dropping in and out of
conversation with Poe.

Death was a running thread during these talks. Poe had spoken of an
attempt on his life, and then he told Sartain it might be best if he committed suicide. After a lengthy silence, he suddenly told Sartain, "If this
moustache of mine were removed I should not be so readily recognized.
Will you lend me a razor, that I may shave it off?" Sartain naturally feared
that Poe might try to kill himself. He told Poe that he didn't have a razor
on the premises, but, if he wanted the mustache removed, he could do his
best to shear him "almost as close" with scissors. Poe agreed, and Sartain
guided him to the bathroom "and performed the operation successfully."
This clipping operation has also been called into question, since Poe's
last daguerreotypes, taken in Richmond, show him wearing the familiar mustache. If Sartain is wrong on such a distinct memory, his entire
account might be doubted. But the last daguerreotype would have been
taken almost three months after Sartain's shearing, and scissors wouldn't
have provided the closest of shaves anyway.

As evening fell, Poe readied himself to go out, and Sartain asked him
where he was heading. Poe said he felt drawn to the city's Fairmount District and the Schuylkill River. A concerned Sartain thought it best to accompany him. Poe's worn-down shoes were causing him pain, so Sartain

gave him slippers to wear for the evening excursion. They walked to the corner of Ninth and Chestnut, where they waited for a horse-drawn bus. Death remained much on Poe's mind. He asked the artist-engraver to be sure that, after his death, the portrait Samuel S. Osgood had done of him, probably in 1845, would go "to his mother" (meaning his mother-in-law, Maria Clemm). The bus took them to a tavern on the north side of Callowhill Street, near the Fairmount Bridge and the district's waterworks and reservoir. It was a popular recreation spot, with fountains and cascades. "At this place there was light enough, chiefly from what shone out through the door of the tavern," Sartain wrote, "but beyond was darkness, and forward into the darkness we went." His description of this journey into darkness is notable for its mood and details:

> I kept on his left side, and on nearly approaching the bridge I guided him off to the right by a gentle pressure until we reached the foot of the lofty flight of steep wooden steps that ascended almost to the top of the reservoir. Here was the first landing, and with seats, so we sat down. All this time I had contrived to keep him in conversation, which never ceased except while we were on our way up that breakneck flight of stairs. I had reckoned on the moon's rising, but it did not: I had forgotten that each evening it rose so much later. There we sat at that dizzy height in perfect darkness, for clouds hid the stars, and I hoping for the moon which came not.
>
> Here he related to me his late experiences, or what he believed to be such, and the succession of images that his imagination created he described in a calm, deliberate, measured voice as facts, that were as wild and fantastic as anything I have met with in his writings. He said he was in Moyamensing Prison, and through the grated window of his cell he could see the battlemented stone tower, and on the topmost point of the coping stood a young female figure, so radiant, either in herself or in her surrounding atmosphere, that the light on the wall of his room was crossed by the shadows thrown from the window-bars. From this remote

position she addressed him in words not loud, but clear, and spoken slowly. Not a word failed to reach his ear, because of his astonishing faculty of hearing. It was necessary that he should bear every question she put and make apt response, or the consequences would be fatal to him. He repeated the words she spoke, imitating the tone and manner.

In his addled state, Poe was likely combining vivid hallucinations with actual hazy memories of a prison cell. What exists of a record indicates that Poe, on his way to Richmond, was always intending to stop in Philadelphia, arriving there on Saturday, June 30. Maria Clemm knew what route he was taking, and said so in a letter written July 9. "Eddy has been gone ten days, and I have not heard one word from him," she wrote. "Eddy was obligated to go through Philadelphia, and how much I fear he has got into some trouble there."

Her concerns were justified, and her instincts were correct. He fell to drinking in Philadelphia, staggering into a sorrier and sorrier state. He was taken to Moyamensing, the Philadelphia County prison, for being drunk. Poe also lost his valise, which held the two lectures he hoped to deliver in Richmond and other cities on his subscription tour for the magazine.

A week later, he admitted in a letter to Muddy: "I have been taken to prison once since I came here for spreeing drunk; *but then I* was not. It was about Virginia." Poe could be extremely manipulative in his letters, and here he was blaming his sorrowful condition on sorrow for his deceased wife—Muddy's daughter. He knew what excuse would touch her heart. To Sartain, Poe claimed that he had been taken to Moyamensing because he "had been suspected of trying to pass a fifty-dollar counterfeit note." Sartain had no doubt that Poe was trying to pass a counterfeit excuse. He knew the real reason was "what takes so many there for a few hours only, the drop too much." Individuals charged with public intoxication were brought before the mayor to be fined. When Poe's turn came, he was recognized. Someone said, "Why, this is Poe, the poet," and the mayor decided to release him. He was dismissed without having to pay the usual fine. One theory that attempts to reconcile the timeline and Sartain's account has Poe traveling from New York to Philadelphia, arriving on the Saturday, getting drunk, ending up in prison, being released, and then, in such rocky shape, deciding it was best to return to Muddy and the Fordham cottage. He boards a train to New York, and this is when he either hears or imagines the plot to kill him. He gets off that train and heads back to Philadelphia, seeking refuge and protection with Sartain Monday afternoon. There are no witnesses to verify where he was much of Sunday and Monday, so this is a plausible scenario, if not provable. Whatever timeline is correct, alcohol remains the overwhelming prime suspect for Poe's paranoia and unsteady condition, with his hallucinations the result of delirium tremens or withdrawal or his acute sensitivity to alcohol.

But Sartain was still in the dark about all of this as he sat in that perfect darkness at the top of the reservoir. Poe continued to share his hallucinatory visions of Moyamensing, which grew stranger and more nightmarish. After communicating with the radiant young woman outside his cell, he told Sartain, he was asked if he would like to take a stroll around the prison. Poe and his prison guides arrived at a great cauldron containing "boiling spirits." He was invited to take a drink but declined. "If I had said yes, do you guess what they would have done?" he asked Sartain. "I should have been lifted by the hair of my head and dipped into the hot liquid up to my lip, like Tantalus [the mythological Greek king who was punished by Zeus to go forever thirsty while standing in a pool of water in Hades]."

"Yes, but that would have killed you," Sartain said.

"Of course it would," Poe replied. "That's what they wanted, and why they tried to catch me; but you see I escaped the snare. At last, in order to torture me, they brought out Mrs. Clemm and compelled me to have my sight blasted and my heart grieved by seeing them first saw off her feet, then her legs at the knee, her thighs at the hips, and so destroy her piecemeal, all to torture me."

Decades later, the solicitous Sartain offered these as examples of what he listened to in that lofty setting. He remembered that Poe, while describing the horrors so vividly, was thrown into a kind of convulsion. With Poe's earlier talk of killing himself, Sartain feared a suicidal jump into the blackness and oblivion. He also feared that Poe might cause him to fall. Enveloped by darkness, they descended the steep stairway "slowly and cautiously," mindful to keep a good hold on the handrails. Sartain trembled all the way down. His goal was to keep Poe talking, no matter how fantastic the talk grew. He guided Poe back to the tavern, where they boarded the omnibus. When Poe hesitated, Sartain gently pushed him forward and said, "Go on." When they were seated, Sartain urged his friend to continue talking. Poe resumed his rambling recitation. In this manner, Sartain recalled, "I took him safe home to Sansom Street, gave him a bed on the sofa in the dining-room, and slept alongside him on three chairs, without undressing."

Staying with Sartain, Poe gradually recovered, physically and mentally. "On the second morning he appeared to have become so much like his old self that I trusted him to go out alone," Sartain wrote,

Regular meals and rest had had a good effect; but his mind was not yet free from the nightmare. After an hour or two he returned, and then he told me that he had arrived at the conclusion that what I said was true, that the whole thing had been a delusion and a scare created out of his own excited imagination. He said that his mind began to clear as he lay on the grass, his face buried in it, and his nostrils inhaling its sweet fragrance mingled with the odor of the earth; that the words he had heard kept running through his mind, but somehow he tried in vain to connect them with who spoke them, and thus his thoughts gradually awakened into rational order and he saw that he came out of a dream.

Poe was ready to go on his way, although it's unclear if Sartain thought he was heading on to Richmond, back to New York, or just somewhere else in Philadelphia. Sartain lent him "what was needful." He closed his account with five words: "I never saw him more."

In these few days, and the months that preceded them, those looking for answers to how Poe died find clues to support a wide variety of possible causes: alcohol, murder, suicide, "brain congestion," "heart disease," infection. The hallucinations could have been the result of delirium tremens, but many things can cause hallucinations. Is the answer lurking in the days between when he left New York and when he left Sartain? Or can it be found buried deep in his past? It is believed he had left New York with a miniature portrait of his mother, Eliza Poe. He had attached a scrap of paper on the back, noting the day he was leaving for Richmond, adding the words, "My adored Mother! E.A. Poe, New York." Moving toward the end, he was carrying a picture that recalled where it all started, in Boston.

"FROM CHILDHOOD'S HOUR"

JANUARY 1809–MARCH 1827

The problem with establishing an accurate biographical record for Edgar Allan Poe begins with him, and it begins at the beginning, with his birth. An autobiographical note he composed in May 1841 opened with the words: "Born January, 1811." He started with a lie, shaving two years off his age. What followed was a mix of fact and fancy, much like the kind of brief "biographies" Hollywood studios crafted for their stars in the 1920s, '30s, and '40s. And, along with a casual disregard for accuracy, Poe shared something else with those later masters of puffery generating enhanced life stories in their Tinseltown public relations offices: the idea to create a more romantic and dramatic image for the public. One standing rule for the silver-screen stars during the film industry's so-called golden age was the younger, the better. Once you crossed the Los Angeles County border, ages were routinely reduced with impunity. This was just one more way Poe was ahead of his time. Among the apocryphal incidents he included were a quixotic attempt to join Greeks fighting for freedom in the rebellion against the Ottoman Empire and his rescue by an American consul after being stranded in St. Petersburg, Russia. He was romanticizing, dramatizing, exaggerating, and, yes, fabricating for his public—the reading public. Although this was clearly Poe's intent, many of the specious elements found their way into his obituaries and the early biographies. Indeed, it took decades after Poe's death to definitively nail down the correct birth year. The autobiographical sketch designed to make himself appear younger, more precocious, and more adventurous was mailed to Rufus W. Griswold for use in his anthology *The Poets and Poetry of America* (1842). Griswold repeated the fabrications in his biographical works on Poe, adding many more ugly ones of his own. So, right from the start, interested readers who went searching for this fellow named Poe were guided by authentic-looking signs that sent them down false trails.

Edgar Poe was born in Boston on January 19, 1809, the second child of David Poe Jr. and Elizabeth (Eliza) Arnold Hopkins Poe, both actors. He was born on a chilly, moonless night in a boardinghouse on Carver Street, near the Boston Common. As recently as three months before Edgar's birth, Eliza and David had been playing Cordelia and Edmund in a production of Shakespeare's *King Lear*. The second sentence of that unreliable but intriguing autobiographical sketch claimed the Poe family was "one of the oldest and most respectable in Baltimore." It was another lie, or exaggeration, if you will. The family did settle in Baltimore but hardly qualified as one of the city's oldest. Poe's great-grandfather, John Poe, and his wife, Jane (née McBride), immigrated to Lancaster County, Pennsylvania, around 1750. The son of a tenant farmer in Dring, County Cavan, Ireland, John moved to Baltimore around 1755 and died there in 1756. John's oldest son, David, was born in Ireland and established himself as a maker of spinning wheels and clock reels in Baltimore. Poe's autobiographical note says that his paternal grandfather, General David Poe, "was a quarter-master general, in the Maryland line, during the Revolution, and the intimate friend of Lafayette, who, during his visit to the U.S., called personally upon the Gen.'s widow, and tendered her his warmest acknowledgments for the services rendered him by her husband." Another fabrication? No, this one is largely truthful. Although David Poe Sr. held the rank of major during the American Revolution, he commonly used and was known by the courtesy title of "General." He served as the deputy quartermaster general of Baltimore during the war. The General was highly regarded in that city, having spent $40,000 of his own money to support the cause of independence. And, yes, he was a good friend of the Marquis de Lafayette, who did visit the General's grave and his widow during an 1824 tour of the United States. The French hero of the American Revolution recalled how his old comrade had "out of his own very limited means supplied me with five hundred dollars to aid in clothing my troops, and whose wife, with her own hands, cut five hundred pairs of pantaloons, and superintended the making of them for the use of my men." David Poe's grandson liked to claim that the revered General was the quartermaster general for the U.S. Army, yet Edgar resisted giving him that promotion in the note for Griswold's collection.

After the war, the General operated a dry goods business in Baltimore. He had hoped that his son and namesake, born July 18, 1784, would become a lawyer. David Poe Jr. tried to dutifully follow the course mapped out for him. He studied law in the office of William Gwynn, an esteemed Baltimore attorney and editor of the *Federal Gazette*, but it wasn't long before he was contemplating a drastic change of course. He and his friends formed a Thespian Club, meeting each week to read and perform plays for themselves and occasional guests. It's difficult to say whether the General was more surprised or angry when his son, not yet twenty, announced he was giving up the law to become an actor. During a business trip to Norfolk, Virginia, he saw a play featuring the young and pretty Eliza Arnold Hopkins. Already bitten by the theater bug, he was now smitten with an actress. David made his stage debut on December 1, 1803, beginning a whirlwind apprenticeship as a roving player. By December 7, he was appearing in his fourth role in seven days, playing a character named Harry Thunder in a play titled *Wild Oats*. Harry, intriguingly enough, breaks with his father to join an itinerant theater troupe. During his first season on the boards, David Poe undertook no fewer than twenty-four roles. On June 30, 1804, it was announced that he would play the ploughman Henry and that Eliza Arnold Hopkins would portray Susan Ashfield in a Richmond production of English playwright Thomas Morton's 1798 comedy, *Speed the Plough*.

Unlike David, Eliza came from a theatrical family. The daughter of English actors Henry and Elizabeth Arnold, both of whom had appeared at London's Covent Garden Theatre, she was born in the spring of 1787. Her father died when she was two. Her mother soldiered on, grooming little Eliza to follow in the profession of her parents. The widowed actress decided to try her luck in the United States, arriving with her daughter in Boston on January 3, 1796. Three months later, nine-year-old Eliza made her American stage debut at Boston's Federal Street Theatre singing English composer William Reeve's "The Market Lass," which had first been performed two years earlier by the songwriter's wife at London's Lyceum Theatre.

> *Health reigns, and rewards daily toil;*
> *I rise at the lark's early song,*
> *And, meeting my swain at the stile,*
> *To market I trip it along.*

A few months later, her mother married singer-musician Charles Tubbs. When Eliza was eleven, she, her mother, and Tubbs were touring with a group called the Charleston Comedians. During a typically rigorous run of bookings that took the company to North Carolina, Eliza's mother fell ill and died. Yellow fever has been cited as the likely cause.

By example and instruction, Elizabeth Arnold had been preparing her daughter for the grueling life of a professional actor. Eliza's mother, a product of the English repertory school of theater, had stressed that actors needed to be both incredibly disciplined and versatile if they wished to find any degree of success. They needed to know a wide variety of roles, and they needed the ability to quickly move with great speed from one part to another, because theater managers made a profit by offering a new play night after night. Company members were required to be comedians, tragedians, singers, dancers, pantomime artists, and character actors, all the while helping out with costumes, scenery, set pieces, props, ticket sales, you name it. And they had to be tough to endure the rigors and brutal conditions of being a wandering player. Remaining in Tubbs's care for about two years, Eliza dedicated herself to not just adding but also mastering valuable talents to her theatrical repertoire. Like her mother, she was made of stern stuff, and the hard work paid off. By the age of fifteen, when she married comedian and character actor Charles Hopkins, also a teenager, Eliza knew an astounding seventy roles. By the age of seventeen, when she was cast with David Poe in *Speed the Plough,* she was well on her way to becoming one of the most popular and promising performers in the country.

David Poe saw a good deal of Eliza and Charles Hopkins throughout the rest of 1804 and into the next year when Charles, also presumably a victim of yellow fever, fell ill in October 1805, dying at twenty in Washington, D.C. A widow at eighteen, Eliza was soon being courted by David. They were married in the spring of 1806, making Boston their home base for three years. After so many years of constant traveling and little in the way of stability, Eliza grew to love the city where, half her lifetime ago, she had launched an American stage career with "The Market Lass." She and David became good friends with another acting couple, Noble Luke and Harriet L'Estrange Usher. And an arrival of a son, William Henry Leonard, called Henry, on January 30, 1807, helped to heal the breach between David and his father. Eliza's fondness for their chosen city found expression in her watercolor painting, *Boston Harbour, morning, 1808.*

But the years in Boston continuously emphasized that her star was burning brighter and brighter while her husband's could barely manage a brief glimmer or two. Eliza was a favorite with American critics and audiences impressed by her remarkable versatility, charmed by her sweet singing voice, beguiled by her graceful dancing, delighted with her willingness to play it for laughs, and captivated by her great beauty. She was described as having raven-black hair, large luminous eyes, a fair complexion, a round face, and a delicate but full figure. The popular and pretty Eliza was lauded for playing everything from Shakespearean roles and romantic leads to comic juveniles and melodramatic heroines. She could appear one night as a distinguished lady of title and the next as a rambunctious tomboy. David looked like her equal. He was handsome and blessed with a good build and a strong voice. But he lacked training, and, according to the overwhelming consensus of the critics, he lacked talent. While Eliza was invariably praised and celebrated, David was lambasted as a dull, inept, and wooden actor. One critic dismissed him as "literally nothing," a judgment that, no matter how warranted, would wreak havoc with the psyche of any actor, no matter how secure. And David Poe hardly was one to endure such criticism with anything resembling equanimity. He was hypersensitive, his temper on a hair trigger. He would threaten to attack the critics who so harshly put down his acting. He would loudly insult audiences who hissed and booed his performances. And he would drink.

The second son, Edgar, might have been named for a Mr. Edgar, an actor and manager with the Charleston Comedians who seemed to have recognized Eliza's abilities and encouraged her. If so, there's something symbolically appropriate there. In many profound ways, theater and a theatrical nature are so much a part of Edgar Poe's heritage. It's deep, deep in his DNA. It is more than just an early and enduring influence on his personality and his writing. It is a birthright.

"When you ponder where the writing came from, I think you start right here," said Poe scholar and English professor Carole Shaffer-Koros. "And it can't be underestimated. His background with both parents, the theater, opened his mind and brain to the arts and the glory of language and the use of words to create a picture. I'm certain he inherited those genes for that capability and inclination. He has the right early environment and the right inheritance to set him on the right path. And the theatrical background never went away. It informs his writing and his personality, and, as an adult, he wins his share of acclaim for his lectures and poetry readings."

Following their third theatrical season in Boston, the Poes moved to New York, beginning their run at the Park Theatre on September 6, 1809, with a play that might have somehow seemed appropriate to their second son as an adult. Eliza had the leading role of Angela in *The Castle Spectre*, a 1797 five-act romantic drama by Matthew Gregory Lewis, perhaps best known today for *The Monk* (his 1796 Gothic novel that was so successful, he was often referred to as Monk Lewis). A proven crowd-pleaser on both sides of the Atlantic, it was packed with most of the standard Gothic elements: a mysterious and foreboding castle, a stalwart and virginal heroine, a wickedly villainous nobleman, a dashing hero, comic supporting characters, melodramatic plot twists, and a resident ghost. No matter what roles the Poes played in New York, however, things for David rapidly turned into a depressing case of different city, same story. Eliza won glowing reviews for most of her performances, particularly those involving singing, dancing, and comedy. David was panned by the critics, some of whom he threatened. And he drank. After six weeks of this, he left the New York theater company and, apparently, the theater. He eventually would leave his wife and his children, but precisely when is unknown. Also in question are the reasons for his departure. The more charitable speculation casts him as an ailing, disillusioned, doomed man in his mid-twenties. In this scenario, he left to safeguard his family and spare them the final months of a fatal illness, presumably tuberculosis. But there is no evidence that he knew he was ill, let alone dying. The more common theory is that he was as ill equipped and ill prepared to shoulder the responsibility of a growing family as he was for a career on the stage. Still, the break with Eliza did not precisely coincide with his break from the acting profession.

And Eliza? She did what she always did, and what her mother always had done: she kept working. Between late October 1809 and her last appearance in New York on July 4, 1810, she had significant roles in about twenty productions. At least five of these plays were by Shakespeare. She played Jessica in *The Merchant of Venice,* the Prince of Wales in *Richard III,* Ophelia in *Hamlet,* Juliet in *Romeo and Juliet,* and Regan in *King Lear.* She then returned to Richmond, opening the season as Angela in *The Castle Spectre* on August 18. A daughter, Rosalie, was born in December, although the precise date has never been determined. Also in doubt is whether David Poe was present for the birth. If he hadn't already deserted his family, he soon would.

Little is known about the care of the Poe children while Eliza was valiantly trying to keep things going as a single mother. What eyewitness tes-

timony does exist was set down well after Edgar Allan Poe's death, when
the witnesses were elderly and decades removed from the memories being
recalled. The Poe children, for instance, were described as both "very pretty
and lively and playful" and "thin, pale and very fretful." There are stories
of an elderly nurse who quieted the children by taking them upon her lap
and feeding "them liberally with bread soaked in gin, when they soon fell
asleep." No doubt. The nurse supposedly admitted that she, "from the very
birth of the girl, freely administered to them gin and other spirituous li-
quors, with sometimes laudanum . . . to put them to sleep when restless."

Eliza, well loved by audiences in the South, continued to find work in
Richmond, Norfolk, and Charleston. She was back on the boards, taking
on arduous parts, just weeks after Rosalie's birth. But by the summer
of 1811, it was clear to reviewers and theatergoers that something was
terribly wrong. She looked gaunt. She looked ill. She was. Although Eliza's discipline and commitment kept her going into what would be her
last theater season, she was fading fast. On October 11, she played the
Countess Wintersen in *The Stranger,* Benjamin Thompson's popular English adaptation of the German melodrama by August von Kotzebue. It
was her final stage appearance. The future social historian of Richmond,
Samuel Mordecai, described what her last days were like in a November
2 letter to his sister:

> A singular fashion prevails here this season—it is—charity. Mrs.
> Poe, who you know is a very handsome woman, happens to be
> very sick, and (having quarreled and parted with her husband)
> is destitute. The most fashionable place of resort, now is—her
> chamber—And the skills of cooks and nurses is exerted to procure
> her delicacies. Several other sick persons also receive a portion of
> these fashionable visits and delicacies—It is a very laudable fash-
> ion and I wish it may last long.

Richmond's *Enquirer* newspaper carried the announcement of a benefit performance for her on November 29. "To the Humane Heart," it

read, "On this night, *Mrs. Poe,* lingering on the bed of disease and surrounded by her children, asks your assistance and *asks it perhaps for the last time.* The Generosity of a Richmond Audience can need no other appeal."

Eliza died on December 8. "By the death of this Lady the Stage has been deprived of one of its chief ornaments," the *Richmond Enquirer* noted in its December 10 edition. "And, to say the least of her, she was an interesting Actress; and never failed to catch the applause and command the admiration of the beholder." She was buried at St. John's Episcopal Church in Richmond.

The cause most often given for her death is tuberculosis, the first signs of which appeared earlier that year during a performance. She was twenty-four. Tradition places Edgar and his siblings at the deathbed. It is likely true, since William Henry Leonard, soon to turn five, remembered her dying farewell. Whether or not they actually watched their mother die, William and Edgar certainly watched her dying. It would have been up close and intensely personal for a delicate child, which Edgar was thought to be. They lived in cramped quarters, and he would have seen the coughing up of blood, the hemorrhaging, and the awful wasting away that would return to haunt him again and again during his life. Not yet three, Edgar had not only been exposed to but also surrounded by four possible causes that would be given for his own death: drink, drugs, poverty, and tuberculosis.

It is believed that David Poe died three days after his estranged wife in Norfolk. His death is shrouded in more mystery than that of his second son, but consumption (tuberculosis), aggravated by alcoholism, has been given as the probable cause. Although, perhaps foolishly, he tried to jump into the acting profession without adequate preparation, he still played 127 roles during his six years on the stage. Biographer Arthur Hobson Quinn estimated that Eliza ended her tragically short career with more than 200 roles to her credit, not counting the many chorus and dancing parts, and she would have played many of those roles multiple times. All of this was during an era when there was no shortage of Americans who viewed actors as lowly, disreputable, immoral types. Yet Edgar, who as a young man had hopes of joining Virginia aristocracy, never disowned his theatrical ancestors. Edgar, who frequently fudged his biography to make his lineage seem more noble and impressive, always spoke of his mother and her standing in the theater with great pride. Typical of these sentiments was a passage he wrote for a piece of theater criticism in 1845: "The writer of this article is himself the son of an actress—has invariably made it his boast—and no earl was ever prouder of his earldom than he of the descent from a woman who, although well-born, hesitated not to consecrate to the drama her brief career of genius and of beauty."

There was much of his mother in Poe. Quinn had no doubt Poe inherited "a spark of genius," as well as "courage and charm," from Eliza. There also was a bit of his father.

"You look at his life and career, and you can see that he inherited a great deal from both parents," said Poe biographer and American literature professor James M. Hutchisson. "Like his father, Poe was hypersensitive, he picked fights that were bad for his career, and he had trouble with alcohol. He never really knew his father, yet he repeats the patterns. From his mother, he inherited that incredible work ethic, her drive, her professional approach to her art, and that versatility. As an actress, she apparently moved from one kind of part to another with the same skill he later moved from genre to genre as a writer. Poe's output as a writer is amazing in its quantity and quality and versatility. The industry and discipline and drive to accomplish all of that is just astonishing, and you see those same qualities in Eliza."

About two years before his own death, Poe confided to a friend that he owed "every good gift of his intellect, & his heart" to his mother. One of the few tangible things Eliza could leave her middle child was her watercolor of Boston Harbor. She had written on the back, "For my little son Edgar, who should ever love Boston, the place of his birth, and where his mother found her *best,* and *most sympathetic friends.*" He didn't. He would, in fact, have an often-troubled relationship with the city of his birth. Instead, he probably reserved the kind of affection his mother described in that inscription for the city where she died. "Richmond remained very dear to him," Hutchisson said. "And it's not as if things always go well for him in Richmond. It's not as if there aren't negative associations with Richmond. But I do think it became and stayed the city of his heart."

Edgar was also given a miniature portrait of his mother and a few of her letters. She was the first of the idealized women in his life he would lose. As has been noted and discussed by many a Poe scholar and biographer, frail but strong-willed women who die young figure in many of his stories and poems.

The most pressing question after Eliza's death was what would become of her three orphaned children. William Henry Leonard was taken in by David Poe's parents in Baltimore. Rosalie, about a year old when her mother died, was immediately taken in by Richmond merchant William Mackenzie and his wife, Jane. And Edgar became the foster child of a Richmond couple known for their benevolence, John and Frances "Fanny" Allan. They had Edgar baptized on January 7, 1812, with themselves as his godparents (which is how Allan became his middle name). The section of his autobiographical note dealing with this time was another exercise in falsification and fabrication: "Mr. John Allan, a very wealthy gentleman of Richmond, Va., took a fancy to me, and persuaded my grandfather, Gen. Poe, to suffer him to adopt me. Was brought up in Mr. A's family, and regarded always as his son and heir."

Not quite. First, it was Allan's wife who genuinely took a fancy to him. It is believed that Fanny was one of the charitable women who cared for Eliza in her dying days, bringing her food and delicacies. Second, the Allans were not yet very wealthy by Richmond society standards, but they were well off, and they promised Edgar's grandparents that they would give him a good liberal education. The General, who was not well off, was willing to be persuaded. How much John Allan needed to be persuaded to take in young Edgar is unclear. He may have been pushed by the Mackenzies as well as by his wife. Certainly the childless Fanny's heart went out to the boy who had lost both parents and was being separated from both of his siblings. John Allan's feelings likely were more ambiguous and complicated. Although he believed in helping the poor and hungry, Allan despised dependency, which he saw as weakness of character. Although himself an orphan who greatly benefited from others' help and support, he viewed himself as a self-made man and, as such, was fond of quoting proverbs and maxims about piety, fortitude, and perseverance. He was also a cautious man, and that caution seems evident in his calculated decision to never formally adopt Edgar. Nor was Edgar Poe regarded as Allan's son and heir.

Even though the Allan name got placed between Edgar and Poe, it was a name given with reservations by the foster father and ultimately rejected by a young man made to feel that he had never been fully accepted. Edgar, who had an aching need for unconditional love, had been taken into the home of a man incapable of either recognizing that need or providing it. As Poe biographer Kenneth Silverman put it, "In being John Allan's ward, he became dependent on the care and generosity of someone who despised dependence and felt that he had been cheated of care and generosity himself." It was a bad combination and a guarantee that, the older Edgar got, the more the emotional gulf and bitterness between them would grow.

John Allan was born in Irvine, a town on the west coast of Scotland, in 1779. He immigrated to Richmond in January 1795. Five years later, he formed a partnership with Charles Ellis, exporting Virginia tobacco. They also dealt in wheat, cornmeal, paint, clothing, coffee, wine, and many other goods. They imported tombstones. And they hired out older slaves to work in coal mines—work in a kind of buried-alive state until they died.

In 1803, Allan married Frances Keeling Valentine, who was eighteen years old, delicate, pretty, sweet-natured, and high-spirited. Fanny's letters to her husband reveal a playfulness that is endearing, especially when teasing or kidding the rough, hot-tempered merchant. She was also nervous, accident-prone, and often ill. They lived above the Ellis & Allan store on the corner of Main and Thirteenth Streets, and it was in this home that Edgar turned three in January 1812. The early years with the Allans gave little hint of the stormy times to follow. Edgar was petted and doted on by Fanny and her sister, Nancy. Fanny, also an orphan, seems to have persuaded her husband to share in the spoiling of the boy described by Richmond neighbors as "a lovely little fellow, with dark curls and brilliant eyes, dressed like a young prince, and charming every one by his childish grace, vivacity, and cleverness." Given the affection lavished on him by Fanny and the material comforts provided by John Allan, Edgar naturally would have believed he had found a family and a home where he was considered a true son and heir.

Edgar grew into a precocious "rosy-faced boy" with a "wonderfully rich and splendid imagination." In his preteen years, he often proved a delight to both of his foster parents.

Already exhibiting a great curiosity and a flair for the dramatic, traits he would nurture throughout his life, he was not dissuaded by the Allans from performing for amused and enchanted visitors. He would recite passages from poems he had committed to memory, impressing guests with his earnest and moving delivery. He'd stand on the dining room table in his stocking feet, toasting the ladies with sweetened wine. And he could read the newspaper by the age of five.

Yet, for all of the early advantages he enjoyed, Edgar was denied the emotional stability of a consistently close and reliable parental relationship. There was a distance between each of the Allans and Edgar. With the loving and devoted Fanny, this was due to her frequent illnesses and periods of confinement. With John Allan, it was because of his aloof and exacting personality. Allan likely viewed himself as more of a benefactor than a father, congratulating himself on taking in and then providing so generously for an orphaned child. Hardly a model of constancy, Allan must have confused Edgar with bewildering mixed signals. He was bolstered by praise and coddling one moment, then crushed by scolding and reprimanding the next.

Allan did, however, make good on his promise that Edgar would receive an education. The day after the boy's fifth birthday, Allan paid a four-dollar tuition bill to a teacher named Clotilda Fisher. The next year, Edgar was attending the Richmond school run by William Ewing, who would describe him as "a charming boy."

The War of 1812 was still raging when Edgar started his formal education, and a nervous Richmond, although concerned about threats of a possible British raid, was spared armed conflict. But the war had badly hurt trade for merchants like Allan, and, in September 1814, British troops were unsuccessfully trying to take Baltimore. The old patriot David Poe Sr., then in his early seventies, was ready and willing to help organize the city's defenses. Hostilities with Britain officially ended with the Senate's February 1815 ratification of the Treaty of Ghent, and Allan moved quickly to open a London office of Ellis & Allan. It was a bold step to greatly increase the business and prestige of the company. In May, he paid two dollars for a new suit of clothes for Edgar. In June, he auctioned off many of the family's household furnishings and personal items, including rugs, mirrors, and a spyglass. On June 22, he wrote to Charles Ellis, instructing him to sell Scipio, a slave, for six hundred dollars and to hire other slaves out at fifty dollars a year. The next day, he boarded the steamship *Lothiar* with Fanny, Nancy, and six-year-old Edgar, who asked that it be recorded that he "was not afraid of coming across the Sea." Fanny was apprehensive, though, and the thirty-four-day voyage from Norfolk to Liverpool did little to calm her fears. Fanny, predictably enough, was very sick. Water was tightly rationed. Their cabin conditions were cramped and uncomfortable, with Allan forced to sleep on the floor. And digestible meals were an iffy proposition. Allan complained that the stingy Captain Stone denied his wife and sister-in-law "the privileges of Fire to broil a slice of Bacon." They bid a relieved farewell to the *Lothiar* on July 28, and, after visiting relatives in Scotland, settled in London.

In April 1816, enrolled as Edgar Allan and assumed by most to be the Allans' adopted son, Edgar entered the Chelsea boarding school run by the Misses Dubourg. He studied spelling, history, and geography. He also latched on to the name Dubourg, using it for one of the witnesses in "The Murders in the Rue Morgue." In 1818, Edgar switched to the Manor House boarding school run by the Reverend John Bransby. It was four miles north of London, in the village of Stoke Newington. And it was here that Edgar's gift for languages blossomed. He excelled at Latin and Greek. Bransby would describe him as "intelligent, wayward and willful." The adult Poe would use both the school and Bransby for one of his finest short stories, "William Wilson." The school is described as solemn and gloomy. The principal, the Reverend Dr. Bransby, has "a sour visage" and dresses "in snuffy habiliments." Asked by a later pupil for his recollections of the student he knew as Edgar Allan, Bransby steered clear of his unflattering depiction in "William Wilson," allowing that "Edgar Allan was a quick and clever boy and would have been a very good boy if he had not been spoilt by his parents, but they spoilt him, and allowed him an extravagant amount of pocket-money, which enabled him to get into all manner of mischief—still I liked the boy—poor fellow, his parents spoilt him!"

While Bransby may have found Edgar willful, Allan, at this point, found much to praise in his foster son. In a March 1818 letter, Allan wrote, "Edgar is a fine Boy and I have no reason to complain of his progress." A month later, he wrote, "Edgar is a fine Boy and reads Latin pretty sharply." The tone of approval and pride continued in Allan's letters home to Richmond: "Edgar is growing wonderfully, & enjoys a good reputation and is both able & willing to receive instruction . . . he is a verry fine Boy & a good scholar."

The five incredibly formative years Edgar spent in England had a profound effect on his imagination, and echoes from that time can be found again and again in his fiction. For instance, the Allans moved to better living quarters at 39 Southampton Row in September 1817, and he'd use that precise address for the narrator of his 1840 story "Why the Little Frenchman Wears His Hand in a Sling." But he also saw his share of impressive and ruined mansions, cemeteries, estates, and abbeys. What he experienced from ages six to eleven provided him with a marvelous storehouse of names, addresses, and settings that he could draw on for tales of horror, humor, and mystery.

"They're living near the British Museum," said Poe scholar J. Gerald Kennedy. "He's surrounded by antiquities, Egyptian mummies, the church with the churchyard where Bransby took the boys to hear the weekly sermon. It's also during this time that there's the first sense of a youthful alienation. This is going to deepen as he gets older."

Edgar's great curiosity and imagination were further stirred by an introduction to the works of Shakespeare and a fascination with Daniel Defoe's 1719 novel, *Robinson Crusoe*. The precocious reader carried the influence of Defoe back to America, launching his own fantastic voyages, making the wondrous utterly absorbing and seemingly possible. Shipwrecks frame the narratives for such tales as "MS. Found in a Bottle" and "A Descent Into the Maelström," as well as Poe's only novel, *The Narrative of Arthur Gordon Pym*. Poe scholar Kennedy believes it's probable that, during the English sojourn, Edgar also read Sir Walter Scott and issues of the new *Blackwood's Magazine*, with its popular mix of essays, satirical pieces, stinging criticism, and, eventually, horror stories. Each was a form Poe would tackle, and, in the case of the terror tales, satirize with the comic piece "How to Write a Blackwood Article."

Reading also provided Edgar with a necessary means of escape as things became increasingly difficult for John and Fanny Allan in London. Unhappy in England and missing her Richmond friends, Fanny succumbed to one illness after another. Some might have been imagined, but almost all resulted in long periods when she was unavailable to Edgar. Meanwhile, John Allan, distant under the best of circumstances, was working long hours to put the London office on solid footing. At first, this effort seemed destined for success. Stormy conditions beyond his ability to control or avoid, however, were hurtling him toward his own disastrous shipwreck. The financial panic of 1819 in the United States, coupled with the collapse of the London tobacco market, made failure inevitable. Allan was saddled with inventory he couldn't sell and mounting debts he couldn't pay. Still, he faced the financial storm with admirable stoicism and resolve. His stated conviction was, "If we are doomed to Fall let us Fall like men." He maintained his composure, but he could not save his business. With the fall of the house of Allan upon them, Fanny rallied, responding with uncharacteristic fortitude and reassurance. Allan noted with a mix of pleasure and surprise that she remained calm and optimistic, even as collapse seemed imminent. It was, however, time to admit defeat and head home; the Richmond part of the business might still be saved. They left England in June 1820, boarding the *Martha* at Liverpool for a thirty-one-day voyage to New York.

Back in Richmond on August 2, the family moved into the home of John Allan's business partner, Charles Ellis. Edgar, again using the last name of Poe, was enrolled that fall in the school of Joseph H. Clarke, described by Poe biographer Jeffrey Meyers as "a hot tempered and pedantic Irish bachelor." Eleven-year-old Edgar arrived feeling more than a little vain about his travels and English education, both of which made him feel superior to the boys around him. Clarke quizzed him on his Latin and was immediately impressed with the new student's ability to decline an adjective. Edgar had also returned from England an aspiring poet, and here, too, Clarke was impressed. During his time at Clarke's school he read Ovid, Caesar, Virgil, Cicero, and Horace in Latin, as well as Homer in Greek. Clarke recalled that Edgar had no great love for mathematics, but his poems were widely regarded as the best in the school. While most of the students "wrote mere mechanical verses, Poe wrote genuine poetry: the boy was a born poet." In an 1876 letter written to Poe biographer E. L. Didier, Clarke gave a summary of Edgar's personality:

> As to Edgar's disposition and character as a boy, though playful as most boys, his general deportment differed in some respects from others. He was remarkable for self-respect without haughtiness, strictly just and correct in his demeanor with his fellow playmates, which rendered him a favorite even with those above his years. His natural and predominant passion seemed to me, to be an enthusiastic ardor in everything he undertook; in his difference of opinion with his fellow students, he was very tenacious, and would not yield till his judgment was convinced. As a scholar he was ambitious to excel, and tho' not conspicuously studious

always acquitted himself well in his classes. His imaginative powers seemed to take precedence of all his other faculties. . . . He
had a sensitive and tender heart, and would strain every nerve to
oblige a friend.

To Clarke, Edgar's "nature was entirely free from selfishness, the pre-
dominant quality of boyhood." The teacher's recognition of a prodigy
prompted Edgar to show him a collection of poems he wished to have published. "Even in those early years," the schoolmaster recalled, "Edgar Poe
displayed the germs of that wonderfully rich and splendid imagination,
which has placed him in the front rank of the purely imaginative poets
of the world." Yet Clarke advised Allan against having them published: "I
told him that Edgar was of a very excitable temperament, that he possessed
a great deal of self-esteem, and that it would be very injurious to the boy
to allow him to be flattered and talked about as the author of a printed
book at his age." Allan followed his advice. When Clarke left Richmond in
1823, William Burke's Seminary for Boys welcomed most of his students,
including fourteen-year-old Edgar.

No brooding, sickly loner during these years, Edgar was athletic,
playful, and popular. One classmate, John S. L. Preston, described him
as "the swiftest runner, the best boxer, and the most daring swimmer at
Clarke's school . . . a generous, free-hearted boy, kind to his companions,
and always ready to assist them with his hand and head." More than
twenty-five years after Poe's death, another classmate, Andrew Johnston,
recalled, "At the time, Poe was slight in person and figure, but well made,
active, sinewy, and graceful." In athletic exercises, Johnston said, Edgar
was "the most daring," and his poetry, admired by them all, could have
a satirical edge.

The stories of his athletic prowess suggest a stronger constitution than
Poe is credited with in the stereotyped imagery. His most notable athletic
achievement, which gained him some local celebrity, was swimming six
miles in the James River, part of it against a strong tide. Done because of
a wager made under a blazing sun on an oppressively hot June day, the

feat began at Ludlam's Wharf near Mayo's Bridge and ended at a location known as Warwick Bar. Poe recalled this happened in 1824, meaning he was fifteen. Although he emerged from the James River badly sunburned, with a blistered back, neck, and face, he did not seem at all fatigued to his friends who had accompanied him in boats. In fact, he walked back home to Richmond. The adult Poe would compare the feat to Lord Byron swimming from Abydos to Sestos in Turkey, which the English poet said was inspired by the Greek myth of Leander.

Another display of athleticism was remembered by fellow Burke student Creed Thomas. It apparently got back to Edgar that a classmate named Miles C. Selden had told someone Poe was a liar and a rascal. Fighting words, to be sure. And a fight was arranged. The bigger, heavier Miles pummeled his adversary for a while, cruising to what the spectators believed would be an easy victory. Edgar was employing a tactic Muhammad Ali would later dub the rope-a-dope. He allowed his opponent to flail away, wearing himself out. When the unsuspecting Miles grew tired, Edgar pounced, administering a sound beating and "showing him a few things in the art of fighting."

Small wonder that Edgar was regarded so highly by so many classmates and neighborhood boys. "No boy ever had a greater influence over me than he had," Thomas Ellis, the son of John Allan's business partner, said in a statement that appeared in the *Richmond Standard*. "He was, indeed, a leader among boys, but my admiration for him scarcely knew bounds." Thomas was particularly impressed when Edgar, a lieutenant in the Junior Morgan Riflemen, a volunteer company of boys, was chosen to participate in the procession for the Marquis de Lafayette's October 1824 visit to Richmond. Edgar and his fellow riflemen were reviewed by Lafayette, who, earlier in the month, had visited the grave of David Poe Sr. in Baltimore. Edgar's grandfather had died in 1816. Recalling his friend in the riflemen uniform during Richmond's ceremonies honoring Lafayette, Thomas would say, "Never was I prouder of him."

Among many of his comrades, however, the admiration and recognition came with qualifications and reservations. He lived in a class-conscious world where he would be accepted but only so far, which was the same attitude suggested by Allan's treatment of him. And adolescence is when a sensitive soul is most likely to feel—or be made to feel—unworthy, alienated, excluded, marginalized, insecure, disrespected, different. Behind all the praise for poetic and athletic prowess, there were whispers and inferences that, increasingly, Edgar could not ignore.

John S. L. Preston, the classmate who cheered Edgar's running, swimming, boxing, and generosity, also delved into the dark side of these years:

> At the time of which I speak, Richmond was one of the most aristocratic cities on this side of the Atlantic. . . . A school is, of its nature, democratic; but still boys will unconsciously bear about the odour of their fathers' notions, good or bad. Of Edgar Poe it was known that his parents had been players, and that he was dependent upon the bounty that is bestowed upon an adopted son. All this had the effect of making the boys decline his leadership and on looking back on it since, I fancy it gave him a fierceness he would otherwise not have had.

Differing from most accounts of Poe at this age, Preston said he found his intellectual classmate to be "self-willed, capricious, inclined to be imperious, and though of generous impulses, not steadily kind, or even amiable." Ability, accomplishment, and intelligence weren't enough in the Richmond Preston described, and the unfairness must have gone down with especial bitterness to someone with such a drive to succeed, to excel, to be recognized.

"Growing up in Richmond, Poe would have been exposed to the culture here, and greatly shaped by it," said Chris Semtner, curator of the Edgar Allan Poe Museum in Richmond. "The planter class, which gave us so many of our first presidents, was still on the top in terms of status in Virginia, and Poe aspired to be part of that class. During this time, he wrote a poem ridiculing another kid who had affections for the same girl. He wrote this poem basically saying how dare this kid from the merchant class have such feelings. It's incredibly pretentious since he's not part of the planter class. He's living with foster parents who haven't legally adopted him, and his foster father is a Scottish immigrant and a merchant. The planter class still looks at the merchant class with some suspicion and looks down on them. So here's Poe trash talking someone for being basically what he is. Poe is of Richmond, but he's not. He's of the merchant class, but he's not. He always seems to be straddling different worlds. He seems to have the ability to be on the inside yet remain the outsider at the same time."

The sense of youthful alienation first evident in London was magnified in Richmond. The teenage Edgar responds to this with a duality that sets in motion a pattern we see again and again throughout his life. He begins to romanticize the role of the loner, taking on the imperious stance Preston noted. The dynamic and free-thinking poet Lord Byron increasingly becomes a hero and role model to him. He views himself as separated from the masses not by class but by intellect, sensitivity, and genius. Yet, at the same time, he craves a place in the august circles where he is granted admittance but never full acceptance. This is true in Richmond. And it will be true when he feels both superior to and shunned by the leading guardians of literary tastes later in his life. He is, at the same time, as Semtner notes, an insider, allowed to participate and observe to some extent, and an outsider, made to feel he's not truly of those worlds. It's a terrible place to be for an orphan coping with the angst and anxieties of being a teenager, just as it is for a struggling writer who fully understands how good he is. The insider-outsider dynamic, however, can be an ideal place for a creative writer. If Shakespeare was an actor and poet allowed into the inner circles of earls and dukes, he occupied the very same type of insider-outsider role. After Poe, Mark Twain will be the comedian permitted enough access to mature into a deceptively versatile literary artist as yet another kind of insider-outsider. Almost all of the barriers that Poe saw as curses for an aspiring Southern aristocrat were unrecognized blessings for a fledgling writer.

"Poe is mingling with all different classes in Richmond," said Semtner, author of *Edgar Allan Poe's Richmond: The Raven in the River City.* "There are his classmates in the school. There are neighborhood boys. He's in the junior rifleman company. There are even reports that he was in a boy gang. And there are descriptions of him putting on amateur stage productions, and this would have greatly upset the rising class that John Allan is part of. So it's possible that Poe is trying to occupy a lot of different worlds at the same time. It allows him to observe a lot of human nature across a wide spectrum."

As part of him imagined a future in the Virginia aristocracy, another part clung tenaciously to the proud realization that his last name was Poe and that he was the son of actors. Worshipful boyhood comrade Thomas Ellis recalled Edgar leading schoolmate Creed Thomas in a theatrical performance staged under a tent on a vacant lot—admission, one cent. It would have been the kind of venture certain to raise John Allan's blood pressure several points, but the more Edgar progressed into his teen years, the fewer complimentary things his foster father had to say about him. In fact, in his letters, Allan often falls to complaining about Edgar. To Henry Poe, Edgar's brother, Allan describes the fifteen-year-old as "miserable, sulky & ill-tempered to all the Family." Allan writes that "why I have put up so long with his conduct is little less than wonderful." He then adds, "The boy possesses not a Spark of affection for us not a particle of gratitude for all my care and kindness toward him. I have given him a much superior Education than I ever received myself." He finds solace in the notion that, despite the boy's ingratitude, he finds his own behavior beyond reproach. "Had I done my duty as faithfully to my God as I have to Edgar," Allan tells Henry, then death would have "no terrors for me."

Allan was not the first or the last parent to have watched bewildered as a delightful child turned into a morose and moody teenager. Yet more than being utterly perplexed by Edgar's dark moods, he resented them. There is a self-serving coldness in what he writes to Henry, largely because his complaints are those of someone who has offered charity, not the love and understanding of a parent. Edgar's great crime, after all, is not being grateful. Edgar is categorized as a duty. A parent may be patient and understanding with a cross and melancholy adolescent, but a bene-factor is apt to lose patience with a ward viewed primarily as the recipient of largesse. John Hamilton Mackenzie, the son of the Richmond couple who had provided a home for Edgar's sister, recalled that Allan never let Edgar forget "his dependence on his charity."

It's also clear that Edgar held significantly more affection toward Fanny Allan. While her chronic illnesses surely deprived him of the closer relationship he needed, there is no record of anything like an es-trangement between them. Indeed, his genuine devotion to Fanny greatly increased his antipathy toward her husband. By this time, the youth with romantic notions of ideal love probably would have heard about John Allan's infidelities. The cheating, perhaps justified in Allan's mind by Fanny's health problems, began soon after their marriage, and an illegitimate son, Edward Collier, was born before Edgar.

It was during this period that Edgar suffered another loss that un-doubtedly triggered fits of melancholia. In April 1823, the then fourteen-year-old was invited to visit the home of his friend Robert Craig Stanard. He was introduced to Robert's mother, Jane Stanard. Poe described the moment to Sarah Helen Whitman, who recorded it in her 1860 book, *Edgar Poe and His Critics*: "This lady, on entering the room, took his hand and spoke some gentle and gracious words of welcome, which so penetrated the sensitive heart of the orphan boy as to deprive him of the power of speech." To the infatuated Edgar, she was "the first purely ideal love of my soul" and "the truest, tenderest of this world's beautiful most womanly souls, and an angel to my forlorn and darkened nature." She was the sympathetic mother figure Fanny Allan couldn't be. She was a confidante, and her home became a refuge where he could be consoled and comforted. In Jane, who suffered from depression and bouts of melancholy, he found a kindred spirit. He was devastated when she died at the age of thirty-one, about a year after they'd met. Diagnosed as mentally unbalanced, she slipped further and further into insanity over the last few months of her life. The cause of her mental illness is unknown, as is the cause of her death. What is known is that Poe gave way to the grief over losing another loving and idealized woman. After her death, he began to suffer from nightmares in which an icy hand would touch his face in a completely dark room. Or he would be haunted by the fear of awakening to find a ghastly face just inches from his own. He took to visiting Jane's grave in Shockoe Hill Cemetery, "where the object of his boyish idolatry lay entombed," Whitman wrote. "The thought of her—sleeping there in her loneliness—filled his heart with a profound incommunicable sorrow. When the nights were very dreary and cold, when the autumnal rains fell and the winds, wailed mournfully over the graves, he lingered longest and came away most regretfully." Her memory inspired the poem "To Helen."

Although it is a mistake to confuse Poe with his deranged, often unreliable narrators, there's no question he drew on experience and deep emotions for some of his best poems and stories. It is difficult not to feel the growing sense of alienation in the stanzas of a poem he wrote in 1829, at just twenty, titled "Alone":

> From childhood's hour I have not been
> As others were—I have not seen
> As others saw—I could not bring
> My passions from a common spring—
> From the same source I have not taken
> My sorrow—I could not awaken
> My heart to joy at the same tone—
> And all I lov'd—I lov'd alone—

Allan was not the man to have much tolerance for such sentiments. Buck up and apply yourself to work—anything else was weakness of character. Allan had been trying to stare down adversity ever since his company's London office went bust. The company's debt was enormous, and Allan got out from under it only through the support and help of his fabulously rich uncle, William Galt. The partnership with Ellis was dissolved, and, when Galt died on March 26, 1825, he left his nephew an immense fortune. Three months later, Allan purchased Moldavia, a brick mansion on the corner of Main and Fifth Streets.

"It was symbolic of the rise of the merchants over the planter class," Semtner said. "When one of the oldest and most prestigious families in Virginia, the Randolphs, had to sell one of their mansions in Richmond, Moldavia, it was purchased by a Spanish merchant named Joseph Gallego, who then sold it to John Allan. There are merchants in a planter's house, and the letters written at the time expressed how scandalized the planters are that these people are taking over their property and, really, taking over their world."

Edgar had left Burke's school in March and then started attending a school run by Dr. and Mrs. Ray Thomas. That summer, sixteen-year-old Edgar fell in love with Sarah Elmira Royster, a fifteen-year-old neighbor. She would remember him as "a beautiful boy" whose "general manner was sad." She also recalled that he "was devoted to the first Mrs. Allan [Fanny] and she to him." Elmira apparently was just as smitten with him, and they were secretly engaged when, in February 1826, Edgar left Richmond to attend the University of Virginia in Charlottesville. But James Royster, Elmira's father, disapproved of the relationship. Learning of the engagement and determined to sabotage it, he intercepted Edgar's letters to Elmira, allowing his daughter to reach the bruising conclusion that she had been callously dumped and forgotten. Believing that to be the case, she married successful Richmond businessman Alexander Shelton in 1827. She was seventeen. Edgar responded with one of his earliest published poems, "Song," which saw print the same year as Elmira's marriage:

> *I saw thee on thy bridal day—*
> *When a burning blush came o'er thee,*

A romantic flourish born of imagination and hurt pride? Perhaps, but Elmira would later say, "I married another man, but the love of my life was Edgar Poe. I never loved anyone else."

Opened the previous October, the University of Virginia was a rough, unfinished campus where professors had good reason to fear attacks by rowdy, spoiled students from aristocratic families. Drinking, gambling, brawling, dueling, pranking, and the occasional student riot had given Thomas Jefferson's brainchild a dangerous reputation when seventeen-year-old Poe showed up to take residence in room 13 of the West Range dormitory. There probably is some justification to Poe's accusations that his foster father had set him up to fail. Whether deliberate or not, Allan, now wealthy beyond his dreams, had sent Poe to Charlottesville on a tight budget. He was surrounded by classmates from affluent families, and they had no problem finding extra cash to support the niceties and necessities of a privileged student's lifestyle. Poe, on the other hand, lacked sufficient funds to pay his school fees and living expenses. He also lacked the kind of resources needed to keep up with the sons of Virginia's rich and famously class conscious. "I will boldly say that it was wholly and entirely your own mistaken parsimony that caused all the difficulties in which I was involved at Charlottesville," he wrote Allan a few years later. "The expenses of the institution at the lowest estimate were $350 per annum. You sent me there with $110." Perpetually short of money, he made the disastrous mistake of taking to gambling, which only resulted in mounting debts. His losses at card playing were reported to be more than $2,000, although the precise number has been debated. He also experienced his first debilitating encounters with alcohol, and it is here we get the earliest reports of him quickly getting drunk after charging down one glass of wine.

But his classes allowed him to pursue a passion and talent for language, ancient and modern. "He was only at the University of Virginia for nine months, but all his courses were language courses: French, German, Spanish, Latin, and Greek, and he must have been doing some Italian as well," said Jerome McGann, a University of Virginia professor emeritus and the author of *The Poet Edgar Allan Poe: Alien Angel*. "The gambling and drinking are what dominate the discussion, but his intellectual life at the University of Virginia has been largely ignored. Poe was studying with the first professor of modern languages teaching at any university in the United States. George Wilhem Blaettermann was a German scholar, and he introduced Poe to the most advanced theoretical school of German romanticism at the time. It had a profound influence on the poetry as well as the fiction."

Descriptions by classmates range from "pretty wild" to "sober, quiet and orderly." An account given by one of those classmates, Miles George, suggests both extremes could be true:

> Poe, as has been said, was fond of quoting poetic authors and reading poetic productions of his own, with which his friends were delighted & entertained, then suddenly a change would come over him & he would with a piece of charcoal evince his versatile genius by sketching upon the walls of his dormitory, whimsical, fanciful & grotesque figures, with so much artistic skill, as to leave us in doubt whether Poe in future life would be Painter or Poet; He was very excitable & restless, at times wayward, melancholic & morose, but again—in his better moods frolicksome, full of fun & a most attractive and agreeable companion.

Allan refused to pay Poe's gambling debts or to continue subsidizing a university education for an ingrate he felt unworthy of such magnanimity. After exams in December, Poe was expected to return to Richmond and work for free in one of Allan's counting houses (the offices where the financial books of a business are kept). He also returned to learn that Elmira was engaged to someone else. The relationship with his foster father, already bitterly strained, hit its breaking point in March. Poe had either determined to leave Moldavia or was being thrown out by Allan. He poured his hot feelings into a letter listing his grievances with Allan, saying, "My determination is at length taken—to leave your house and indeavor to find some place in this wide world, where I will be treated—not as you have treated me." There undoubtedly was more than some truth in a later passage: "Again, I have heard you say (when you little thought I was listening and therefore must have said it in earnest) that you had no affection for me." Typical of later angry letters sent to Allan and others, he manages to slip in a request for money. He had a knack for following insults, accusations, and recriminations with a plea for badly needed funds. Perhaps not the wisest of strategies. He also had the habit of melodramatically adding darks hints about how, if aid was not forthcoming, some dark fate was certain to overtake him.

"I MUST DIE"

JULY 7–13, 1849

Poe seemed to be settling down after his agitated Monday appearance at artist John Sartain's Philadelphia studio. The patient and caring Sartain kept watch over Poe, relieved that Poe's distressed ramblings had given way to rational conversation. A couple of days after their evening excursion into the darkness, Sartain believed his friend was much improved and well on his way to recovery. Before the week was out, however, Poe was again in sorry shape, physically and emotionally. He was still in Philadelphia, and death was very much on his mind as he wrote to his mother-in-law on Saturday, July 7, 1849: "I have been *so* ill—have had the cholera, or spasms quite as bad, and can now hardly hold the pen. . . . It is no use to reason with me *now*; I must die." He also related to Maria Clemm that he had "no desire to live since I have done 'Eureka,'" a forty-thousand-word rumination on cosmology that he considered his crowning achievement. Was he still suffering from the delirium tremens or some other condition caused by yet another disastrously timed encounter with alcohol? Had he contracted cholera? Or was there some underlying health problem that the drinking had exacerbated?

"It sure looks like at some point he was treated for cholera, whether he actually had it or not," said Stephen Macko, a University of Virginia professor whose areas of specialty include biogeochemistry, marine organic chemistry, stable isotope geochemistry, isotope geometry, and isotopic hair analysis. Known as "the hair detective," Macko has tested the hair of everyone from George Washington to Ötzi the Iceman (the natural glacier mummy of a man who lived between 3400 and 3100 BC). In 2017, he used the latest scientific testing techniques to analyze a sample of Poe's hair cut from his head immediately after his death.

"The custom was to save snips of hair when someone died, and several people cut snips of Poe's hair," Macko said. "The mercury was there from the medicine he was given during the cholera epidemic [of 1849]. Mercury was a catch-all for a lot of diseases, from cholera to syphilis. And, actually, the mercury might have killed you as well as the disease. It wasn't improbable that you could die from mercury poisoning instead of the disease. It was probably not only useless, it was dangerous. But it shows up in Poe's hair."

Cholera outbreaks hit several cities in the United States that year, with thousands dying in New York, St. Louis, Nashville, and New Orleans. It was believed to have been spread by Irish immigrant ships. Poe would have been given calomel, a mercury chloride mineral that was a widely prescribed medicine during the Victorian era. It was used to treat not only cholera and syphilis but also typhoid fever, mumps, dysentery, and constipation. An earlier test on Poe's hair, designed by Baltimore environmental health engineer Albert Donnay, was performed in 2002 by Dr. John Ejnik and Dr. Jose Centeno at the Department of Environmental and Toxicologic Pathology, United States Armed Forces Institute of Pathology, in Washington, D.C. It showed that Poe's mercury level had increased during the last months of his life by 264 percent. Although that might sound alarming, it nonetheless was about thirty times below the level where mercury poisoning symptoms typically develop. The two-inch hair sample used in this 2002 test was from a cutting taken after his death. There is a significant range to normal hair growth, however, so the estimate is that the two-inch strand represented about three to five months of his life. But we can't be sure which three to five months, since there's no way of knowing how close to the scalp the cutting was made. Still, given the strong likelihood that he took calomel in Philadelphia about three months before his death, the reason for the mercury spike detected in 2002 seems obvious.

Those who have put syphilis forward as a possible cause for Poe's death might argue that the presence of mercury supports their case. But, despite the malicious rumors and charges made by enemies after his death, there never has been any evidence that Poe was sexually promiscuous. There's also no record of Poe complaining of the symptoms of syphilis in its early stages, like sores, rash, ulcers, and hair loss. Cholera, or the threat of it all around him in Philadelphia, remains the best-guess reason for the presence of mercury in his hair. Typically spread through infected water supplies, the bacterial disease of the small intestine causes severe vomiting and diarrhea. If he'd had cholera, he sure would have known it. Both because of the summer heat and epidemic, the city streets Poe wandered were anything but crowded. While it wasn't, by any means, a ghost town, it was a city on edge. Wandering the sparsely populated streets in the summer heat, Poe would have encountered one window after another with cholera warnings, notices, and bulletins. When the epidemic was over, the death toll in Philadelphia was relatively small compared to other cities. Credit for this was given to the expansion of the water system in the Fairmount District Poe and Sartain had visited. So while it's entirely possible that Poe contracted cholera, the 2002 tests rule out that he died of mercury poisoning.

How long Poe stayed with Sartain is uncertain, so there's no way of knowing where he was when the despairing letter of July 7 was written. Around July 10, he rebounded more fully from the nightmare state he now was willing to admit had been fueled by alcohol. "All was hallucination, arising from an attack which I had never experienced—an attack of *mania-á-potu*," he wrote to Muddy, using the Latin phrase for madness from drinking (usually taken to mean delirium tremens). "May Heaven grant that it prove a warning to me for the rest of my days. If so, I shall not regret even the horrible unspeakable torments I have endured."

His missing valise turned up at the train depot. But the two lectures he had packed for presentation in Richmond were missing. "Oh, Mother, think of the blow to me this evening, when on examining the valise, these lectures were gone," he lamented to the ever-sympathetic Muddy. "All my object here is over unless I can recover them or re-write one of them."

But had Poe endured a bout of delirium tremens? It was an easy assumption for many biographers to make, just as it would have been an easy assumption for Poe to make. There's no way of knowing if Poe had such classic symptoms as temperature elevation, tremors, rapid heartbeat, heavy sweating, and light sensitivity. He did have the severe confusion, agitation, and hallucinations often caused by the abrupt withdrawal from alcohol in a system physically dependent on its presence. Still, many of the candidates suggested for Poe's death have a similar effect on the central nervous system. "I think the symptoms suggest some kind of neurological infection," said Scott Peeples, the College of Charleston professor who coedited *The Oxford Handbook of Edgar Allan Poe*. "There are the hallucinations, which he was not prone to throughout his life."

There's no question that alcohol was a continuing problem for Poe throughout his adult life. Yet we have no idea whether, during this period of his life or any other, he was drinking enough to cause the kind of physical dependency that results in the DTs. Another problem with this assumption is that withdrawal symptoms typically begin two to four days after alcohol consumption starts. If Poe had been drinking as soon as he arrived in Philadelphia, and the wild visions he described began in Moyamensing Prison, then the delirium and the hallucinations were immediate. Poe's nervous system very well could have been under attack before he started drinking. The uncertainty of the timeline makes any Dupin-like deduction tricky business.

What does seem fairly certain is that he saw more of Sartain during his unexpectedly prolonged stay in Philadelphia. Henry Graham Ashmead, eleven at the time, remembered being in the office of *Sartain's Union Magazine* that July. He was looking at one of the imported steel prints reproduced in the periodical, headquartered in a building on the northwest corner of Walnut and Third Streets. He noticed a fellow, looking rather the worse for wear, in conversation with the magazine's literary editor, John S. Hart.

[A] gentleman of distinguished bearing but somewhat seedily attired, who had been talking with Prof. John S. Hart, approached me and noticing the print I held in my hand delightfully explained its story. I thanked him and told him I must be going. He asked me where I lived; when I told him, he replied, "I am going that way and will walk with you, my lad." . . . I was charmed by the strangers delightful conversation and flattered, as a child would be, by his considerate attention. . . . That afternoon a lady, calling on my mother, chanced to remark she had seen me talking with a person evidently in needy circumstances from his attire. Mother inquired who I had been with; I could give no information, but that I had met him in the magazine office. . . . That very evening Mr. Sartain called and Mother asked him who the stranger was, and she was told that he was no less a personage than Edgar Allan Poe.

Seedy and perhaps still a bit rocky, Poe was sufficiently recovered to pitch Sartain a new poem for his magazine, "Annabel Lee," as well as a third version of "The Bells." After Poe's death, the January 1850 edition of *Sartain's* featured the first authorized appearance of "Annabel Lee" (although it already had been printed in the *New-York Tribune*, with his obituary, and the *Southern Literary Messenger*). Poe's physical condition noticeably deteriorated during the last two years of his life, but it was during this time that he wrote many of his best regarded poems, among them, "Ulalume," "To Helen," "A Dream within a Dream," "Eldorado," "For Annie," and, of course, most majestically, "The Bells" and "Annabel Lee."

"He's rejuvenated as a poet at the end," Peeples said. "His career begins and ends with the poetry, so the end finds him returning to his first love, poetry."

The shabbiness of Poe's appearance described by the young Henry Ashmead likely isn't an exaggeration. He had been drinking and imprisoned. He had been hallucinating and paranoid. He had been ill and despondent. By July 12, you could add homeless and hungry. It was in this miserable condition that he made his way to the newspaper office of twenty-seven-year-old George Lippard, the editor of the weekly *Quaker City*. A novelist and a great admirer of Poe, he was one of many acquaintances who noticed that "When he drank, the first drop maddened him; hence his occasional departures from the line of strict propriety." On this hot Thursday, Poe climbed the four flights of stairs to the printing office, toward Lippard, who recalled that he was wearing only one shoe. "He came stealthily up stairs, as if conscious that the world had forsaken him, and that he was an intruder anywhere." Lippard also noticed he was "poorly clad." Poe wearily sat down near the table where his young friend was working. He told Lippard that he had nothing to eat, nowhere to sleep, and "not one friend in God's world."

"You are my last hope," Poe said. "If you fail me, I can do nothing but die."

Lippard's heart "sickened within him, to see a man like this in want of bread—in want of a bed to sleep upon." A writer who appreciated Poe's genius while holding the upper classes in low regard, Lippard was deeply offended that years of brilliant work as a poet, short story author, and critic had brought a true artist so little in the way of financial reward. To him, the saddest of all sights was "a great man whose genius had enriched publishers, begging his bread in Philadelphia, on a hot summer's day." Lippard, though, had just parted with his last quarter to pay the rent and was in no position to help Poe with a loan. Instead, he set forth into the heat, feeling ill himself, seeking out publishers who might be good for a few dollars. "Tell them that I am sick," Poe told him. "That I only want enough to get me out of Philadelphia." With the "hot sun pouring down over half-deserted streets," Lippard set about on what proved a fruitless task. The combination of cholera and wretched heat had driven the publishers out of town. Too sick to continue, he had just enough strength to reach his home. Early the next morning, he hurried to the printing office and found Poe sitting at a corner table, his head buried in his hands. "I thought *you* had deserted me," he said, tears in his eyes.

The destination remained Richmond. There he would find receptive audiences for his lectures. There he would find subscribers for his magazine. There he would find the path that finally would lead him away from poverty and struggle. Philadelphia was supposed to be a quick stop, probably to conduct a little business. It had turned into a detour that was beginning to feel like a trap.

"Get me out of Philadelphia," Poe implored him, hoping for a little bit of luck on that Friday the thirteenth. "I'm heart-sick for Virginia. I'm freer there than in any other place. If I can only feel my boot upon Virginia soil, I'll be a new man."

Lippard went out again, this time locating five men willing to help Poe: magazine publishers Louis A. Godey and Samuel D. Patterson, Sartain, editor and author Reverend Charles Chauncey Burr, and Sartain's clerk, William F. Miskey, who gave all he had—one dollar. Lippard returned to the *Quaker City* with the good news. Moved beyond words, Poe grasped his hand, the look on his face saying "much more than words." Lippard, whose stories included Gothic horror tales and historical fiction, would live just five years and four months longer than Poe, dying of tuberculosis at the age of thirty-one on February 9, 1854. The writer and social reformer's last words, spoken to his doctor, were, "Is this death?" When death had come to Poe, Lippard responded with a sympathetic obituary for the *Quaker City*. It included a passage that could be viewed as a challenge and an indictment of Griswold and all those bent on twisting Poe's memory. "As an author, his name will live," Lippard correctly predicted, "while three-fourths of the bastard critics and mongrel authors of the present day go down to nothingness and night. And the men who now spit on his grave; by way of retaliation for some injury which they imagine they received from Poe living, would do well to remember, that it is only an idiot or a coward who strikes the cold forehead of a corpse."

That last day with Poe was much on Lippard's mind in October 1849, and he shared memories of it in the obituary. The kindly Reverend Burr insisted Poe accompany him to his home on Seventh Street, and he bought him a train ticket that would take him to Baltimore, where he could book passage on a ship to Richmond for seven dollars. Poe, some of his optimism restored, spoke to them a great deal about his plans for the future. He talked about the importance of "Eureka," which had been published in March 1848. And Poe recalled the first time he met Lippard, welcoming the worshipful younger writer into his Philadelphia home on Seventh and Spring Garden Streets. That evening, Burr and Lippard went with him to the train depot at Eleventh and Market Streets. Lippard noted in the obituary, "He held our hand for a long time, and seemed loth to leave us—there was in his voice, look and manner, something of a Presentiment that this strange and stormy life was near its close."

Poe boarded the 10 P.M. train for Baltimore. They heard his last words, Lippard recalled. They watched him depart. "They never saw him again."

"SAVE ME FROM DESTRUCTION"

MARCH 1827–MAY 1836

After leaving John Allan's house and Richmond in March 1827, Poe made his way to Boston, where he may have picked up some journalistic assignments and worked as a store clerk. He also arranged for the publication of his first book, *Tammerlane and Other Poems*. In late May, he signed up for a five-year hitch with the army, enlisting as a private under the alias Edgar A. Perry. He was assigned to Battery H of the First Artillery in Fort Independence, Boston Harbor. The book appeared in July, credited to "a Bostonian" (maybe because he was avoiding debt collectors or maybe because he didn't want Allan to be aware of his location). The hero of the title poem is the Turco-Mongolian conqueror born in 1336, but the inspiration may have been the romance with Elmira Royster. Biographer Arthur Hobson Quinn identified four major themes in the poem that Poe continued to explore: pride, love, beauty, and death. About fifty copies of the forty-page book were printed by Calvin S. F. Thomas, just a year older than Poe. It attracted little notice. Its author was eighteen.

Also of note on the literary front, several pieces by Poe appeared in 1827 issues of the Baltimore publication the *North American or, Weekly Journal of Politics, Science and Literature*. That would be William Henry

Leonard Poe, not Edgar. By the time Edgar had joined the army, the older Poe brother had already seen a bit of the world, sailing on an American frigate and landing in such places as the West Indies, South America, Montevideo, the Mediterranean, and Russia. And he was the first of the Poe brothers to have a short story published. One of them printed that year, "The Pirate," is based on his brother's romance with Elmira Royster. The hero of that tale was named Edgar Leonard, after both brothers. Henry probably also told the details of this teen attraction to Baltimore editor and writer Lambert A. Wilmer, who used the Edgar-Elmira amour as inspiration for his 1827 three-act poetic drama, *Merlin*.

Henry Poe also had poems accepted for publication, two of which are nearly identical to verses in his brother's first book, *Tamerlane*. Although they'd seen very little of each other after their mother's death, Henry and Edgar had a strong brotherly bond. Edgar would later appropriate some of his brother's experiences for the autobiographical sketch written in 1841. Edgar told the world that, after leaving the University of Virginia with "some debts of *honor*" that John Allan had refused to pay, he "ran away from home" on a "quixotic expedition to join the Greeks, then struggling for liberty." As this bit of romanticized fiction goes, he failed to reach Greece and ended up in St. Petersburg, Russia, where he was rescued from difficulties by that American consul. It sure made a better story than the truth, and all that Greece and Russia stuff made it into many of the early biographies of Poe.

Poe never left the country during this period of his life . . . or ever again, for that matter. From late May to early November 1827, he was stationed at Fort Independence in Boston. His company was ordered to Fort Moultrie, located on Sullivan's Island, near Charleston, South Carolina. He spent about thirteen months at this location, later using it as the setting for his immensely popular mystery story "The Gold-Bug." He also used it in "The Oblong Box" and "The Balloon Hoax." He described the island in "The Gold-Bug," the story that achieved the widest readership during his lifetime:

This Island is a very singular one. It consists of little else than the sea sand, and is about three miles long. Its breadth at no point exceeds a quarter of a mile. It is separated from the main land by a scarcely perceptible creek, oozing its way through a wilderness of reeds and slime, a favorite resort of the marsh hen. The vegetation, as might be supposed, is scant, or at least dwarfish. No trees of any magnitude are to be seen. Near the western extremity, where Fort Moultrie stands, and where are some miserable frame buildings, tenanted, during the summer, by fugitives from Charleston dust and fever, may be found, indeed, the bristly palmetto, but the whole island, with the exception of this western point, and a line of hard, white beach on the seacoast, is covered with a dense undergrowth of the sweet myrtle . . .

"Very little is known about his time here," said James M. Hutchisson, author of the 2005 biography *Poe* and a professor of American literature and southern studies at the Citadel in Charleston. "We know he was stationed at Fort Moultrie and he set 'The Gold Bug' there, and, other than that, it's a period for which there is very little information or documentation."

Although Poe found army life excruciatingly dull, he proved himself a good soldier. His superiors praised him for "promptly and faithfully" performing his duties, as well as his exemplary deportment, which included the avoidance of drink. He was given the duties of company clerk, then, after his company moved from Fort Moultrie to Fortress Monroe at Old Point Comfort, Virginia, he was promoted to the highest rank for a noncommissioned officer, sergeant major. "What most people don't understand is that Poe was in robust health for much of his life," said Patrick Hansma, a forensic pathologist, Poe scholar, and author. "As a teenager, he was known for his abilities as a swimmer, boxer, and long jumper. Sergeant Major Poe was slim, fit, and had a soldier's stride. And later, when he's living in Philadelphia and New York, he's walking everywhere all the time. He's quite fit and athletic, which, obviously, is not how most people view him."

By December 1828, however, he was wearying of army repetition and regimentation. He began to lobby for a discharge. Providing a sympathetic ear was a superior officer with the company, Lieutenant J. Howard, who probably was told everything, including his real name and actual age, that he had been orphaned, that his university experience had not ended well, and that he had broken with his foster father under acrimonious conditions. The fatherly and compassionate Howard agreed to support the discharge, provided he reconcile with John Allan. Howard tried to act as intermediary, sending a letter to Allan, who clearly wasn't in any mood to forgive or to forget the bitter feelings expressed by a charity case he also viewed as an ingrate and a wastrel. Holding all the cards and knowing Poe would be trapped in an occupation where he couldn't do much to aggravate a Richmond merchant, Allan handed down a devastating decree. It would be best if Poe remained "as he is until the termination of his enlistment." While it was a tall order, Poe attempted to sway Allan with a letter of reconciliation, sending it December 1, 1828, from Fort Moultrie. Addressed "Dear Sir," it was a temperate, carefully worded missive. His aim was to persuade Allan that his heart was not in army life and that "the prime of my life would be wasted" after three more years of military service. He feared Allan "believed me degraded & disgraced, and that any thing were preferable to my returning home & entailing on yourself a portion of my infamy." He also hoped that the praises of his superiors would prove that "I am altered from what you knew me, & am no longer a boy tossing about on the world without aim or consistency." He closed with "dearest love to Ma," signing it "Yours respectfully & affectionately." It was the type of letter that would have swayed most men. It did not sway John Allan, who probably felt his answer had already been given, and, in his view, it was an entirely correct one. He did not answer Poe's letter. Poe was dealing with someone who, as biographer Kenneth Silverman shrewdly observed, "encouraged independence but resented individuality."

Poe tried again from Fortress Monroe on December 22, this time with a slight change of tactics. "I wrote you shortly before leaving Fort Moultrie &

am much hurt at receiving no answer," he began. "Perhaps my letter has not reached you & under that supposition I will recapitulate its content." He was giving Allan the out, while, at the same time, giving himself another chance to plead his case. He also upped the guilt factor and emotional manipulation by a few notches. He mentioned the kindness shown him by Lieutenant Howard and Colonel James House. "It must have been a matter of regret to me, that when those who were strangers took such deep interest in my welfare, you who called me your son should refuse me even the common civility of answering a letter," he wrote. "My father do not throw me aside as *degraded*[.] I will be an honor to your name . . . If you determine to abandon me—here take [I my] farewell—Neglected—I will be doubly ambitious, & the world shall hear of the son whom you have thought unworthy of your notice. But if you let the love you bear me, outweigh the offence which I have given—then write me my father, quickly." This time, he signed the letter, "Your affectionate son."

The "son" did not rise in Allan's estimation. He again was unmoved. Again he chose not to respond. Allan, after all, didn't truly view him as a son. And whatever affection he may have expressed for the young Edgar probably didn't lead to any feelings of genuine parental love.

Having been promoted to sergeant major and turned twenty, Poe tried yet again on February 4, 1829. Now he was taking blame for his conduct at the University of Virginia, offering youth and inexperience as reasons for going astray. He also offered a new reason for seeking a discharge. He wished to enter the United States Military Academy at West Point. Nothing seemed capable of softening Allan's iron resolve, but then something did—Fanny Allan died of tuberculosis on February 28. She was forty-four. Although he had repeatedly asked after "Ma" in his letters to Allan, Poe seemingly was unaware that she was so seriously ill. She had expressed a longing to see him, and this was not to be. Granted leave, he raced to Richmond, arriving the night after her funeral. He learned she had been buried in Shockoe Hill Cemetery, also the final resting place of the idolized and doomed Jane Stanard, who had died five years before.

First Eliza Poe, then Jane Stanard, and now Fanny Allan . . . three loving maternal figures, three deaths in Richmond, three graves where his great sense of loss and abandonment could not be buried and left behind.

Perhaps, as many have suggested, Fanny Allan's dying wish was that John Allan would patch things up with Edgar. For a while, there was something resembling rapprochement. Allan purchased a suit of black clothes, a hat, gloves, and a knife for Poe. He also agreed to support his discharge from the army and the plan to attend West Point. On March 10, back at Fortress Monroe, Poe again was beginning letters with, "My dear Pa." One last hurdle needed to be cleared for him to leave the army. A soldier seeking a discharge before his enlistment was up was expected to pay for a substitute. Overeager to leave the service, Poe foolishly agreed to pay an ex-soldier the excessive amount of seventy-five dollars to take his place, giving him twenty-five dollars and a note for the rest. He was officially released on April 15, 1829, and returned to Richmond. Armed with letters of recommendation from Lieutenant Howard, two other officers, and Allan, he left in early May for Washington, D.C., then Baltimore, where he was welcomed by several family members, including his grandmother, the General's widow; his aunt Maria Clemm and her six-year-old daughter, Virginia; and his twenty-two-year-old brother, Henry. On May 20, he was thanking Allan for sending him one hundred dollars. Getting into West Point proved far more difficult than supposed, however, and he sent along explanations for the delays, along with requests for money, to Allan. The era of good feeling between them could not survive. It began to crumble with snarky comments and complaints here and there, building to sharper and angrier exchanges. By August, Allan was expressing his displeasure. "I was afraid you were offended & although I knew that I had done nothing to deserve your anger," Poe responded. "I was in a most uncomfortable situation—without one cent of money . . . My grandmother is extremely poor & ill (paralytic). My aunt Maria if possible still worse & Henry entirely given up to drink & unable to help himself, much less me."

By October, Allan's frustrations with delays regarding West Point, along with the usual requests for money, got his temper going. Poe wrote him: "I am sorry that your letters to me have still with them a tone of anger as if my former errors were not forgiven—if I knew how to regain your affection God knows I would do any thing I could." Allan continued to send money, though, and, in December, Baltimore's Hatch & Dunning published a second volume of poetry from the writer who had declared himself "irrevocably a poet." About 250 copies of *Al Aaraaf, Tamerlane, and Minor Poems* were printed. Although he was a few years away from writing the first story that can be categorized as horror, two poems written in 1829 indicate where he would be heading—where he would be drawn as a storyteller. There was "Alone," with its dark, foreboding conclusion:

> *From the lightning in the sky*
> *As it pass'd me flying by—*
> *From the thunder, and the storm—*
> *And the cloud that took the form*
> *(When the rest of Heaven was blue)*
> *Of a demon in my view—*

The other, which appeared in the seventy-one pages of *Al Aaraaf, Tamerlane, and Minor Poems,* is "Spirits of the Dead," with its opening:

> *Thy soul shall find itself alone*
> *'Mid dark thoughts of the gray tombstone—*
> *Not one, of all the crowd, to pry*
> *Into thine hour of secrecy.*
> *Be silent in that solitude,*
> > *Which is not loneliness—for then*
> *The spirits of the dead who stood*
> > *In life before thee are again*
> *In death around thee,—and their will*
> *Shall overshadow thee: be still.*

He was also indulging in some early romantic reworking of his biography, claiming that he was a descendant of Benedict Arnold, that his grandfather had been the quartermaster for all of Washington's army during the Revolution, and that his parents had died in the tragic Richmond Theatre fire. None of it was true. The Richmond Theatre fire, which claimed seventy-two lives, occurred on December 26, 1811. Eliza Poe had died on December 8.

The acceptance to West Point finally came through, and, on June 20, 1830, Poe arrived at the academy perched on the high ground above the Hudson River. Although he excelled at French and mathematics, the twenty-one-year-old twice-published poet soon realized that little about life at West Point suited him. His career as a cadet began with a two-month summer encampment. This meant living in a tent with three other cadets. It meant constant drilling and military training in the July and August heat from 5:30 A.M. to early evening. It was in a Camp Eaton tent that he wrote a letter to John Allan, denying the charge he had removed books from Moldavia that didn't belong to him. "I have taken nothing except what I considered my own," Poe maintained in his reply to Allan. The accusation, though, was a harbinger of the storm that soon would obliterate whatever positive feelings remained between them.

Poe moved into 28 South Barracks for the start of classes on September 1. If Edgar Perry had found regular army life stultifying, Edgar A. Poe must have viewed the harsh discipline and rigid regimentation of West Point as positively draconian. Now the routine started with classes before breakfast, which was served at 7 A.M., followed by more classes until 4 P.M., followed by military exercises until sunset, followed by supper, followed by yet more classes until 9:30, and lights out at 10. The cadets were given 304 regulations to follow, and the restrictions were many and, well, strict: no drinking, no gambling, no card playing, no tobacco, no cooking in the rooms, no musical instruments, no novels or plays, no games of chess or backgammon, no leaving the post, no bathing in the river. The rules, famously bent by some of the Point's celebrated graduates, were designed to encourage complete dedication to academic study and military training. Poe obviously was never going to thrive in such Spartan conditions, coping with such exacting expectations and precise standards of conduct. It was the educational inverse of the University of Virginia, where discipline was trampled under the boots of young Southern aristocrats and the reading of novels was one of the milder forms of diversion.

Like many of his classmates at the University of Virginia, however, the West Point cadets often found Poe entertaining and intriguing. He regaled them with the fictional version of his life story, including the romantic adventures and the Benedict Arnold nonsense. They had no reason to doubt his veracity. He delighted them with verses making fun of their instructors. And he impressed them with an entirely truthful autobiographical item—that his poetry had been published. The need to impress was there, as was the sensitivity to slights, both born of being an orphan searching for a place where he was fully accepted, respected, and appreciated—where he knew he belonged. Thomas W. Gibson and Timothy Pickering Jones were his roommates at 28 South Barracks (a structure that was demolished the same year Poe died). Gibson would recall that there was some ribbing about Poe being older than the rest of them: "Poe was easily fretted by any jest at his expense, and was not a little annoyed by a story that some of the class got up, to the effect that he had procured a cadet's appointment for his son, and, the boy having died, the father had substituted himself in his place." Poe, who liked to amuse the other cadets, was not amused to be the butt of the joke.

Gibson also remembered that Poe at twenty-one "had the appearance of being much older." He described Poe as having "a worn, weary, discontented look, not easily forgotten by those who were intimate with him." Also not easily forgotten was Poe's mirthful side. "Very early in his brief career at the Point he established a high reputation for genius," Gibson wrote of him, "and poems and squibs of local interest were daily issued from Number 28 and went the round of the Classes."

It was inevitable that Poe would find his way to the tavern started in 1824 by Benny Havens. Mrs. Havens provided the roast turkey, chicken dinners, and buckwheat cakes, and the gregarious Old Benny provided an endless stream of talk along with the liquor forbidden the cadets. Poe enjoyed his congenial company, as well as the alcohol. Yes, Poe was drinking again, although not to the extent where he couldn't keep up with his studies and duties. He finished third in French and seventeenth in mathematics. He and Gibson became adept at sneaking off the grounds and making their way to the tavern for "supplies." One would keep a lookout while the other made the run to Benny's establishment. The runner would return with a bottle to be kept in the room, and, Gibson recounted, "many a thirsty soul, with not enough of pluck to run the blockade himself, would steal into our room between tatoo and taps to try the merits of the last importation."

One "dark, cold, drizzling night, in the last days of November," it was observed that the brandy bottle had been empty for two days and a tavern run was in order. Poe and Gibson drew straws to see who would go "replenish the stock." Gibson drew the short straw. Benny gave him a full bottle of brandy and a gander, chopping off the goose's head for him. Carrying the bird over his shoulder, Gibson arrived back at the Point covered in blood. Poe was on lookout, of course, and met him outside the barracks. Observing Gibson's appearance, he immediately concocted a prank, providing further proof that, behind the poet's pose, there was lurking both a horror writer and a humorist with a love of jests. The two quickly worked out the details of their "grand hoax." Poe took the bottle from him and went back to their room. Their roommate, Jones, was there studying, and a visitor from the North Barracks was waiting to see if a snort or two would be possible that night. Poe entered, took his seat, and pretended to be absorbed in French lessons. Placing the body of the gander outside the door, Gibson staggered into the room, a bloody spectacle. "My God! What has happened?" shouted Poe, the son of thespians, playing his part with what Gibson described as "well-acted horror." Gibson, appearing to be drunk, ranted about having killed "Old K——."

"He won't stop me on the road any more!" Gibson shouted, producing a bloody knife. "I have killed him!"

"Nonsense," Poe said. "You are only trying one of your tricks on us."

"I didn't suppose you would believe me," Gibson said. "So I cut off his head and brought it into the barracks. Here it is!"

And with these words, Gibson picked up the gander and hurled it at the only candle in the room, plunging them all into darkness. The visitor jumped through the window, making "fast time for his own room in the North Barracks." Jones was sitting in a corner, "his face a blank picture of horror."

Behind such mirthful diversions, there were distant rumblings from the direction of Virginia, warnings that Allan soon would find reasons to break with his foster son. Early October brought a thunderclap that must have shaken the ground under Poe—news that the fifty-one-year-old Allan had remarried. His second wife was Louisa Gabriella Patterson of Elizabethtown, New Jersey. She was twenty years younger and from a wealthy family. The marriage took place in New York, just three months after Allan's mistress in Richmond had given birth to twin sons. His new wife would have three children, but even before the first arrived, Poe realized the dynamic had radically changed, and not in his favor. The chances for an inheritance were dwindling to nothing. There were plenty of hints, none of them good. Allan had sent Poe to West Point with insufficient funds, just as he had sent him to the University of Virginia. Although the wedding took place about sixty miles from West Point, Allan and his bride made no effort to visit him. Then the lightning, in the form of John Allan's indignant anger, struck in late December. He wrote Poe an angry letter declaring himself forever through with the orphaned boy taken into his home twenty years before. Allan wrote that he never wanted to hear from Poe again.

While he may have just been looking to seize on an opportune moment for making the final break, the proud Allan was not without a legitimate complaint. He had heard from Sergeant "Bully" Graves, the substitute Poe had rashly agreed to pay seventy-five dollars to take his place in the army. Graves had first reached out to Poe for the fifty dollars still owed him. Poe had put him off, saying the money was to have come from Allan, but the rich merchant was "not very often sober." The charge of habitual drunkenness got back to Allan, who was understandably furious. One fabrication too many came crashing down on Poe, but he had legitimate complaints of his own, and he poured them into a letter written on January 3, 1831. "I suppose altho' you desire no further communication with yourself on my part, that your restriction does not extend to my answering your final letter," he began, "Did I, when an infant, sollicit [sic] your charity and protection, or was it of your own free will, that you volunteered your services in my behalf?" He opens with the strongest charge to be made against Allan: that he regarded an orphaned boy as a charity case to be supported rather than a son to be loved. He then summarized his problems at the University of Virginia, blaming them, not without some justification, on Allan's stinginess. He wrote of Fanny, saying that he believed "she loved me as her own child." After her death: "You promised me to forgive all—but you soon forgot your promise. You sent me to W. Point like a beggar. The same difficulties are threatening me as before at Charlottesville—and I must resign."

He admitted that he had written the letter to Sergeant Graves, but "The time in which I wrote it was within a half hour after you had embittered every feeling of my heart against you by your abuse of my *family*, and myself, under your own roof—and at time when you knew that my heart was almost breaking." He adds a favorite device in letters: a hint that death soon will find him. He writes that his "future life (which thank God will not endure long) must be passed in indigence and sickness." He closes with his resolve to court dismissal from West Point by neglecting his studies and duties. Poe made good on his resolve, and Allan dismissed his letter as "the most barefaced one sided statement." His verdict was a harsh one: "I do not think the Boy has one good quality . . . I cannot believe a word he writes."

A general court-martial was convened, and Poe left West Point for New York City, living in the Madison Square area, on February 19 (although his dismissal from the academy was not official until March 6). He quickly fell ill with a violent cold, headaches, and a discharge of blood from the ear. He wrote to Allan pleading for money, a letter that apparently was ignored. Poe recovered, and set about arranging for a third volume of poems to be published. He briefly considered heading for Europe and joining the Polish army in battle against Russia, but France's abandonment of Poland as an ally ended that Byronesque dream.

Believing that *Poems by Edgar A. Poe* would feature the satirical verses he had written at West Point, more than half of the cadets supported the publication with a 75-cent subscription, and the 124-page volume was dedicated to the United States Corps of Cadets. Those cadets were perplexed and disappointed with the book. The poems were serious and, to them, confusing. The printing was cheap. It "was received with a general expression of disgust" at West Point, Gibson recalled.

That spring, Poe moved to Baltimore and again joined the household that included his father's widowed sister, Maria Clemm, and her now eight-year-old daughter. The family just managed to get by on his paralytic grandmother's pension and the meager amount of money Maria brought in through sewing. Suffering from advanced tuberculosis and drinking heavily, Poe's brother, Henry, died on August 1, 1831, at the age of twenty-four. It is likely the same combination that led to the death of their father at the age of twenty-seven. It was another cruel loss that Poe felt deeply. Although they had lived most of their lives in different cities, the Poe brothers shared a bond that went beyond common ancestry. They also shared a mutual interest in poetry. And they borrowed from each other's experiences and writing, perhaps viewing it as all-in-the-family communal property. They spent only six months living in the same place—the city where their great-grandfather had settled about seventy-six years earlier. Poe had arrived in time to witness the end. Dying at the same age as their mother, Henry was buried in the churchyard of the First Presbyterian Church.

With the remaining family in dire straits, Poe tried reconciling with Allan in mid-October, going so far as to adopt an apologetic and obsequious tone. He praised Allan's forbearance and generosity, condemning his own "most flagrant ingratitude." He tried again a month later. Two more letters followed in December. Allan looks to have sent some money, but, emotionally, he had nothing to send. There then appears to have been a year and several months with no communication between them.

It was also during this time in Baltimore that Poe seems to have been seeing a great deal of seventeen-year-old Mary Starr. What we know of the romance is from an account she gave to writer Augustus Van Cleef when she was seventy-one. She lived around the corner from Poe and his Baltimore relations. "They were all very poor, but everything was wax neat," she recalled. She had been walking with a companion when Poe approached her, seeking an introduction. The young man striding toward her was five feet, eight inches tall. He had a high forehead, large expressive eyes, and dark brown hair. Even in matters follicle, Poe has been the victim of stereotype. The common assumption is that his hair was black, mostly because the most popular images of him are daguerreotypes, which, of course, were black-and-white photographs. It photographed black, but there are several surviving samples of Poe's hair, and, yes, it's brown. The color of his eyes is less certain. Some said hazel. Some said gray. Some said bluish gray. One witness went with violet.

But Starr added more telling and insightful details, giving us a charming portrait of the aspiring writer in his early twenties:

He was handsome, but intellectually so, not a pretty man. He had the way and the power to draw any one to him. He was very fascinating, and any young girl would have fallen in love with him. . . . Mr. Poe immediately jumped across the balustrades separating the stoops, and sat down by me. He told me I had the most beautiful hair he ever saw, the hair that poets always raved about. It was auburn, and worn with frizzled puffs on the sides, as was then the style. From that time on he visited me every evening for a year, and during that time, until the night of our final lovers' quarrel, he never drank a drop, as far as I knew. Mr. Poe . . . had dark, almost black hair, which he wore long and brushed back in student style over his ears. It was as fine as silk. . . . The expression about his mouth was beautiful. He was pale. . . . He had a sad, melancholy look. He was very slender when I first knew him, but he had a fine figure, an erect military carriage, and a quick step. But it was his manner that most charmed. It was elegant. When he looked at you it seemed as if he could read your very thoughts. His voice was pleasant and musical, but not deep.

She remembered he always wore a black cravat tied in a loose knot and a black frock coat with a military collar. She remembered he despised ignorance and silly small talk. She remembered he was quick to anger and jealousy. She remembered he was extremely proud and sensitive. She remembered he scoffed at all things sacred and never went to church. And she remembered he spoke of marriage, something her brother opposed because of Poe's inability to support himself, let alone a wife and family.

The final lovers' quarrel she mentioned occurred when Poe arrived late at her house one night and admitted he had been drinking. He told her that he had met some cadets from West Point, and they had taken him to Barnum's Hotel for supper and champagne. "A glass made him tipsy," she said. "He had more than a glass that night. As to his being a habitual drunkard, he never was as long as I knew him." They quarreled, and she ran back into the house. Poe followed and was blocked by Mary's mother. While the romance was over, they would reconnect years later and remain friends.

Meanwhile, Poe the poet had turned his attention to a new form: the short story. When he had moved to Baltimore that spring, he was twenty-two years old. He had lived more than half his life, and he had written half his poems. Financially, he had nothing to show for it. Poverty was pushing him in another direction, and while it wasn't a path he would have chosen for himself, it was the one that would take him toward the kind of literary immortality he sought. Fate played its hand in the form of a contest Poe could not resist. The *Saturday Courier,* a Philadelphia publication, announced in late May that it was soliciting entries for a contest "in the promotion of the Cause of LITERATURE." The winning entry would be named the best American tale and its author awarded one hundred dollars. Although he'd only written a handful of short stories, Poe was confident in his genius. He submitted five stories. The committee announced in late December that the best American tale was "strongly characterized by taste, genius and feeling." It was "Love's Martyr," by Delia S. Bacon, author of *Tales of the Puritans*, a recently published collection of three long stories about colonial life. Bacon's story was based on the July 1777 murder of Jane McCrea by two Iroquois escorts while on the way to meet her Loyalist fiancé at Ticonderoga. If Bacon is remembered at all, it is for the years she spent trying to prove that Shakespeare didn't write the plays attributed to him. She contended there were several authors, including Francis Bacon (no relation), Walter Raleigh, and Edmund Spenser. Two years younger than Poe, she died ten years after him.

While favoring Bacon's story, the six judges for the *Saturday Courier* added that many of the other entries were "distinguished by great merit." They certainly meant Poe's submissions because the *Courier* published all five throughout 1832: "Metzengerstein," "The Duc de L'Omelette," "A Tale of Jerusalem," "A Decided Loss," and "Bon-Bon" ("The Bargain Lost").

As Poe was approaching his twenty-third birthday in January 1832, there were developments at West Point that undoubtedly would have greatly amused him. On January 12, his roommate and prank partner Thomas W. Gibson was dismissed from the U.S. Military Academy after his second court-martial. The charges against him were technically worded, but, essentially, he was kicked out for setting fire to a building too close to the barracks for the faculty's comfort. Two days later, the *Saturday Courier* published Poe's first short story, "Metzengerstein," a Gothic fantasy tale that, in mood and theme, foreshadowed much of what was to come in his fiction. A horror tale in the German tradition, or perhaps a spoof of the German horror tale, Poe's nightmarish spooker follows young Baron Frederick Metzengerstein, whose shameful debaucheries and flagrant treacheries "out-Heroded Herod" (a pet phrase that he used again in two of his finest horror stories, "William Wilson" and "The Masque of the Red Death"). When the stables of his family's rivals, the Berlifitzings, burn, causing the death of the elderly count, the remorseless baron becomes haunted by the appearance of "a gigantic and fiery-colored horse." At the same time, the head of a gigantic horse appears to have moved in a tapestry depicting a battle between the Metzengersteins and the Berlifitzings. Its publication is a significant moment in American literature and the history of horror fiction: Poe has started his career as a purveyor of frights and chills. He had found a storytelling form that would take him to extraordinary heights.

The Gothic tradition was already well established in Europe, flourishing in the second half of the eighteenth century thanks to the success of such novels as Horace Walpole's *The Castle of Otranto* (1764), Ann Radcliffe's *The Mysteries of Udolpho* (1794), and Matthew Gregory Lewis's *The Monk* (1796). In America, scary and supernatural tales were among Washington Irving's most popular. Poe, by this point, was also well acquainted with the lurid Gothic storytelling featured in *Blackwood's* and other magazines.

"There are a lot of people writing this kind of stuff when Poe first tries his hand at it," said Poe scholar Scott Peeples. "It's a pretty crowded field, and it continues to be, with lots of magazines seeking this type of material. So Poe was treading in familiar and well-worn territory. He was just doing it so much better than anyone else. You see stories similar to what he wrote, and there's no comparison. He's that good. They can't touch him."

Peter Ackroyd, a biographer of William Shakespeare and Charles Dickens, as well as Poe, believed that, with the publication of "Metzengerstein," "he had found his true vocation."

At the same time Poe found a storytelling form that suited him so well, he found the family he so desperately yearned for and needed. His aunt, Maria Clemm, provided the steady and steadfast motherly presence he had again and again been denied by death and illness. By the spring of 1833, she had moved into a small two-and-a-half-story brick house on Amity Street, now open to today's public as a museum. Poe joined the household that included his grandmother, aunt, and two cousins. The ailing grandmother's pension was crucial to meeting the rent for this new home. A paralytic who, according to Poe, never left her bed, the General's widow, Elizabeth Cairnes Poe, was patiently and tenderly cared for by Maria with a dedication that impressed neighbors and relatives. It was one of many reasons that Poe praised Maria's character. In his own way, he was also becoming dependent on her care.

"The idea of your chosen family is a more modern idea, but you see that with Poe," said Enrica Jang, executive director of Poe Baltimore and the Edgar Allan Poe House & Museum. "In Richmond, he ultimately finds rejection. The message is, 'You don't really belong here.' Then he goes to Baltimore and finds the family that says, 'You're one of us.' He finds his chosen family here. This is the house where Poe sought refuge. Maria, no stranger to poverty, welcomed him into her household. He goes dark here and begins to write those short stories. This tiny little house is where a huge literary career has its real start. Tremendously great things can come of humble places, and this house is proof of that."

Poe had also gone dark in manner of dress, with black remaining a favorite color for clothes (although this might have been a choice born of practicality, as well). Still, it certainly played into the view of himself he took to Baltimore—that of the romantic poet doomed to a life of suffering and unhappiness. And it certainly suited his emulation of Byron, one of the few poets for whom he regularly expressed admiration (the others included Samuel Taylor Coleridge and Alfred Tennyson). It has been suggested that his mood at this time matched his choice in clothing, but that's difficult to assert with any certainty. It was, to be sure, a difficult time as far as financial prospects were concerned, and Poe was coming to terms with a galling collection of disappointments: that he had hopes of joining the Virginia aristocracy and was now facing a life of poverty; that he had attended both the University of Virginia and West Point but failed to stay more than a few months at either, let alone graduate; that he had published three volumes of poetry and that they had brought him neither fame nor fortune; that he had twice spoken of marriage to women who would marry others. These Baltimore years, however, are among the least documented of Poe's life. What day-to-day life was like for him falls largely in that all-too-familiar realm of speculation. We know he was increasingly turning his attention to stories, both horrific and humorous. He followed "Metzengerstein" with "The Duc de L'Omelette," published by the *Saturday Courier* on March 3, 1832. Changing gears, Poe gave readers an overtly comic tale about a self-important aristocrat who engages the devil in a game of cards. It's as if, right from the start of his career as an author of short stories, he was driven to prove his versatility. In June, the *Saturday Courier* published "A Tale of Jerusalem," a humorous piece about Roman soldiers attempting to play a joke on the Pharisee and Gizbarim of Jerusalem.

Determined to make a living as a writer, he continued to turn out stories, which brought in little money. He carried on in a humorous vein with the stories "Bon-Bon" (first published under the title "The Bargain Lost") and "Loss of Breath" (originally published as "A Decided Loss"), an over-the-top satire of a *Blackwood's* story. Although obviously in no way meant to be taken seriously, most of these early comic efforts do share an element of wild fantasy with the horror tales.

Poe vainly pursued jobs as an editorial assistant and a teacher in the fall of 1832. What kind of employment he might have actually found is unknown, although there is speculation that he was a kiln worker for a while in a brickyard. In April 1833, he was desperate enough to make an appeal to John Allan. "It has now been more than two years since you have assisted me, and more than three since you have spoken to me," he wrote. "I am perishing—absolutely perishing for want of aid. And yet I am not idle—nor addicted to any vice . . . save me from destruction."

As was often the case with Poe's pleadings for money, he tried his favorite one-two combination of pity and guilt. They were dead spots in Allan, at least as motivating factors for helping his onetime ward. Allan had reached the irreversible conclusion that Poe was an ingrate "destitute of honor & principle." Yet, on the back of a letter from Poe, Allan did remark with a kind of pity for the young man who considered himself a poet, and it carried the haunting hint of something like insight: "his Talents are of an order than can never prove a comfort to their possessor."

Those who study Poe's life have a tendency to describe the writer as needy. It was a trait that the stoic and proverb-quoting Allan would have viewed as weakness. Yet it was a neediness Poe recognized in himself, well aware of its source. When Nathaniel Beverly Tucker, an author and a professor of law at William and Mary College, mentioned having encountered his mother, Poe wrote to him: "In speaking of my mother you have touched a string to which my heart fully responds. To have known her is to be an object of great interest in my eyes. I myself never knew her—and never knew the affection of a father. Both died (as you may remember) within a few weeks of each other. I have many occasional dealings with Adversity— but the want of parental affection has been the heaviest of my trials."

After the deaths of his parents, as well as those of Jane Stanard and Fanny Allan, along with John Allan's inability to be the "beloved Pa," was it any wonder Poe was clinging to those who dwelled in the Amity Street house, where Maria and her ten-year-old daughter, Virginia, increasingly doted on him?

A month after sending what would be his final letter to Allan, Poe found a local outlet for his writing, the *Baltimore Saturday Visiter*. Its editor was Lambert A. Wilmer, the author, poet, and journalist who had befriended Poe's brother. In June 1833, the weekly publication announced its own contest to encourage literature, offering a fifty-dollar prize for the best story and twenty-five dollars for the best poem. Poe set himself to the task of taking first place in both categories. He submitted one poem, "The Coliseum," and then demonstrated how impressively he had dedicated himself to the task of mastering the short story. He sent the judges six stories grouped under the heading of "The Tales of the Folio Club." They included the first of his gripping stories about terrifying voyages, "MS. Found in a Bottle," in which Poe reached back to the lessons absorbed from reading Dafoe. Here was the incredible crafted into a narrative that was as convincing as it was powerfully engaging.

The judges were John H. B. Latrobe, James H. Miller, and, most significantly for Poe, Baltimore lawyer and novelist John Pendleton Kennedy, who would become a devoted friend and adviser. The committee met on October 7, after dinner, at Latrobe's home on Mulberry Street. Latrobe recalled in 1852 that the judges "were wholly unprepared" for what Poe had sent them. His stories were "so far, so very far, superior to anything before us, that we had no difficulty in awarding the first prize to the author," Latrobe remembered. "Our only difficulty was in selecting from the rich contents of the volume. We took the 'MS. Found in a Bottle.'" Their selection was marked by the influence of not only *Robinson Crusoe* but also Coleridge's "The Rime of the Ancient Mariner." Kennedy sent for Poe at once. The judges were as impressed by the writer as they had been by his writing. From his appearance, Latrobe said, "the world was then going hard with him," but when "he warmed up, he was most eloquent," and "his appearance was forgotten." Latrobe was particularly struck by Poe's fanciful yet earnest description of a trip to the moon. He left them with the impression "that he had himself just returned from the journey which existed only in his imagination."

The committee's official report to the publishers of the *Saturday Visiter* was extravagant in its praise of an exciting literary discovery. It was, they said, "the singular force and beauty" of "The Tales of the Folio Club" that "left us no ground for doubt." These tales, they continued, "are eminently distinguished by a wild, vigorous and poetical imagination, a rich style, a fertile invention, and varied and curious learning." Poe later claimed that he had, in fact, won first place for both stories and poetry, but, having won the fifty-dollar award for his story, he was given second place in poetry. While, yes, it sounds like another one of those Poe-esque exaggerations, this one was confirmed by Latrobe. The poem that claimed the twenty-five-dollar prize was submitted under an assumed name by the new editor of the *Visiter,* John Hill Hewitt. Poe, according to Hewitt, accosted him in the street, accusing him of using underhanded means to cheat him out of the poetry prize. Hewitt's reply was "a blow which staggered him, for I was physically his superior." With Poe about to reply in kind, friends stepped in and separated the prize winners. Years later, they ran into each other in Washington, D.C., Poe proposing they let bygones be bygones.

"MS. Found in a Bottle" was published in the *Visiter* on October 19. Two days later, Poe called on Latrobe, who recalled the encounter in an address at the Poe Memorial in 1877:

> His figure was remarkably good, and he carried himself erect and well, as one who had been trained to it. He was dressed in black, and his frockcoat was buttoned to the throat. . . . Not a particle of white was visible. Coat, hat, boots, and gloves had very evidently seen their best days, but so far as mending and brushing go, everything had been done, apparently, to make them presentable. On most men his clothes would have looked shabby and seedy, but there was something about this man that prevented one from criticizing his garments. . . . The impression made, however, was the award in Mr. Poe's favor was not inopportune.

The committee strongly advised Poe to publish "The Tales of the Folio Club" in book form. In many a biography of a writer, this would be the rags to riches moment, or, at least, the moment where the shadow of poverty would have eased somewhat. The prize recognition was a welcome and stirring endorsement of his decision to pen short stories, and the *Visiter* was willing to publish the "Folio Club" collection as a book. But privation continued to be the order of the day for Poe, who nixed that plan. In early November, Kennedy sent the stories to a Philadelphia publisher, Carey & Lea, for consideration. Henry C. Carey sat on the manuscript for a couple of years and decided against publishing it. Still, as frustrating as the end result was, Poe had gained a steadfast friend, mentor, and patron. Kennedy proved himself all this and much more.

Poe was coming into his own as a writer in Baltimore, but, back in Richmond, John Allan neither noticed nor cared. Now completely gray, Allan had been in rapidly deteriorating health for about a year. He and Louisa Allan welcomed a son, Patterson, on January 26, 1834. By the middle of February, it was clear that John Allan was dying. Exercise meant leaning on a cane and walking across a room, assisted by his wife and a servant. There is a dramatic account of Poe showing up at the Richmond house around this time, asking if he could see Allan. When told by Louisa that this was not possible, he supposedly pushed her aside and rushed up the stairs. He burst into Allan's bedroom, only to have the dying man raise a cane and threaten to strike him if he came near. There is no evidence that Poe made any such trip, and many Poe biographers doubt this melodramatic scene took place. Yet it may well have been Allan's response to seeing Poe, and Louisa Allan certainly had worked up a distaste for someone then held in such low regard by her husband. Allan died on March 27 and was buried in Shockoe Hill Cemetery. He left an immense fortune and an estate that included eight houses, stocks in banks and railroads, land holdings, a lumber house, and more than two hundred slaves. His widow and three children were the main beneficiaries, and even the illegitimate children were provided for with inheritances. Poe was not mentioned in the will.

Running true to form, Poe played fast and beyond loose with the facts. He rewrote history, claiming Allan had remarried when he was about sixty-five years old. The quarrel, he said, was with the new Mrs. Allan. In Poe's sham account, John Allan took Louisa's side, writing him an angry letter that he answered in kind. It certainly shows that flights of fantasy were not confined to his short stories. Allan was only fifty-four when he died, and, while Louisa Allan would have had nothing flattering to say about Poe and probably did speak against him, there were no actual quarrels between them. The fabrication is meant to cast himself in the role of a legitimate heir done out of his inheritance in stock melodrama fashion by the manipulating presence of a second wife. The one thing Poe gets right in his fanciful retelling is that Allan "bequeathed me nothing," and, yes, it's certainly possible Louisa had a hand in this.

Inheriting just a portion of that vast wealth would have underwritten the young Poe's dream of joining the Virginia aristocracy. The truth is that this dream had died well before Allan's demise, and Poe had started crafting nightmarish tales as a way of throwing "myself upon literature as a resource." While John Allan didn't do Poe any favors by cutting him off so coldly from any chance at wealth and station, he did do horror literature, mystery fans, and generations of readers an enormous good turn by leaving a maturing writer out of his will. If Allan had given Edgar Poe everything he wanted, it's doubtful we would today have the Edgar Allan Poe who has exerted so much influence over so many genres. Allan consigned Poe to a life of struggle but, inadvertently, also to one of brilliance.

"I think the dynamic with John Allan was doomed from the start," said Poe biographer James M. Hutchisson. "Poe deluded himself into thinking he would inherit some money and position when John Allan died. He saw himself becoming the comfortable, well-heeled man of letters. And if that had happened, I think he would have largely been a gentleman poet. I think he also would have written essays and letters, but it's entirely possible and probably likely that he wouldn't have written the mystery and horror stories. There would have been no need to exploit a popular genre. There would have been no financial incentive to write the stories that have kept him alive."

Struggle is key to Poe's productivity and his development as a writer, said author Daniel Stashower: "So much of what he wrote was forged in adversity, including the horror and mystery stories. He's being shaped by struggle. You take away that struggle, and we don't know what would have happened, but he's definitely not the Poe we know."

In March of 1835, Poe again was hoping to land a teaching job, and he asked for John Pendleton Kennedy's help. Kennedy, who twenty-five years later would be mentioned as a possible running mate for Abraham Lincoln, invited Poe to dinner. Poe's response reflects his low spirits and precarious financial situation. He couldn't accept the "kind invitation" because of "reasons of the most humiliating nature." His clothes had become too shabby for social calls. "You may conceive my deep mortification in making this disclosure to you—but it was necessary," Poe wrote. "If you will be my friend so far as to loan me $20 I will call on you to morrow—otherwise it will be impossible, and I must submit to my fate."

Poe could combine requests for money with self-abasing comments and foreboding hints of dire consequences. Yet this time, he doesn't appear to have been exaggerating his situation. Kennedy recorded that he found him "in a state of starvation." Would he be a friend? Kennedy had a gift for friendship, and among the writers who considered him a friend were Washington Irving, James Fenimore Cooper, Charles Dickens, and William Makepeace Thackeray. He was more than a friend to Poe that spring. He was a lifesaver. "I gave him clothing, free access to my table and the use of a horse for exercise whenever he chose; in fact brought him up from the very verge of despair," Kennedy recalled, and he, too, probably was not exaggerating the situation.

Kennedy also made sure that Maria Clemm and her daughter were amply provided with food. He had been corresponding with Thomas Willis White, the Richmond printer who had founded the *Southern Literary Messenger* in August 1834, and suggested Poe for an editorial position. Poe had already been contributing criticism and short stories to the new publication. His first appearance in the *Southern Literary Messenger* was a January review of a collection of poems by William Cullen Bryant. It was followed in March by one of his more lurid shockers, "Berenice," which, in turn, was followed by the April publication of "Morella." Both horror stories featured favorite Poe elements: haunted narrators and beautiful young women doomed to a trip to the crypt. The short, red-faced, congenial White was not completely comfortable with "Berenice" and some of the indignant response to it. The tale pushed well past the magazine proprietor's notions of propriety, with an ailing bride entombed alive, a monomaniacal narrator whose obsession drives him to grave desecration, and a grisly payoff where we learn that dental instruments have been used to extract thirty-two teeth from the unfortunate young woman's mouth. Poe explained that there was a method to his morbidity, and that his approach would be to the benefit of the *Messenger*:

A word or two in relation to Berenice. Your opinion of it is very just. The subject is by far too horrible, and I confess that I hesitated in sending it to you. . . . The history of all Magazines show plainly that those which have attained celebrity were indebted for it to articles *similar in nature to Berenice* . . . You ask me in what does this nature consist? In the ludicrous heightened into the grotesque: the fearful coloured into the horrible: the witty exaggerated into the burlesque: the singular wrought out into the strange and mystical. You may say all this is bad taste. I have my doubts about it. . . . But whether the articles of which I speak are, or are not in bad taste is little to the purpose. To be appreciated, you must be *read,* and these things are invariably sought after with avidity. They are, if you will take notice, the articles which find their way into other periodicals, and into the papers, and in this manner, taking hold upon the public mind they augment the reputation of the source where they originated. . . . To be sure originality is an essential in these things—great attention must be paid to style, and much labour spent in their composition, or they will denigrate into the turgid or the absurd.

Right from the beginning of his career as a spinner of terror tales, Poe is the careful craftsman with a clear vision of what the form should be. Like "MS. Found in a Bottle," "Berenice" and "Morella" are promises of the greater horrific delights to come. But Poe also contributed a humorous piece, "Lionizing," and a balloon-hoax story considered an early science-fiction effort, "Hans Pfall" (later published as "The Unparalleled Adventure of One Hans Pfall"). Along with the criticism, they demonstrate how versatile a writer Poe was, something that couldn't have been lost on White. Kennedy's endorsement also carried a great deal of weight, as did Poe's willingness to accept about five dollars for each contribution. White offered him a position at the *Southern Literary Messenger,* and Poe responded on June 22, "You ask me if I would be willing to come on to Richmond if you should have occasion for my services during the coming winter. I reply that nothing would give me greater pleasure . . . Indeed I am anxious to settle myself in that city."

Poe's financial prospects in Richmond had seemed to die with John

Allan in March 1834, but he was drawn back to the city of his youth by the *Southern Literary Messenger* in August 1835.

"Richmond always plays a key role in Poe's life," Peeples said. "But there's always the qualifier. The Allans were not quite his family and Richmond was not quite his hometown. It's almost but not quite, but Richmond comes as close as he's going to get to a hometown."

Separating from Maria and Virginia would be difficult for him, but White's offer of a salary of fifteen dollars a week quickly became even more attractive. Poe's grandmother, the General's wife, died on July 7 at the age of seventy-nine. It meant the loss of her annual pension of $240, which, as little as it may have been, was essential to the family economy. Poe was even more extravagant in his praise of Maria's care for the General's widow, who had been confined to her bed for eight years: "never in any instance leaving it during that time. She had been paralyzed, and suffered from many other complaints—her daughter Maria attending her during her long & tedious illness with a Christian and martyr-like fortitude, and with a constancy of attention, and unremitting affection, which must exalt her character in the eyes of all who know her."

Perhaps leery after being warned that Poe's presence might hurt his publication, White didn't give him an official title. Poe was being brought on as a staff writer, literary critic, and catchall editorial assistant. In addition to writing reviews and stories, his duties included planning and proofreading, as well as overseeing whatever correspondence came in. To Kennedy, Poe accurately reported that he had been hired by White and was "assisting him in editorial duties." To his cousin William Poe, he indulged the need for self-aggrandizing fabrication by writing, "I have lately obtained the Editorship of the Southern Messenger."

So Poe is almost but not quite the editor of the *Messenger*. He moved into a boardinghouse on Bank Street, and the homecoming must have stirred plenty of mixed emotions. He was surrounded by reminders of his life in the Allan household and a time when his prospects seemed so lofty. The *Messenger* offices were above a shoe shop at the corner of Main and Fifteenth, next door to where the company of Ellis & Allan had been

located. But he had hopes—hopes that his association with White's magazine would improve his circumstances, hopes that he could regularly send
badly needed money to the Amity Street house in Baltimore, hopes that
he might land a job teaching English at the Richmond Academy.

Although he again failed to secure a position as a teacher, Poe applied
his great industry to learning the magazine business. While he had no
practical experience as an editor, he was a quick learner, a gift inherited
from his mother. In theater terms, Eliza Poe was what's called a quick
study: she had the ability to swiftly absorb roles and keep them in her
memory banks. Her son had a similar ability to read widely on an astonishing array of subjects and retain what he read.

Still, as busy as he was at the *Messenger,* Poe was lonely, missing the
security and loving support provided by Maria and Virginia, who turned
thirteen on August 22. Richmond may have been the closest thing he had
to a hometown, but he had come to think of home as being where Maria
and Virginia were. The pleasant, middle-aged White was impressed by
Poe's intelligence, talent, and activity. Already emotionally vulnerable,
however, Poe was plunged into a state of despair by a letter in late August
from Maria Clemm. She was seeking his advice. His cousin, Baltimore
lawyer and newspaper editor Neilson Poe, had offered to take Virginia
into his home, seeing to her welfare and education. Financially and socially, what he could offer Virginia and her mother was extremely attractive. Poe viewed his cousin's offer as an act of treachery. He read Maria's
letter with a growing sense of panic. It would mean the loss of the home
he had found in Baltimore. It would mean, he realized, the loss of his aunt
as a surrogate mother. And it would mean the loss of Virginia. He was
more than deeply attached to Virginia. He was in love with her.

Perhaps no aspect of Poe's biography has raised more eyebrows than
his declaration of love for a first cousin just turned thirteen. It did not
carry quite the ick factor then that it would in the twenty-first century,
but, even in an era when very young brides and marriages among cousins were not matters of certain scandal, Virginia's age might have given
some concerned observers justifiable pause. It's entirely possible that

Poe viewed Virginia as a chaste and idealized soulmate. Passion did not mean physical love. It was something finer, truer, far beyond physical love. What is beyond doubt is the sincerity and depth of his feelings for the sweet-natured Virginia, and that she adored him, as well. He poured those feelings into the anguished letter he wrote to Maria on August 29:

> *My dearest Aunty,*
> *I am blinded with tears while writing this letter—I have no wish to live another hour. Amid sorrow, and the deepest anxiety your letter reached [me]—and you well know how little I am able to bear up under the pressure of grief—My bitterest enemy would pity me could he now read my heart—My last my last my only hold on life is cruelly torn away—I have no desire to live and* will not. *But let my duty be done. I love, you know I love Virginia passionately devotedly. I cannot express in words the fervent devotion I feel towards my dear little cousin—my own darling . . . All [my] thoughts are occupied with the supposition that both you & she will prefer to go with N. Poe; I do sincerely believe that your comforts will for the present be secured—I cannot speak as regards your peace—your happiness. You have both tender hearts—and you will always have the reflection that my agony is more than I can bear— that you have driven me to the grave—for love like mine can never be gotten over. It is useless to disguise the truth that when Virginia goes with N. P. that I shall never behold her again—that is absolutely sure. Pity me, my dear Aunty, pity me. I have no one now to fly to—I am among strangers, and my wretchedness is more than I can bear. It is useless to expect advice from me—what can I say? Can I, in honour & in truth say—Virginia! do not go!—do not go where you can be comfortable & perhaps happy—and on the other hand can I calmly resign my—life itself . . . What have I to live for?*

He added a sentence for Virginia: "My love, my own sweetest Sissy, my darling little wifey, think well before you break the heart of your cousin Eddy." Having pleaded his case in a manner he hoped would touch the hearts of the two people closest to him, Poe began drinking to an extent that alarmed the easygoing White. His "rather dissipated" state shook White's confidence in him. Poe might have been fired or might have quit on the point of being fired. What we know for certain is that he couldn't endure the uncertainty any longer. He bolted for Baltimore, where his ardor, and perhaps his vulnerability, won over Aunty and Sissy. A marriage license was taken out on September 22, and there might have been a secret ceremony. A week later, Poe wrote White, asking to be reinstated at the *Messenger*. White's response shows a touching degree of affection and concern for the talented young writer, combined with his version of tough love. Poe could have his job back under one condition: he must give up drinking. "You have fine talents, Edgar—and you ought to have them respected as well as yourself," White wrote to him. "Learn to respect yourself, and you will very soon find that you are respected. Separate from the bottle, and bottle-companions, for ever! Tell me if you can and will do so—and let me hear that it is your fixed purpose never to yield to temptation. If you should come to Richmond again, and again should be an assistant in my office, it must be expressly understood by us that all engagements on my part would be dissolved, the moment you get drunk." He then added two sentences that showed just how unnerved he had been by seeing the effects of alcohol on Poe: "No man is safe who drinks before breakfast! No man can do so, and attend to business properly." White closed the letter with the words, "I am your true friend."

Poe agreed to White's altogether understandable demand. He returned from Baltimore, with Virginia and Maria, on October 3. Virginia would forever be his beloved Sissy. Maria, though, was no longer Aunty. She was Muddy or Mother. And Poe, Maria said, was "indeed a son to me." With his family with him, Poe turned to his work at the *Messenger* with increased vigor and a renewed spirit. White was pleased, not only in the turnaround, but in how loudly Poe's voice was reverberating through the country as a powerful literary critic. Poe reprinted stories and poems in the *Messenger* and took care of a wide variety of editorial duties, but his reviews were gaining the attention that he'd hoped would have been given to first his poetry and then his stories. Although there wasn't the time for many new stories or poems, criticism was providing a dynamic new outlet for his literary voice. By February 9, Kennedy could observe with satisfaction "that you have entirely conquered your late despondency." Poe responded by noting that White, who had increased his salary, was "exceedingly kind in every respect."

Poe was taking his stand as a critic, demanding that American literature be nurtured and encouraged by being held to the highest possible standards. Another publication observed at the time that Poe's reviews "will teach writers to value the praise and dread the censures of the critic." Poe, in fact, was becoming the de facto editor of the *Southern Literary Messenger*. On Monday, May 16, 1836, Poe and Virginia were married by a Presbyterian minister in the presence of White, his daughter Eliza, Maria Clemm, and others. Virginia was still thirteen, and Poe wasn't taking any chances on her age becoming a subject for gossip or scandal; her age was given as twenty-one. Soon after, Elmira Royster Shelton encountered her onetime fiancé and "his lovely wife" in Richmond. They seemed the picture of happiness, and her reaction was telling. "I never shall forget my feelings at the time," she said. "They were indescribable, almost agonizing." In an instant, however, she brushed those pangs aside. "I remembered that I was a married woman, and banished them from me," she recalled in a letter written to Muddy on September 22, 1849, "as I would a poisonous reptile."

"CONSIDERABLE FEVER"

JULY 14–SEPTEMBER 27, 1849

Before leaving Philadelphia on Friday, July 13, 1849, Poe had predicted that his health and state of mind would improve once he planted his feet on Virginia soil. It wasn't a bad bit of prophecy, at least of the short-term variety. He reached Richmond on July 14, taking a room at the recently opened American Hotel, located on the southwest corner of Eleventh and Main Streets. It was a pricey selection, given his recent financial woes in Philadelphia, and he moved to more affordable lodgings at the old Swan Tavern, which had stood on Broad Street, between Eighth and Ninth, since the 1780s. A letter from Maria Clemm did much to lift his spirits: "Oh, if you only knew how your dear letter comforted me! It acted like magic." He was eager to start drumming up support for his magazine, *The Stylus*. And a description of him calling on twenty-seven-year-old poet Susan Archer Talley stands in sunny contrast to his fearful state in Philadelphia.

Poe was accompanied by his sister, Rosalie, who had remained in Richmond in the care of the Mackenzie family. Although characterized as "backward," she had managed to teach writing for nine years at a school run by one of the Mackenzies. Her mental development was roughly that of a twelve-year-old, but she was proud of her brother's accomplishments and doted on him. The visit to the Talley family farmhouse, Talavera, was just a "day or two" after his arrival in Richmond. Talley recalled that Poe's "attitude was easy and graceful." She got the impression that he was a "refined, high-bred, and chivalrous gentleman." His eyes brightened when she offered him her hand, and she "felt that we were no longer strangers."

His reviving optimism received a further boost by the realization that his financial backer in the magazine, Edward Patterson, had forwarded fifty dollars for him to editor John Reuben Thompson at the *Southern Literary Messenger.* He also either found one of his missing lectures, "The Poetic Principle," or was able to rewrite it to the point that a presentation could be announced for the middle of August. Exchanging letters with Patterson on plans for *The Stylus,* he hoped a lecture in Richmond would raise some funds in support of the magazine. The newspaper articles noting his presence in the city and the upcoming lecture must have been immensely gratifying to Poe. They welcomed and celebrated him as a returning son—one of their own, one who belonged. It was in Richmond where press treatment of him was most laudatory. He had become an orphan in the city. He had been exiled by John Allan, who cut him off emotionally and financially. And now he was reading *The Richmond Whig* brag about how "this gentleman," Edgar A. Poe, "who is a native of this city," was gaining literary recognition in France. In announcing the lecture, the city's *Daily Republican* stated that Poe, "who is now in Richmond, the place of his nativity, on a visit, is about to afford our citizens an intellectual feast, in the way of a lecture; and such as all, who are familiar with the genius of the man, can readily imagine will be of a high order."

He wasn't a native of the city, of course, but the eagerness to claim him spoke volumes. Poe had also been renewing acquaintances with the woman he had hoped to marry when they were both teenagers. Elmira Royster Shelton was now a widow and quite a wealthy one. Her husband, Alexander Shelton, had died at thirty-seven, leaving her an estate worth $100,000. His will stipulated that, were she to remarry, she would forfeit three-quarters of the estate. His goal seemed to be to keep the fortune largely intact for their children. Still, when Poe called on her home in the Church Hill section and proposed marriage, probably in late July, she didn't dash his hopes. She asked for time to consider it. He resolved to visit her frequently, and, apparently, he did.

At this point, Poe almost derailed all of his hopes by drinking. He got inebriated fast and he recovered slowly, often indisposed for many days. Two incidents of intoxication, believed to have occurred in early August, were devastating to his already weakened system. After the first, he was treated in his Swan Tavern rooms. Susan Archer Talley saw him a few days later looking pale and tremulous. She had no doubt "that he had been seriously ill." The second bout, even more debilitating, set off alarm bells with two friends, Dr. Gibbon Carter and Poe's boyhood chum John Mackenzie, son of the couple who had taken in Rosalie. Mackenzie had Poe transported from his rooms at the Swan Tavern to his family's home, Duncan's Lodge. His friends believed "his life was in imminent danger." Poe improved under their care, but Carter warned him that "another such attack would prove fatal." He must stop drinking. Moved to tears while recounting his many attempts to quit, Poe resolved to "withstand any temptation." He demonstrated this determination by taking the pledge. On the evening of August 27, he was initiated into the Shockoe Hill Division of the Sons of Temperance. According to several friends, no one saw him take a drink for the remainder of his stay, about four weeks, in Richmond.

This was his last recorded binge, but alcohol had been a problem for Poe off and on for twenty-two years, starting with his University of Virginia days in the fall of 1827. "He had trouble with booze, no question about that, and well knew the imp of the perverse," Poe scholar Dennis Eddings said. But how much did he drink and how often? There have been in the realm of Poe scholarship the alcohol deniers, who say the incidents of intoxication are exaggerated and overstated. There also have been those who argue that alcohol is clearly the curse that hangs over his adult life, making it the leading suspect for the cause of his death. The truth probably falls somewhere between these two viewpoints.

"There are years of sobriety for Poe, and there's also overwhelming evidence that alcohol was a problem," Poe Baltimore executive director

Enrica Jang said. "And over the years, that takes a toll. Alcohol is an underlying issue with Poe, and it never can be dismissed or discounted. I think there was a temptation to underplay the drinking for anyone trying to get away from the idea of Poe being an alcoholic, because it was a shameful thing to people before we became more and more aware of the need for treatment and the need for understanding what an addictive personality means."

Yet the image of a constantly intoxicated Poe viewing much of life through the bottom of a wineglass not only is erroneous but also hinders our understanding of the writer, the writing, and how the writing, which took many forms, was accomplished. Novelist Matthew Pearl, author of *The Poe Shadow,* believes that the romanticizing of Poe's problem with alcohol has been as reckless as the denial of it. "What drives me a little crazy is the treatment of his drinking," he said. "There has been a tendency to glamorize it, and that's dangerous. There's something unsettling about his relationship with alcohol. The evidence suggests that Poe had a constitution that didn't react well to even small amounts of alcohol. That's supported again and again by many contemporary witnesses. And this was a time when social expectations were that you'd drink. But the drinking has become part of the romanticized stereotype of Poe. It feels like a caricature, and that's because it is. And it's a caricature that obscures the real writer."

From this caricature, it's not too much of a leap to the absurd notion that he wrote under the influence of alcohol—that the horror stories were, like the nightmare visions he suffered in a Philadelphia prison cell, fueled by drink.

"It's clear that Poe drank, but it's also clear he didn't drink while he was writing," novelist and biographer Daniel Stashower said. "He needed to summon enormous powers of concentration and willpower to write as much as he did at such a high level. You constantly ask yourself, 'Where did he find the time? Where did he find the time to do all of this sensational work in so many genres when everything was such a struggle and he always was fighting to keep body and soul together?' And he produced that vast amount of writing in a very short amount of time. He was a true professional. He never seems to be dogging it. It's all really good. You can't produce that kind of work under the influence of alcohol, which, again, is not to say he didn't have a problem with alcohol."

Without question, many friends and acquaintances encountered Poe when he had been drinking. The eyewitness accounts are too numerous and detailed to be discounted. But it's also true that many who knew him over a long period of time never saw him drunk. One such colleague was author and journalist Lambert A. Wilmer, who had known Henry Poe and witnessed the older brother's descent into alcoholism. When an early biographer claimed that intemperance was the younger Poe brother's master passion, Wilmer asked, "How then did it happen, that during an intimate acquaintance with him, which continued for more than twelve years, I never saw him intoxicated in a single instance[?]" Wilmer added, "The purpose of these statements is merely to contradict the assertion that Poe was, *at every period of his life,* an habitual drunkard."

Sticking to the temperance pledge would have been difficult during his remaining weeks in Richmond. There were many social engagements, and alcohol would have been a constant. This was also a time and place where the refusal of drink might even be considered an insult. On August 7, he wrote to Patterson, acknowledging that he was just getting around to replying to a June 7 letter. "The fault, Heaven knows, has not been mine," he wrote. "I have suffered worse than death—not so much from the Cholera as from its long-continued consequences in debility and congestion of the brain." Is this confirmation that he actually had contracted cholera in Philadelphia? Is there a hint of a lurking condition, considering that, precisely two months hence, his dying delirium will be attributed to "congestion of the brain"?

What we do know is that, about two weeks after doctors and friends feared for his life, he was in fine form for the lecture delivered to a packed audience in the Concert Room of the Exchange Hotel. Despite the large turnout, he didn't raise much money for the magazine. Tickets were only twenty-five cents. Still, the audience response was overwhelmingly positive, as were the write-ups in the local newspapers. "The lecture of this talented gentleman . . . was one of the richest intellectual treats we have ever had the good fortune to hear," raved the *Daily Republican*. "The clearness and melody of his voice, and the harmonious accentuation of his words, were soul inspiring. . . . The effect on the audience was perceptible. . . . Mr. Poe, in conclusion, favored the audience with his own beautiful production, 'The Raven.'" *The Richmond Whig* declared, "We must say that we were never more delighted in our lives." There was a dissenting voice in the *Semi-Weekly Examiner*, which expressed disappointment in his recitations and the sing-song nature of his delivery. It should be noted, as Poe did in a letter to Muddy, that the *Semi-Weekly Examiner* review, which included words of praise for his theories on poetry, was written by John M. Daniel, an editor Poe had challenged to a duel during the previous year's visit to Richmond. Overall, Poe couldn't have been more pleased. "I *never* was received with so much enthusiasm," he told Muddy. "The papers have done nothing but praise me before the lecture & since."

Reports that Poe and Elmira would be married started making the rounds in Richmond in late August, although no announcement had been made and no agreement had been reached. Certainly his continued sobriety could only have improved his chances with Elmira. Her children, Ann and Southall, however, hardly made it a secret that they disapproved of their mother's suitor. When Poe would visit the Grace Street house, ten-year-old Southall would mimic him behind his back, much to Ann's giggling delight. Ann, nine years older than her brother, later admitted that neither of them lost a chance to run him down in her eyes. Both resented the idea of their late father being replaced.

In early September, Poe traveled to Norfolk and lectured on "The Poetic Principle." He spent a few days with friends at the ocean resort of Old Point Comfort. One evening, sitting with a little group on the veranda of the Hygeia Hotel, one member of the party said, "This seems to be just the time and place for poetry, Mr. Poe." He agreed, reciting "The Raven," "Annabel Lee," and "Ulalume" for them. Back in Richmond, he wrote to Muddy on September 18 that he had cleared enough in Norfolk to settle his bill at the Swan Tavern and move to the Madison House, another inexpensive boarding establishment. It was around this time that Elmira, persuaded by his earnestness and despite the objections of her children and family, reached an understanding with him. Both children cried and begged her not to marry him. If Poe was aware of their feelings, he never acknowledged them. "I think she loves me more devotedly than any one I ever knew & I cannot help loving her in return," he wrote to Muddy. "If *possible* I will get married before I start—but there is no telling."

Poe encouraged Elmira to send Muddy a reassuring letter, which she did, on September 22. "I am fully prepared to *love* you, and I do sincerely hope that our spirits may be congenial—There shall be nothing wanting on my part to make them so," she wrote. "I have just spent a very happy evening with your dear Edgar, and I know it will be gratifying to you to know, that he is all that you could desire him to be, sober, temperate, moral & much beloved—He showed me a letter of yours, in which you spoke affectionately of me, and for which I feel very much gratified & complimented . . . Edgar speaks frequently & very affectionately of your daughter & his Virginia, for which I love him but the more."

Doing his share to hearten the lonely and isolated Muddy, Poe wrote her, "I showed your letter to Elmira and she says 'it is such a darling precious letter that she loves you for it already.'"

About twenty-five years after these sentiments were expressed, Elmira claimed that she and Poe were not engaged when he left Richmond but that there was what she called "a partial understanding." She further confused matters by adding, "I do not think I should have married him under any circumstances." It has been suggested that she was hedging in 1875 because of her children's opposition to the marriage. Yet it's clear from the letters by Poe and Elmira in September 1849 that they were making plans. These talks about the future included some discussion of where they would live. Poe was ruling out a return to New York. Richmond might have seemed the logical choice, given how warmly he had been received. She already had a lovely house there. And, as he once wrote to his cousin George Poe, "Richmond is my home, and a letter to that City will always reach me in whatever part of the world I may be." Still, Poe wondered if they—or, more to the point, he—would be happy in Richmond. As ardently as he had pursued and persuaded Elmira, Poe now recognized the shadow of doubt hanging over him. The shadow reached all the way from New England and took the form of a woman he probably would have flown to if she were free. So, even while making plans for married life with Elmira, he was thinking of the unattainable Annie Richmond in Lowell, Massachusetts. He had been smitten with Annie since meeting her in October 1847. Eleven years younger and married, she was idealized and idolized by Poe, who knew he couldn't have her and yet couldn't imagine living without her. "Could we be happier in Richmond or Lowell?" he asked Muddy. "I *must* be somewhere where I can see Annie . . . I want to live *near Annie.*" For two years, he had gloried in the friendship with Annie, even as other women came in and out of his life. It was a platonic friendship, but he yearned for more, even though there was no question of her leaving her husband, Charles. He was deeply in love with her. He addressed her in letters as "My Sweet Friend and Sister," but the feelings he expressed for Elmira, however genuine, paled in comparison to those inspired by Annie. While there was obviously great mutual affection between him and Elmira, he sometimes seemed to be viewing the impending match in distinctly practical terms. And then there's the ominous line in a letter to Muddy: "I confess that my heart sinks at the idea of this marriage." What if Annie was suddenly free? We get some glimpse at his thoughts in a letter he wrote to Muddy in late August, when, presumably, Elmira hadn't yet made up her mind about reaching an understanding. "Do not tell me anything about Annie," he implored her. "I cannot bear to hear it now—unless you can tell me that Mr. R. is dead."

Indeed, he had idealized Annie the same way he had Virginia. There's no sense of that with Elmira. The depth of his feelings is revealed in the final lines of his tribute to Annie, the 1849 poem "For Annie":

> *But my heart it is brighter*
> *Than all of the many*

Stars in the sky,
For it sparkles with Annie—
It glows with the light
Of the love of my Annie—
With the thought of the light
Of the eyes of my Annie.

Mr. Richmond continued in fine health, though, and the best Poe could hope for would be to live near Annie and maintain a close friendship. Blissfully unaware of Poe's chilling wishes for him, Charles Richmond probably would have continued genially supporting the friendship. Also unaware of the dark and anguished thoughts confided to Muddy, Elmira suggested they start off living in her house. They'd have Muddy join them and make plans from there. Elmira at one point suggested a trip to New York and the Fordham cottage, but Poe wrote Muddy that it would probably be best for her "to give up everything there" and join them in Richmond.

During his last weeks in Richmond, Poe happened to pass by William A. Pratt's Daguerreian Gallery at 145 Main Street. Standing at the street door, Pratt engaged the writer in conversation, reminding him that he often promised to sit for a picture. When Poe protested that he wasn't dressed for it, Pratt said he'd gladly take him just as he was. Thus Poe agreed to sit for what would be his last two photographs. Thompson of the *Southern Literary Messenger* dated the sitting to two weeks before Poe's death.

Around the same time, on September 24, Poe again gave the "Poetic Principle" lecture in the Exchange Hotel's Concert Room. This time, tickets were fifty cents and the audience smaller. And this time, Elmira attended, as did Susan Archer Talley, with her mother and sister, and Rosalie Poe. More than half a century later, the poet and author then known as Susan Archer Weiss recalled, "I noticed that Poe had no manuscript, and that, though he stood like a statue, he held his audience as motionless as himself—fascinated by his voice and expression. Rose pointed out to me Mrs. Shelton, seated conspicuously in front of the platform." After the lecture, Poe descended from the platform and went to his sister. Weiss recalled the scene: "Rose, radiantly happy, stood drawn up to her full height, and observed, 'Edgar, only see how the people are staring at the poet and his sister.' I believe it to have been the proudest moment of her life, and one which she ever delighted to recall."

If this account is reliable, then Elmira apparently attended both of the Richmond lectures. The letter to Muddy was written September 22, two days before the second lecture, and it contains the passage, "Edgar's lecture a few weeks since, on the Poetic Principle, was very beautiful, he had quite a full and very fashionable audience—He will repeat his lecture on Monday next, when I sincerely hope he will be patronised by a very large audience."

The following evening, he visited Talavera and had a long talk with Susan Archer Talley. He would be leaving for New York in a couple of days. The reason he gave was business for *The Stylus*. He said he would be back in less than two weeks. "He declared that the last few weeks in the society of his old and new friends had been the happiest he had known for many years," she recalled, "and that when he again left New York he should there leave behind all the trouble and vexation of his past life. On no occasion had I seen him so cheerful and hopeful as on this evening."

Poe called on Thompson at the offices of the *Southern Literary Messenger* on September 26, giving him a manuscript of "Annabel Lee." Thompson gave him five dollars for traveling money. He told Thompson that his plan was to stop in Philadelphia, where he would earn one hundred dollars for editing a volume of a local woman's poetry.

Was Poe in bad shape when he left Richmond? The strongest eyewitness testimony for this was provided by Elmira Shelton: "He came up to my house on the evening of 26th Sept. to take leave of me.—He was very sad, and complained of being sick; I felt his pulse, and found he had considerable fever, and did not think it probable that he would be able to start the next morning, as he anticipated.—I felt so wretched about him all of that night, that I went up early the next morning to enquire after him, when much to my regret, he had left in the boat for Baltimore." Later that night, about nine thirty, he visited the office of John F. Carter, a young doctor. The two talked pleasantly, Poe looking over the papers and playing with the handsome Malacca sword-cane a friend had recently given the physician. Poe abruptly stood up and announced that he was going over to Sadler's Restaurant for dinner. He absentmindedly took Carter's cane with him, leaving his own behind, along with a copy of Thomas Moore's *Irish Melodies*. If Poe was there to ask for medicine or if he even looked feverish, Carter made no mention of it in his recollections of the evening. Sadler later told Carter that Poe had left about midnight, heading for Rockett's Landing and "the Baltimore boat" with some companions. Again, no mention of illness. And just days after Poe's death, Thompson wrote, "The evening before his departure from Richmond he was with me and spoke in the highest spirits of his resolves and prospects for the future." So it's impossible to say what condition Poe was in, physically or psychologically, when he boarded a steam packet for Baltimore at four in the morning. Was he feverish, sad, and confused as the vessel began its journey north? Or was he buoyant, optimistic, and sober, as Thompson and others described him?

Certainly during the last few days in Richmond, many friends and acquaintances described his mood as upbeat. That seemed to be the case when he bid farewell to the Talley family on September 25. He was the last to leave the party at Talavera that night. The parting image was for Susan Archer Talley both symbolic of his life and sadly prophetic of his death: "We were standing on the portico, and after going a few steps he paused, turned, and again lifted his hat, in a last adieu. At that moment, a brilliant meteor appeared in the sky directly over his head."

"EXTREMITY OF TERROR"

MAY 1836–JANUARY 20, 1842

Settled in Richmond with his beloved "Mother," Maria Clemm, and his adored "Sissy," Virginia, newlywed Poe generated a ferocious amount of copy in his position as editor at the *Southern Literary Messenger*. A substantial portion of these pieces consisted of reviews. First a poet and then the promising author of both humorous and terror-tinged short stories, he had entered upon the phase of his career for which he'd be most famous in his lifetime. Given that his duties also included evaluating articles submitted for consideration, editing and proofreading copy, soliciting contributions, and writing items for fillers in each issue, it's no wonder that he had little time for short stories and poetry. It is a wonder that he managed to produce as much penetrating and finely polished criticism as he did. His industry, stamina, and dedication were as admirable as his attempts to provide for his family.

By most accounts, it was a happy household. "He was unquestionably of an affectionate disposition, of which he gave the best kind of proof when he labored cheerfully for the maintenance" of Muddy and Sissy, wrote his friend Lambert Wilmer. "While he was editor of the *Southern Literary Messenger* he devoted a large part of his salary to Virginia's education, and she was instructed in every elegant accomplishment at his expense. He himself became her tutor at another time, when his income was not sufficient to provide for a more regular course of education. I remember once finding him engaged, on a certain Sunday, in giving Virginia lessons in Algebra."

Wilmer grew positively indignant at the accusation that Poe was anything but devoted to, solicitous of, and caring toward Virginia. Of all the malicious charges hurled at Poe after his death, this one struck Wilmer as particularly despicable:

> One of his severe chroniclers says, "It is believed by some that he really loved his wife; if he did, he had a strange way of showing his affection." Now it appears to me that he showed his affection in the *right* way, by endeavoring to make his companion happy. According to the opportunities he possessed, he supplied her with the comforts and luxuries of life. He kept a piano to gratify her taste for music, at a time when his income could scarcely afford such an indulgence. I never knew him to give her an unkind word, and doubt if they ever had any disagreement. That Virginia loved him, I am quite certain, for she was by far too artless to assume the appearance of an affection which she did not feel.

If and when the marriage was consummated is unknown. Poe's sexuality is yet another mystery and, thus, another source of endless speculation. It has been theorized that Poe may have been impotent and love to him meant a pure kind of adoration. Was there something telling in his pet name for her, Sissy? Was she more of a devoted and petted sister than a wife? There is testimony that they initiated a true married life when she turned sixteen. So, it's all theory, of course, and can never be anything more than that. Those seeking to speculate on the state of things in Eddy and Sissy's bedroom must do so from outside a closed door. His affection and devotion, however, were confirmed by many witnesses.

Wilmer was equally impressed with Poe's work ethic. "He appeared to me to be one of the most hard-working men in the world," he wrote in a remembrance published in 1866. "I called to see him at all hours, and always found him employed."

Prolific with his pen, Poe was also a voracious reader, constantly pursuing a staggering variety of subjects. Vincent Price, who would star in several movies inspired by or loosely based on Poe stories and poems, once declared, "A man who limits his interests limits his life." The actor wasn't specifically talking about Poe at the time, but he certainly was voicing a sentiment the writer he so admired would have wholeheartedly endorsed. Poe's corollary might have been, "The artist who limits his interests limits his art." Price as an actor, like Poe as a writer, was branded a horror specialist, but, like Poe, he had many interests and an antic sense of humor.

"Do you want to know what made Poe such a master of the horror story?" Price once asked. "In addition to being a great observer of human nature, he had great curiosity. He was intensely interested in everything, so everything informed his art: history, science, languages, criminology, flora, anything, everything, and, above all, the human psyche. It all informed his work, and that's what you need if you're going to write well in this deceptively complex area we call horror. You must have that driving curiosity and sense of wonder about the great things we're capable of . . . and the bad, as well. You can't just be interested in scaring people or sending chills down their spine. That's what separates the best horror stories and makes them literature. You have to know that about Poe the man in order to appreciate Poe the writer."

Or, you might say, the person who limits his or her interest in Poe limits Poe's life, and our understanding of that life. Poe excelled in the chills department, but not because he spent all of his spare time haunting graveyards, mourning lost loves, and communicating with gaunt and ghastly ravens.

"This isn't a different writer working in these different genres," said Paul Lewis, English professor at Boston College and past president of the Poe Studies Association. "There is no difference between Poe the book reviewer and critic and Poe the creative writer and poet. You've got to break down that wall. The same intellectual and emotional impulse is at play in these very different kinds of works."

That great curiosity Price referred to served Poe well as a critic. During his tenure at the *Southern Literary Messenger,* Poe was reviewing novels, poetry, and biographies, as well as works about naval history, phrenology, botany, philosophy, religion, navigation, geography, natural history, music, and exploration. Poe was making his name as a critic, and making no shortage of enemies with the high standards and searing insights he brought to his literary criticism. Those looking for proof of Poe's humorous abilities logically head for his comic pieces and hoaxes, but his wit runs through many of the horror stories and the criticism as well. Indeed, many of his funniest lines can be found in the reviews.

"The book is a public imposition," Poe wrote in 1836 of a volume titled *Ups and Downs in the Life of a Distressed Gentleman.* "The 'Introduction' . . . is by much the best portion of the work—so much so, indeed, that we fancy it written by some kind, good[-]natured friend of the author. . . . [The book] is written, we believe, by Col. Stone of the New York Commercial advertiser, and should have been printed among the quack advertisements in a spare corner of his paper." That same year, he had this to say about Joseph Robinson's *The Swiss Heiress; or The Bride of Destiny:* "The Swiss Heiress should be read by all who have nothing better to do. We are patient, and having gone through the whole book with the most dogged determination, are now enabled to pronounce it one of the most solemn of farces. Let us see if it be not possible to give some idea of the plot."

Although he drew blood with rapier thrusts, his harsher reviews earned him the nickname "the Tomahawk Man." Summarizing his approach in an 1841 letter, Poe wrote: "In criticism I will be bold & sternly, absolutely just, with friend & foe. From this purpose nothing shall turn me. I shall aim at *originality* in the body of the work, more than at any other especial quality."

"The level of detail and specificity in some of those reviews anticipates modern literary criticism," Poe biographer James M. Hutchisson said. "He deserves more credit for his amazing gifts as a critic."

Poe has been claimed as an iconic figure by writers of horror, mystery, science fiction, and fantasy, or as Poe scholar Scott Peeples said, "Everybody wants Poe on their team." That's not so much true with critics, though, perhaps because, a century after his death, his reputation as a critic had faded into obscurity. One Nobel Prize–winning writer who celebrated all of Poe's gifts, including the criticism, was George Bernard Shaw, an influential critic, essayist, and playwright. "He was the greatest journalistic critic of his time, placing good European work at sight when the European critics were waiting for somebody to tell them what to say," Shaw wrote in a January 1909 tribute marking the centennial of Poe's birth. Like Shaw, and Shaw's hero, Mark Twain, Poe was capable of turning that slashing wit inward and poking fun at himself. "I have great faith in fools—self-confidence my friends will call it," Poe wrote. It's the kind of playful self-putdown that, to the casual observer, will sound more like Twain than Poe.

Those also looking for Poe's literary influences will find them celebrated in his criticism. He used a January 1836 review to charmingly repay a childhood debt to Daniel Defoe and *Robinson Crusoe*. Poe's positive review of a Defoe biography makes the point that, while the English author was a versatile and gifted writer who remained a household name, his immense fame rested on the massive popularity of one book. And that one book, *Robinson Crusoe,* had completely overshadowed his many other accomplishments. "While Defoe would have been fairly entitled to immortality had he never written Robinson Crusoe, yet his many other very excellent writings have nearly faded from our attention," he wrote in the *Southern Literary Messenger*. He also makes the point that even *Robinson Crusoe* was not fully appreciated because readers all caught up in the book's wonders failed to grasp the art and careful craft involved: "Not one person in ten—nay, not one person in five hundred, has, during the perusal of Robinson Crusoe, the most remote conception that any particle of genius, or even of common talent, has been employed in its creation. . . . The powers which have wrought the wonder have been thrown into obscurity by the very stupendousness of the wonder they have wrought!" In discussing the perception of Defoe and the effect of *Robinson Crusoe* on that perception, Poe the critic, in many ways, is anticipating what will happen to his own literary reputation. The greater body of work will be overshadowed by a relatively small group of stories, and the power that wrought those wonders will be thrown into obscurity.

But the review finds Poe looking not forward in any prophetic sense but into the past, indulging in a giddy bit of nostalgia for the thrill of being shipwrecked with Defoe's hero. The adult Poe is joyously recalling that youthful first encounter with *Robinson Crusoe* in England and the monumental effect it had on him: "How fondly do we recur, in memory, to those enchanted days of our boyhood when we first learned to grow serious over Robinson Crusoe!—when we first found the spirit of wild adventure enkindling within us, as, by the dim light, we labored out, line by line, the marvelous import of those pages, and hung breathless and trembling with eagerness over their absorbing—over their enchanting interest!"

Most of the poems and stories Poe published in the *Southern Literary Messenger* during his time as editor were reprinted pieces, like "To Helen," "Loss of Breath," and "Bon-Bon." Excerpts from his unfinished blank-verse play, *Politian,* based on the 1825 killing of Kentucky attorney general Solomon P. Sharp, ran in the December 1835 and January 1836 editions, but the majority of that work had been completed before he settled into the editor's chair in Richmond. When Poe had asked John Pendleton Kennedy for his opinion of *Politian,* Kennedy's response had been that Poe should continue putting his efforts into short stories and poems.

While keeping up with his editorial duties, Poe was spending an enormous amount of time reading and then writing about what he had read. It has been argued that, compensating for having completed just one semester of college, Poe read widely but not all that deeply—that he claimed an erudition that wasn't truly earned, that, under the immense pressure of writing so much copy, he sometimes made up quotations and didn't always read all of the works he reviewed. There is evidence for some of these charges, to be sure, yet the bulk of his criticism bears out Shaw's evaluation of him. Like Shaw, Poe knew the value of a well-turned and extremely sharp critical point. As with the stories, he wanted to be entertaining, and he wanted to be read.

As usual, Poe wasn't making it easy on himself. He leveled charges of plagiarism and sloppy grammar against many a writer, even some of the country's best-loved and most well-known literary figures. He also condemned the practice of "indiscriminate puffing," where one writer would lavishly praise the work of another, expecting the same soft treatment in turn. Also known as logrolling, this chummy swapping of favors has never disappeared from the literary landscape.

Of course, being a creature of contradiction, duality, and ambiguity, Poe left himself open to these very same charges. Quick to pounce on grammatical errors, he committed more than his share. That's understandable, given the speed and quantity that magazine work demanded. And while Poe might have asked for that understanding, he wasn't inclined to offer it to others. He also violated his anti-puffing rule on occasion. And given how Poe defined plagiarism, which included the borrowing of tone and techniques, he sometimes put himself on shaky ground in this territory too. Still, if not always pure on the details, his overall intentions were as sound as his spot-on judgments.

"He also had a lot of enemies because he was such an insightful and brilliant critic," Harry Lee "Hal" Poe said. "He could be vicious, but usually the targets were deserving ones. A lot of what he was reviewing was complete garbage. And his assessments have stood the test of time. The stuff he put down as junk has faded and been blessedly forgotten. The writers he praised, like Dickens and Hawthorne, deserved to be remembered. He's been proved right on all of his literary assessments."

This did not go completely unrecognized as Poe was gaining prominence as a critic at the *Southern Literary Messenger*. The *Richmond Whig* praised his reviews for "lashing dullness, as it always deserves to be lashed, with a cat-o'-nine tails." The *National Intelligencer* declared, "The tone of the criticisms differs widely from puffery, and is perfectly independent."

And the *Philadelphia Saturday Evening Post* noted that "the editorial criticism and reviews appear to be written in a spirit of candor quite unusual for the American press."

Other publications viewed Poe's style of criticism with alarm, denouncing him as a ruthless self-promoter, more interested in boosting his own fame than the country's literary standards. The critics of the critic also winced when Poe got personal with his reviews, where he questioned a writer's character or education.

Poe answered his detractors by indicting the kind of national pride that praised an inferior work simply because it was written by an American—"forcing our readers to relish a stupid book the better because sure enough its stupidity was American." As for his approach to criticism, "It is folly to assert, as some at present are fond of asserting, that the Literature of any nation or age was ever injured by plain speaking on the part of the Critics. As for American letters, plain-speaking about *them* is, simply, the one thing needed. They are in a condition of absolute quagmire."

It was a stand that gained him notoriety but not popularity. "Poe was a great critic of American nationalism," Poe scholar J. Gerald Kennedy said. "He resisted the notion of an ordained dominance over the North American continent. That also was something that didn't go over very well. Poe also had an absolute obsession with being the arbiter of literary tastes and judgment. He wanted to be the preeminent critic and the impresario."

To George Rex Graham, a later publisher who provided a forum for his criticism, "Literature with him was religion; and he, its high-priest, with a whip of scorpions scourged the money-changers from the temple. In all else, he had the docility and kind-heartedness of a child. No man was more quickly touched by a kindness—none more prompt to return for an injury."

Southern Literary Messenger publisher Thomas Willis White may have been uncomfortable with an editor regularly courting controversy, but Poe was getting results. Under his guidance, the journal enjoyed a substantial jump in circulation and recognition. In June 1836, Poe wrote to Kennedy,

"Our Messenger is thriving beyond all expectations, and I myself have every prospect of success." By the fall, however, the relationship between proprietor and editor was showing a decided strain. They were heading for a break, although the reason for it remains in doubt. Poe was growing restless and depressed, unhappy with the long hours, constant duties, and paltry salary. White was anxious and depressed, worried about debt and devastated by the realization that his wife was dying of uterine cancer. It has been suggested that Poe was again drinking, although White never explicitly cited this as the reason for seeking a parting of the ways. White confided in a late December letter, "Highly as I really think of Mr. Poe's talents, I shall be forced to give him notice, in a week or so at farthest, that I can no longer recognize him as editor of my Messenger." The supposition is that he was making good on his promise to dismiss Poe if he again started drinking. It's not an unlikely scenario. Yet it's also clear that White was growing personally disenchanted with Poe and wished to reassert control of the magazine. Both reasons may be true. The January edition of the *Messenger* carried the notice that Poe was retiring as editor. The good-hearted White tried to soften matters with money and the promise to publish chapters from Poe's novel, *The Narrative of Arthur Gordon Pym*. Whatever guilt he may have been feeling, he was clearly relieved to be shut of an editor he viewed as high maintenance. There was also probably some truth in Poe's recollections of the situation: "The situation was disagreeable to me in every respect. The drudgery was excessive, the salary was contemptible. In fact, I soon found that whatever reputation I might personally gain, this reputation would be all. I stood no chance of bettering my pecuniary condition."

Poe stayed in Richmond until late January, then moved to New York, where he had briefly lived in 1831 following his departure from West Point. This time around, he needed to find lodgings that also would accommodate his wife and mother-in-law. He found them at Sixth Avenue and Waverly Place, where they shared a floor with their lodger, a bookseller named William Gowans. Poe's editorial responsibilities at the *Messenger* had kept him from producing much in the way of poetry and short stories, but after Harper & Brothers had turned down his "Tales of the Folio Club" collection in early 1836, he did find time to work on *The Narrative of Arthur Gordon Pym.* In New York, he set about finding work and finding a publisher for his novel.

If Poe had been drinking during his last few months in Richmond, he seems to have entered a long period of sobriety in New York. Gowans left behind an account of this period, stating, "For eight months or more, 'one house contained us, us one table fed!' During that time I saw much of him, and had an opportunity of conversing with him often, and I must say I never saw him the least affected with liquor, nor even descend to any known vice, while he was one of the most courteous, gentlemanly, and intelligent companions I have met with during my journeying and halting through divers divisions of the globe."

In May, Harper & Brothers agreed to publish *The Narrative of Arthur Gordon Pym* (although it would not see print until late July 1838). The family may have lived briefly at 113½ Carmine Street, but, early in 1838, they moved to Philadelphia, hoping for some improvement to what had become increasingly desperate circumstances.

Baltimore and Richmond were the two cities where Poe had found a degree of acceptance and, more importantly, a sense of family. In 1830s America, they were considered Southern cities. And although born in Boston, Poe certainly viewed himself as a Southerner. For the remainder of his life, however, his residences would be in the Northern cities of Philadelphia and New York. Just how deep the Southern identity ran in Poe is one of the more intriguing topics weighed by scholars and biographers.

"He always had the bearing of a Virginia gentleman," Richmond's Poe Museum curator Chris Semtner said. "And he probably carried a Tidewater accent through his entire life. In fact, there are some poems that only rhyme correctly when you factor in a Southern Tidewater accent."

"You do need to consider Poe's Southernness," Poe biographer Hutchisson said. "He was a Southerner. He grew up a Southerner. He talked and thought like a Southerner. He thought of himself as a Southerner. Now, that also means he subscribed to some of the best and worst social views and attitudes of Southerners. He had some extremely elitist, segregationist, and exclusive notions about class and race. Some think he dropped in and out of the Southern identity. It has been argued that he was a Southerner when he wanted to be. But I find it difficult to believe he left all of that behind him when he left Richmond."

Having once aspired to the Virginia aristocracy, Poe certainly attacked the abolitionist movement. Like many Americans of his time, North and South, he believed in the superiority of the white race. And his depictions of Black characters tend to be broadly stereotypical. But while he absorbed those attitudes and views of his Southern upbringing, Hutchisson said, he wasn't necessarily overtly racist, at least not in the twenty-first-century understanding of that term. Any defense or indictment of Poe on these grounds, he cautioned, runs the risk of being overstated.

While Poe's manners and accent marked him as a Southerner, it's possible he never felt fully accepted anywhere. Whether in Richmond or Philadelphia, he was still that outsider gaining inside access by dint of his talent.

"I have sort of mixed feelings about the whole Southern identity thing," Poe scholar Peeples said. "On the one hand, Richmond tends to get under-acknowledged in terms of its effect on him. But if you look at the trajectory of Poe's life and career, I think he was someone who could change his spots when necessary. He was fairly cosmopolitan, and I don't buy the whole misplaced and exiled Southerner in a hostile Northeastern land. It's not as if he grew up in the deep South. Quite frankly, I don't think he identified that strongly with any one region. The idea of Poe as a Southern refugee stuck. It's not completely untrue, but it's often exaggerated."

Poe, in fact, looked beyond sectional and national boundaries, very likely viewing himself as a citizen of the world. There are many intriguing what-if questions surrounding so short a life. What if Poe had lived another twelve years and witnessed the start of the Civil War? Would his allegiances have been with the Old Dominion and, therefore, the Confederacy? An even bigger question, however, is where he would have gone as a writer.

"Much is made of Poe thinking of himself as a Southern gentleman, but the bigger theme, I think, is that he views himself as an unrecognized genius," Poe Studies Association past president Amy Branam Armiento said. "He knew he was really good at something and had something special to offer, and that he was constantly being thwarted. Would he have stayed in the North? You have to be curious, but we'll never know. What we do know is that he never stood still, geographically and artistically. He was always on the move, so who's to say where he would have gone?"

Supporting the idea that he felt isolated by an awareness of his own literary gifts is something Poe wrote near the end of his life:

> I have sometimes amused myself by endeavoring to fancy what would be the fate of any individual gifted, or rather accursed, with an intellect *very* far superior to that of his race. Of course, he would be conscious of his superiority; nor could he . . . help manifesting his consciousness. Thus he would make himself enemies at all points, And since his opinions and speculations would widely differ from those of *all* mankind—that he would be considered a madman, is evident. How horribly painful such a condition! Hell could invent no greater torture . . .

To Kennedy, the path Poe would have taken in the 1850s and 1860s is yet another unsolvable mystery:

> Poe dies right as we start the inevitable slide toward the Civil War. And where would Poe have gone in that process? Inevitably a Southern sympathizer? The party Poe most identified with, the Whigs, became the Republican Party. His politics tended to be conservative. So it's all just so hard to anticipate. Poe was obsessed with the spiritual and intellectual problems that con-

sumed many people at that time, but he also was bound up with the complications of his own tormented existence. That's the inconceivable Poe. It's near impossible to imagine what Poe would have become and who he would have become. He was meant to die at forty always.

Although a Whig, Poe didn't see much logic or sense exhibited in the realms of politics and government. He believed that most political beliefs were "purely personal, rather than considerations of principle." The majority of the people, he wrote, "care hardly more about the characters of their rulers than do the subjects of the sultan." So, like the later writer and critic associated with Baltimore, H. L. Mencken, Poe had little good to say about the merits of the republic. "Poe was dubious about the notion of radical democracy," Kennedy said. "And he recognized the great susceptibility of democracy to corruption."

Politics, though, was not much on Poe's mind when he made the move from New York to a boardinghouse on Mulberry Street in Philadelphia. He was thinking of improved circumstances for himself, Sissy, and Muddy. It did not immediately bring about the hoped-for economic relief. Writer James Pedder lived nearby and found the family suffering from having so little to eat. He recalled that they were living on bread and molasses for weeks at a time. By July, things were so bad, Poe wrote his friend James Kirke Paulding seeking help. A satirist, dramatist, novelist, and longtime friend of Washington Irving, Paulding had recently been appointed secretary of the navy by President Martin Van Buren. Convinced he could not possibly support Virginia and Maria, let alone himself, through just literary work, Poe asked if Paulding could secure him a clerk's position in his department (*"any thing, by sea or land"*). Although Paulding recognized Poe's genius and considered him the country's leading literary talent, the clerkship didn't come through. Eleven days after Poe wrote this letter to Paulding, Harper & Brothers finally published *The Narrative of Arthur Gordon Pym,* which confused and even angered many critics. Despite a supersized subtitle that promised atrocious butchery, mutiny, horrible suffering, famine, shipwreck, massacre, and calamity, it was yet another Poe book that failed to sell many copies. Still, not all of the reviews were negative, and a few grasped what Poe was attempting with *Pym*, which is the title character's account of five fantastic voyages. One of the appreciative reviews appeared in the *Morning Courier*: "There is certainly an array of horrors set forth in the title; but the volume is highly interesting in the story, well written, and to lovers of marvellous fiction will be quite a treasure." Poe went back to refining his take on the short story.

"Poe did not seem to understand what makes a great novel," said Poe scholar Edward G. Pettit. "And he can't write a novel. His novel, *The Narrative of Arthur Gordon Pym*, is a glorious mess. I love it. It's so much fun. It's bizarre and weird, but he can't sustain the grand effects he produces so masterfully in the short stories."

Things were so dire, Poe made an earnest attempt to learn the art of lithography, a method for printing text or illustrations on paper and other surfaces. "He labored long and painfully to make himself practically acquainted with this business," Wilmer recalled. "Confinement in a stooping position affected his health; decided symptoms of consumption made their appearance, and his wife and mother-in-law persuaded him to abandon an occupation which was hurrying him to the grave."

As the family moved to a small house on Sixteenth Street near Locust in early September, there was little to indicate that Poe was about to crank up the volume and produce the mature works that would make him a literary rock star to future generations. It would be his most productive and impressive stretch as a writer, and it began that October when his friends Nathan C. Brooks and Dr. Joseph E. Snodgrass published his short story "Ligeia" in their Baltimore monthly *The American Museum*. Like "Berenice" and "Morella," "Ligeia" tells of a doomed attempt at marriage and the death of a beautiful woman. The raven-haired, dark-eyed Lady Ligeia, however, chillingly demonstrates her belief that human will can be stronger than death. She does this by rejuvenating herself in the body of the narrator's second wife, the fair-haired, blue-eyed Lady Rowena. Such beautiful and ethereal women were something of an endangered species in Poe's stories and poems.

"With reason, of course," Pettit said. "In many ways, the death of a beautiful woman is his biography. At some point he says that the death of a beautiful woman is the most romantic of topics. If you're a woman and Poe loves you, look out, you're doomed."

All three terror tales also feature a haunted and possibly disturbed narrator. But the far more artful and brilliantly crafted "Ligeia" is the work of a horror writer realizing the full extent of his formidable powers. "The story of the Lady Ligeia is not merely one of the wonders of literature: it is unparalleled and unapproached," George Bernard Shaw would write about seventy years after its first appearance in print. "There is really nothing to be said about it: we others simply take off our hats and let Mr. Poe go first."

Poe opens the story with what may be a spurious quotation attributed to seventeenth-century English clergyman, philosopher, and writer Joseph Glanvill. It is entirely possible he made up these four sentences to suit his purposes, especially with the final line about man not yielding "unto death utterly, save only through the weakness of his feeble will." He then makes these the Lady Ligeia's dying words. Her death leaves the narrator "crushed into the very dust with sorrow."

"He's lost all of these women who meant so much to him and died young, so he's always returning to that sense of loss," Armiento said. "In the short stories, the doomed women are quite frightening. In the poems, the doomed women are romanticized. As a writer, he's surrounded by the death culture, and you sense he's trying to work out the many losses in his life."

Horror literature tends to tackle the big themes, giving us metaphorical and allegorical means to wrap our minds around the most difficult subjects. Perhaps the biggest one is death. Poe tackles this one in his poems, short stories, and even the essays. "He's looking at death in a different way and all kinds of ways," Semtner said. "He's grappling with it. What is this transition between life and death? What happens to us? Those are his questions, but they're ours, too."

In late 1838, Poe received a badly needed fifty dollars for assisting Professor Thomas Wyatt in preparing *The Conchologist's First Book* for publication. Harper & Brothers had published Wyatt's *Manual of Conchology* earlier that year, selling it for the exorbitant price of eight dollars. Wyatt wanted a cheap edition that he could sell at lectures, and, in order to get around Harper & Brothers, he had Poe put his name on the inexpensive *The Conchologist's First Book,* which was published in April 1839. Poe did do some original writing for the volume, but it was, for the most part, Wyatt's work. It was the publishing equivalent of the old street hustler's shell game. But similarities to Captain Thomas Brown's *The Conchologist's Text Book,* published in Glasgow in 1833, put Poe in the firing line for charges of plagiarism. He got nothing but trouble for those fifty dollars. Understandably miffed by the deception, Harper & Brothers was not happy with Poe's part in undercutting sales for the expensive edition of Wyatt's work. As Arthur Hobson Quinn observed in his biography of Poe, it was "grimly ironic" that this was the only book published under his name during his lifetime that went into a second edition.

Just as he had followed "Metzengerstein" with a comic story, he now followed "Ligeia" with one of his best humorous efforts, "How to Write a Blackwood Article," and its companion piece, "A Predicament." Both appeared in the November issue of *The American Museum.* But while Poe was building up steam creatively, he wasn't having much luck building up the family's prospects for eating regularly. There hadn't been a steady income since the separation from the *Southern Literary Messenger.* That changed when, in May 1839, Poe wrote to the owner of *Burton's Gentleman's Magazine,* seeking employment as an assistant editor. The publication's colorful English-born owner, William Evans Burton, was a popular character actor who divided his time between playing the clown on stage and playing owner-editor of the magazine he had founded in July 1837. He needed someone who could free him for absences due to theatrical engagements and handle the myriad of editorial duties. Poe, with his experience at the *Messenger* and the reputation he gained in Richmond, fit the bill. But Billy Burton was not one to cede control of a journal bearing his name. Nor was he one eager to court controversy. He kept his new assistant editor on a short leash and a short salary: ten dollars a week. He advised Poe to keep his disregard of other writers to himself, and he justified the low salary by assuring his employee that the workload wouldn't amount to more than two hours a day. Billy was talking utter rot. The drudgery aspects of this position were not dissimilar to those at the *Messenger*, except that he lacked the power and prestige of an editor's title. The money was badly needed, however, and his connection with *Burton's* did bring him into contact with Philadelphia's leading writers and artists.

One of these was *Burton's* contributor Thomas Dunn English, a poet and novelist ten years Poe's junior. They started out as warm friends, and the younger writer was a frequent visitor to the Poe household. "Mrs. Poe was a delicate gentlewoman, with an air of refinement and good breeding," he recalled, "and Mrs. Clemm had more of the mother than the mother-in-law about her." Poe could be a difficult friend, to say the least, and this particular friendship would start to crumble when he mocked English's poetry in 1843. It led to a spectacular all-out literary feud.

"Poe was no saint, and he wasn't always easy to be around," novelist Matthew Pearl said. "He had difficulty with friendships. He could push people away who were genuinely fond of him and wanted to help him. He could be charming, courtly, witty, and gracious, but he also could be sensitive, petty, suspicious, jealous, and resentful. He wanted to be noticed and appreciated, but he had a difficult time with processing appreciation."

Poe scholar Steve Medeiros puts it more vividly: "If you could look through the peephole and see who was knocking, and could see that it was Poe, you wouldn't answer the door, because he would want something. As much of a genius as he is and as charming as he could be, he could also be a real pain in the ass."

By the time Halloween rolled around in 1839, Poe had published two of his greatest horror stories: "The Fall of the House of Usher," which included the poem "The Haunted Palace," and the doppelganger tale "William

Wilson." Poe was on a roll, taking the Gothic storytelling form to scary new heights. And he was far from through. The next few years in Philadelphia would see a steady string of macabre masterworks: "A Descent Into the Maelström," "The Oval Portrait," "The Masque of the Red Death," "The Tell-Tale Heart," "The Pit and the Pendulum," and "The Black Cat." It has been suggested that Poe turned to horror only because there was a market for such stories, but that's undoubtedly an oversimplification. If he could have peered into the future, Poe probably would have been more than a little irked to discover he had been primarily and overwhelmingly identified with the horror genre, but there definitely was something lurking inside him that was irresistibly drawn to the spooky side of the street. He'd have a tough time denying that.

In his 2000 book *On Writing: A Memoir of the Craft,* proud Poe literary descendant Stephen King admitted, "I was built with a love of the night and the unquiet coffin, that's all. If you disapprove, I can only shrug my shoulders. It's what I have." Poe had that too, and much more of course. But, as King suggests, if a writer responds to the sound of the creaking door, he or she should not resist it.

"And Poe didn't," King said. "I suspect he couldn't. He followed the lure of the night and nightmares, and the rest of us have been following him ever since."

There's no question that he responded not only to the sound of the creaking door but also to the tapping at the window of an ominous bird of yore, the bells in towers where dwell the ghouls, the exceedingly musical chiming of a gigantic ebony clock, the hissing of a glittering steel pendulum swinging and descending, the jingling of bells on the caps of walled-up men, and the muffled beating of murdered men's hearts secreted under floorboards. Poe obsessed over the search for the precise sounds in his poetry and prose, and, in his best horror stories, he used these shrieks and groans and roars and whimpers as clarion calls, summoning us to the doomed mansions, ancient catacombs, ancestral crypts, dungeons of the Inquisition, and homes by horror haunted where we come face-to-face with universal fears.

Deep into that darkness peering, long I stood there wondering, fearing
Doubting, dreaming dreams no mortal ever dared to dream before;

Although those lines were written for "The Raven" (1845), they serve as an apt description of Poe as he was about to take the horror story to heights it hadn't been before.

"Poe wasn't brilliant because he had the power to make people fearful," said Wes Craven, the late screenwriter-director who specialized in horror films. "His brilliance stemmed from the recognition and understanding that we're all fearful. He didn't create the fear. He ingeniously tapped into what was already there. . . . He could stunningly articulate that fear in all of us. Poe wasn't drawing on a dark terror in himself. He was masterfully drawing on the darkness that exists in human beings. He also anticipated the techniques of not just the horror stories to come but also the horror films that followed. All of the nuances, all of the techniques, all of the frightening devices are there. He showed us the way, and we're nowhere without Poe."

The director of *A Nightmare on Elm Street* almost sounded like a college English or humanities professor when discussing Poe's art, and, well, that's precisely what he was before turning to filmmaking and responding to his own creaking door. Robert Englund, the actor who played Freddy Krueger in the *Elm Street* movies, said that people introduced to Craven expected to meet a "crazoid, wild-eyed biker type" with tattoos, leather jacket, and greasy hair. Instead, they encountered a soft-spoken, erudite fellow who enjoyed talking about philosophy and literature. Today's readers of Poe's stories probably would have had a similar response if they could have met the real writer.

If not his first literary love, horror presented intriguing possibilities to Poe. He believed that the terror tale could offer more than sensationalism and cheap thrills. With the chillers he served up during the Philadelphia years, Poe had reached, to borrow a phrase from "The Black Cat," an "extremity of terror and of awe." "Yes, he was writing for an audience and for a living," Poe scholar Jeffrey A. Savoye said, "but Poe gives modern horror a kind of historical literary pedigree, which it really doesn't have without him." What concerns King and many Poe scholars isn't Poe's overwhelming association with the horror genre but the horror writer caricature of him that discredits the true genius. "The misconception that bothers me the most is the notion of madness," Pettit said. "It devalues him as a great artist. He was so hard working, so dedicated, so exacting, but some rather believe he had to be insane to write about insane characters. It's the opposite. You have to be in complete command of your art to depict that so effectively."

He certainly was in complete control at the age of thirty as he sent readers to the melancholy House of Usher and its "air of stern, deep, and irredeemable gloom." Poe was realizing the lofty goal he had set for himself. He wasn't just crafting commercial shockers; he was writing masterpieces of the genre. Readers were invited to accompany the young narrator as he journeys to a decaying mansion, the ancestral home of his boyhood friend, Roderick Usher. The unnamed narrator is Usher's "best, and indeed his only personal friend." Usher's twin sister, Madeline, is wasting away, suffering from an illness that has "long baffled the skill of her physicians." One night, the narrator is informed that Madeline has died. Entombed alive, Madeline rises from her coffin during a violent storm, seeks out her brother, and falls on him, dragging him "to the floor a corpse, and victim to the terrors he anticipated." The narrator flees, only to see the mansion collapse. Inside and out, psychologically and literally, he has witnessed the fall of the House of Usher.

Poe again gives us a mysterious young woman buried alive, but he eschews most of the conventions of the haunted house story. By focusing on the disintegrating mental state of the troubled Roderick Usher, he leaves us to ponder the causes behind his "struggle with the grim phantasm, FEAR." Is he the victim of the supernatural? Or is the terror in his crumbling mind rather than within the disintegrating walls of his house? Like Robert Louis Stevenson's later horror masterpiece, *The Strange Case of Dr. Jekyll and Mr. Hyde*, "The Fall of the House of Usher" inspires many fascinating allegorical interpretations. Poe has no literal answers for us. The terror here is in the eye of the beholder.

Washington Irving was so impressed by "Usher," he wrote Poe that a collection of tales, "equally well written, could not fail of being favorably received." Poe tried just that with *Tales of the Grotesque and Arabesque,* a two-volume collection of twenty-five stories, horrific and humorous. He polished and revised many of the entries, bolstered by another letter from Irving, this one praising "William Wilson."

Published by Lea & Blanchard of Philadelphia in early December 1839, *Tales of the Grotesque and Arabesque* featured "Metzengerstein," "Berenice," "Morella," "MS. Found in a Bottle," "Ligeia," "The Fall of the House of Usher," and "William Wilson." Despite Irving's rosy prediction, it failed. Perhaps because the stories had already been printed (and many of them reprinted) in magazines, sales were few. Looking to augment his meager salary at *Burton's,* Poe started contributing to the family news-paper *Alexander's Weekly Messenger.* He challenged readers to send him codes, cryptograms, ciphers, and puzzles to solve. Ultimately, it proved so popular that he was deluged with challenges. The only way to stem the tide was to print a request for readers to cease and desist.

With at least a dependable if not generous source of regular income, the family could settle into a pattern of domesticity that lifted them mercifully beyond a bread-and-molasses diet. They were able to keep a garden. And Poe delighted in telling readers of *Alexander's Weekly Messenger* about his pet cat: "The writer of this article is the owner of one of the most remark-able black cats in the world—and that is saying much; for it will be remem-bered that all black cats are witches. The one in question has not a white hair about her, and is of a demure and sanctified demeanor. The portion of the kitchen which she most frequents is accessible only by a door, which closes with what is termed a thumb-latch; these latches are rude in con-struction, and some force and dexterity are always requisite to force them down. But puss is in the daily habit of opening the door." This lighthearted and engaging tribute to his black cat then described how she jumped from the ground to the latch, holding on with her left paw while using her right to press down the latch. She then would spring from the door, the force of her leap swinging it open. This cat's beloved successor, a large tortoiseshell named Catterina, would join the family in 1844.

Trouble, though, was building between Burton and Poe. Disturbed by persistent rumors that Burton was tiring of the magazine and getting ready to sell, the badly underpaid Poe began making plans to start his own monthly journal, *The Penn*. The rumors were confirmed in May 1840, and Poe decided it was time to start circulating his prospectus for *The Penn*. Furious that such a magazine would reduce the value and asking price for his *Gentleman,* Burton fired him by letter on May 30. Poe, now also furious, responded by calling Burton a bully, a blackguard, and an ass. He explained that, had he not "firmly believed it your design to give up your journal," he never would have pursued one of his own. Burton retaliated by hurling the usual accusation of Poe being a drunk.

"His enemies, and he had no shortage of them, were quick to make this claim about him, loudly and often, usually as an indictment of his moral character," Pettit said. "So it can make it difficult to know how much of a problem alcohol was for him."

For the rest of the year and into 1841, Poe pursued his dream of owning and editing his own magazine. He was in the right city to attempt this. Boston at this point was the nation's unofficial book publishing capital. New York was the most important city for newspapers and daily journalism. But Philadelphia had taken the lead in the magazine trade. Poe had made his name as a great editor and literary critic in Richmond, and he probably knew he had to head north in order to enhance that reputation.

Poe was also in the right city for taking the next significant steps with his horror stories. Philadelphia already had a strong Gothic storytelling tradition, largely established by the influential writer Charles Brockden Brown (1771–1810), a spinner of spooky tales who predates Irving and an American novelist who predates James Fenimore Cooper. Brown planted the Gothic tale in American soil with the kind of intellectual vigor Poe was bound to admire. His influence also was embraced by Philadelphia friends and colleagues of Poe, including young George Lippard.

"During the first half of the nineteenth century, more Gothic works are published in Philadelphia than in any other American city," Pettit said. "And this is important because the type of horror story he writes changes in Philadelphia. Before Philadelphia, he's writing horror stories like 'Berenice' and 'Morella,' which are very traditional European Gothic. In Philadelphia, it's more psychological horror in stories like 'The Tell-Tale Heart' and 'The Black Cat,' and that's very much Philadelphia Gothic in the tradition of Charles Brockden Brown. The horror no longer tends to be a supernatural outside threat. It's now inside the home and inside someone's head. I think if he stays in New York, he doesn't write stories like 'The Tell-Tale Heart' and 'The Black Cat.' I don't think they happen. Philadelphia becomes the crucible for Poe's imaginative genius."

Poe made an earnest attempt to find backers and subscribers for *The Penn,* aiming to launch it in March 1841. A financial crisis hit the Philadelphia banks in February, however, putting his plans on indefinite hold. The magazine dream cruelly yanked away just as it was about to come true, Poe accepted an offer from George Rex Graham to become the book review editor at his *Graham's Magazine.* Burton wanted out of the publishing business, so Graham, only twenty-seven, purchased his magazine in late 1840. Once an editor at Philadelphia's *Saturday Evening Post,* Graham had also bought a magazine called *The Casket* from *Post* publisher Samuel C. Atkinson. So he launched his own magazine in December 1840 with a circulation of about five thousand. Poe's salary was eight hundred dollars a year. But Poe hardly was idle on the writing front. He had been at work on what would be his first great mystery story, or what he would call a tale of ratiocination, "The Murders in the Rue Morgue." Introducing master detective C. Auguste Dupin, it appeared in the April edition of *Graham's Magazine.* Poe, who reveled in the reputation of being able to figure out any cipher, had spotted another popular magazine staple that he believed could stand some improvement: the mystery and murder yarn. In doing so, he created the archetype for the super sleuth—Sherlock Holmes would inherit many of his traits. An amateur detective, Dupin is the master of observation and deduction. He is intriguingly idiosyncratic, relentlessly logical, and supremely confident in his superior intellectual powers. He knows he is smarter than the police, the criminals, and the companion who records his investigations.

So, Poe's fingerprints can be found all over the later detective stories that will feature Arthur Conan Doyle's Sherlock Holmes and Agatha Christie's Hercule Poirot. When Doyle met with reporters in New York during an 1894 visit to America, he was asked by a journalist, "Now, weren't you influenced by Edgar Allan Poe when you wrote Sherlock Holmes?" A hush fell over the room, but, if the members of the press were anticipating an indignant outburst from Doyle, they were to be disappointed. He was, in fact, eager to acknowledge his debt to Poe. "Oh, immensely!" he replied. "His detective is the best detective in fiction." A reporter shouted out, "Except Sherlock Holmes," but Doyle was having none of it: "I make no exception. Dupin is unrivaled. It was Poe who taught the possibility of making a detective story a work of literature." Nor would this be the last time Doyle would shout Poe's praises. In a March 1909 speech at the Author's Club in London, Doyle famously asked, "Where was the detective story until Poe breathed the breath of life into it?" But the creator of Sherlock Holmes was impressed by the whole writer, marveling at all of the accomplishments beyond the detective story: "Just think of what he did in his offhand, prodigal fashion, seldom troubling to repeat a success, but pushing on to some new achievement." From Poe's mind, Doyle said, "have sprung nearly all our modern types of story."

Poe followed "The Murders in the Rue Morgue" with two more stories featuring Dupin, "The Mystery of Marie Rogêt" and, another one of his finest efforts, "The Purloined Letter," as well as the buried-treasure mystery tale that became a sensation, "The Gold-Bug."

"Poe was more than just a horror writer," Kennedy said. "We rightly think of Poe in terms of terror and horror, but there was also an important element of Poe that resisted the psychology of fear and was constantly trying to understand a fearful world and manage his anxieties. It's one of the reasons we get the detective story."

The two forms he crafted into literature have one thing in common: both horror and mystery are an attempt to uncover a truth. The horror story probes the mysteries of the cosmos and human nature, searching for revelations that we may never find. The journey into darkness must be taken, and fears must be faced, but answers are not guaranteed. We may well be on the trail of the unknowable, the insolvable, the impenetrable. The detective story might take us down similarly dark alleys, but it gives us the assurance and comfort that an answer can be found, understood, and revealed. What becomes clear in Philadelphia is that these are two dynamic sides of Poe's complex personality. He is simultaneously drawn to the fathomless depths and the lofty summits that logic and perception can conquer. Both were proper realms of the intellect to Poe.

December 1840 had seen the first appearance of "The Man of the Crowd," Poe's story about "secrets which do not permit themselves to be told." The narrator, a constant and careful observer of the people around him on the streets of London, becomes fascinated with a short, feeble old man whose face wears an expression he has never seen before. He resolves to follow the man. He tails his quarry for an entire day, finally stepping directly in front of him and gazing into his face. The old man takes no notice of him. The narrator resolves that it would be useless to keep following him. He will learn no more than he has already learned. The rest is unknowable. Sometimes a person's conscience takes up a burden "so heavy in horror that it can be thrown down only in the grave," the narrator tells us. "And thus the essence of all crime is undivulged." Or, as Poe reminded us in "Dream-Land":

Never its mysteries are exposed
To the weak human eye unclosed

There is nothing supernatural or specifically eerie about the story, and yet it has been classified as both a mystery and a terror tale. If not strictly a horror story, "The Man of the Crowd" trades on a theme that is emblematic of so much that will follow in the genre. And then, just four months later, Poe gave us "The Murders in the Rue Morgue," with Dupin assuring us he can unravel the seemingly unsolvable mystery.

"Poe always is trying to solve mysteries," said Poe scholar and Boston College English professor Paul Lewis. "His childhood left him with a sense of the world being deeply mysterious and untrustworthy. There was a need to show to himself that he was not the victim of mystery, and that becomes the great creative, motivating impulse. He has great confidence in his abilities. Only he can solve the mystery."

Unlike "The Murders in the Rue Morgue," the sequel story, "The Mystery of Marie Rogêt," was based on an actual crime, the murder of New York cigar store employee Mary Cecilia Rogers.

"There was some criticism after 'The Murders in the Rue Morgue' that amounted to, 'Well, what's the tough thing about writing a mystery story if you start knowing how it will turn out?'" said Daniel Stashower, author of *The Beautiful Cigar Girl: Mary Rogers, Edgar Allan Poe, and the Invention of Murder.* "So here was an opportunity to test his skills with an actual case. The writer is a detective. It's the same skill set. Poe is applying his own detective skills, and he took a pretty good swing at it. Yes, you can say in the simplest terms that Poe invented the detective story with 'Murders in the Rue Morgue,' but then he's very quickly pushing on and testing the limits to see what could be done. He's not repeating himself and now is showing what can be done with what's essentially a true-crime story."

There are some that argue Poe did quite a bit more than just invent the detective story and explore the possibilities of the true-crime genre. One of those is former FBI agent John Douglas, and his testimony is not to be taken lightly. The coauthor of *Mindhunter: Inside the FBI's Elite Serial Crime Unit,* Douglas was the bureau's criminal profiling pioneer and one of the creators of the *Crime Classification Manual.* As he helped develop the bureau's behavioral science and profiling program in the 1970s and '80s, he was surprised to see their work become the inspiration for such crime novels as *Red Dragon* and *The Silence of the Lambs.* Although these works of fiction took liberties ("I would *never* send an FBI Academy

trainee to interview an incarcerated serial killer"), they made Douglas re-
alize "our antecedents actually do go back to crime fiction far more than
crime fact." He said that Dupin "may have been history's first behavioral
profiler."

"Like the men and women in my Investigative Support Unit a hundred and fifty years later," Douglas said, "Poe understood the value of
profiling when forensic evidence alone isn't enough to solve a particularly
brutal and seemingly motiveless crime. 'Deprived of ordinary resources,'
he wrote, 'the analyst throws himself into the spirit of his opponent, identifies himself therewith, and not infrequently sees thus, at a glance, the
sole methods by which he may seduce into error or hurry into miscalcu-
lation.' This is as good a definition as I've seen of behavioral profiling and
proactive criminal strategy. I firmly believe that without the pioneering
work of such inspired storytellers as Poe, English novelist Wilkie Collins
[*The Woman in White,* based on an actual case, and *The Moonstone*],
and Arthur Conan Doyle's immortal creation, Sherlock Holmes, there is
a good chance that modern criminal profiling as we know it would not
exist."

So Poe is the father of both the modern detective story and behavioral profiling? "It really is a case of life imitating art," said Douglas's
Mindhunter coauthor, the novelist and nonfiction writer Mark Olshaker.
"What Poe was doing was this kind of inferential combination of deductive and inductive reasoning: scientific method, relying on experience of
previous crimes, using logic and observation. With both the writer and
the detective, before they can make sense out of what they're contemplating, they must be able to tell it in story form. A detective can't solve a
crime until he or she can tell it as a story—this is what I think happened,
and in this order. In the same way, the writer always is the detective."

Of all the cities associated with Poe, Philadelphia is the one most
likely to get the short shrift in the public imagination. Baltimore has a
football team called the Ravens, for crying out loud, and Richmond can
make the best case for being the city of his tell-tale heart. But it wasn't
where he wrote "The Tell-Tale Heart." That was Philadelphia.

"If Poe had been a baseball player, you'd say his all-star years were in Philadelphia," Pettit said. "You're remembered for the town where you put up the numbers, and Poe unquestionably put up his big numbers here in Philadelphia. Except for the last burst of creativity that starts with 'The Raven,' Philadelphia is pretty much the career."

If you detect a bit of Philadelphia home rooting there, well, there is a good-natured rivalry among the scholars, curators, and museum directors representing the major cities associated with Poe. The sparring caused headlines in 2007 with Pettit and Baltimore scholar Jeff Jerome exchanging arguments over which city had the better claim on Poe. It resulted in the Great Poe Debate marking the writer's bicentennial, with Pettit and Jerome joined by Boston College English professor Paul Lewis. It could have been a five-way tussle if Richmond and New York had gotten into the act.

"Poe begins his writing career in Baltimore," said Enrica Jang, the executive director of Baltimore's Edgar Allan Poe House & Museum. "He found his real family here. And we have the body. We've got the trifecta. We win. You have a writer who is famous for writing about death, and he happens to die under mysterious circumstances in this city and he happens to be buried here. But Poe also helped shape the character of the city. There are plenty of cities that claim to love writers, but none demonstrates it like Baltimore with Poe."

Even Pettit has to concede that "Baltimore decided to make a big thing about that association, and that's one of the things that has kept Poe alive." But as a professor at Louisiana State University with no particular municipal dog in the fight, J. Gerald Kennedy stresses that, "He's in Philadelphia for six years, and there's no question that this is the golden period of his career." He still thinks of himself first as a poet, and the public still thinks of him first as a critic, but he has produced the bulk of the work that will frame his reputation for future generations in a way summarized by a line he had written for "Berenice": "and then—then all is mystery and terror."

Philadelphia, while being the city of great literary triumph, also would be the city of great tragedy. On January 20, 1842, while singing at home, nineteen-year-old Virginia suffered a pulmonary hemorrhage and began coughing up blood. A neighbor recalled that she "ruptured a blood-vessel, and after that she suffered a hundred deaths." Poe, who had turned thirty-three the day before, had no illusions. He knew this was the unmistakable sign of what was then called consumption: tuberculosis.

"They're in a row home, across the street from a sewage lot," said Helen McKenna-Uff, the former National Park ranger often assigned to the Edgar Allan Poe National Historic Site in Philadelphia. "And the idea was that someone collected the contents of outhouses and then brought it to this lot to spread out and let dry and become fertilizer. So they were living across the street from that, and that's where Virginia developed the first symptoms of tuberculosis. There might have been worse places for her to be living at that time, but that was pretty damn bad."

The doctors were not hopeful. For two weeks, it seemed likely that she would die. Struggling for breath, she hadn't the strength to leave a bed that was in a corner where the ceiling was so low, her head nearly touched it.

"Her life was despaired of," Poe recalled. "I took leave of her forever & underwent all the agonies of her death. She recovered partially and I again hoped."

There would be another hemorrhage before the year was out. Four months after the first horrifying appearance of consumption's "scarlet stains," Poe published "The Masque of the Red Death," opening with a description of the fatal pestilence: "Blood was its Avatar and its seal—the redness and the horror of blood."

"RATHER THE WORSE FOR WEAR"

SEPTEMBER 27–OCTOBER 3, 1849

The days after Poe left Richmond on September 27, 1849, are completely shielded from our view. We have no reliable testimony establishing his whereabouts until the afternoon of Wednesday, October 3. If, indeed, he left Richmond on a steam packet, as it is generally assumed, he would have arrived in Baltimore on September 28. No one who made the trip with him came forward to describe his physical condition and emotional state on board. Not one person stepped forward after Poe's death to recall a conversation or brief encounter at the steamer's railing. Did he fall to drinking, reaching Baltimore in a dangerously weakened and inebriated state? The steamers had saloons by then, so alcohol would have been available during the trip.

"Even a very small amount of alcohol had a terrible impact on him, but there's no evidence that he was drinking at that point," Edgar Allan Poe Society of Baltimore secretary and treasurer Jeffrey A. Savoye said. "And it's somewhat simplistic to jump to, well, he started drinking on the boat and he drank himself to death."

He would have disembarked at Spear's Wharf in Baltimore. Did he then walk about eight blocks or so to the station at President Street and catch a train to Philadelphia? He had planned to go there and edit the po- ems of Mrs. Marguerite St. Leon Loud. If he did make the trip, he didn't make contact with the Louds, nor did he make any attempt to collect a badly needed one hundred dollars for his editorial assistance. Was he sick and feverish, as Elmira Royster Shelton had seen him the night before his departure? Was he already dying when he left Richmond? Or was Dr. Gibbon Carter's dire warning a couple of months earlier all too accurate and another bout of drinking did prove fatal? It's not that there's too little evidence to support conjecture. It's that there's almost no evidence. Or as Poe scholar Steve Medeiros summarizes it, "The only thing we're certain of is our uncertainty."

Any eastern city with a seaport area would have had its rowdy and dangerous areas. Even allowing for that, Baltimore had picked up a par- ticularly rough reputation in the 1830s and '40s. It also had picked up a nickname—Mobtown.

"They would riot at the drop of a hat," said Baltimore Poe scholar Jeff Jerome, and indeed, in addition to the 1835 riot, Baltimore erupted into violence in 1777, 1812, 1839, 1856, 1861, and 1877. "We took our riots very seriously back then, making the police hide, chasing the mayor out of town, burning down houses."

He's not exaggerating. Right before Poe left the Amity Street house for Richmond in 1835, the August 6–9 Baltimore bank riot claimed the homes of some of the city's most prominent citizens. The unrest was sparked by the failure of the Bank of Maryland, which resulted in the loss of savings for thousands of depositors. Whipped into a fighting mood after months of accusations of fraud and financial misconduct, outraged citizens took out their anger on the homes of former bank directors. It started with the smashing of windows, then escalated to the burning of houses. In some cases, they left the homes standing and made bonfires of the contents—furniture, drapes, books, rugs, you name it. Even many who disapproved of the lawlessness and disorder expressed sympathy for the victims of the injustices that incited it. "This is the most popular mob I have ever witnessed," one Baltimore resident said, "and I have seen several." The mob took control of the city. The mayor, whose home was a target, accepted the inevitable and submitted his resignation. At least twelve people were shot and killed during three nights of rioting. It took a volunteer army of about three thousand to finally disperse the rioters and put an end to the violence. At the time of these 1835 riots, Poe, Maria Clemm, and Virginia were living about two miles away from the center of the firestorm.

"If he had been drinking and incapacitated himself in a place known as Mobtown, that could have been incredibly dangerous," said Enrica Jang, executive director at the Edgar Allan Poe House & Museum. "And if he was ill when he left Richmond, it was very cold, wet weather when he got to Baltimore. So the elements would have been very bad for someone with an undiagnosed illness or condition. Any way you look at it, he could have been in a bad way in a bad place at a bad time."

Political thuggery and corruption were also not uncommon in Baltimore, and, in the 1870s, this gave rise to a theory that attempted an explanation of Poe's missing days. Political gangs were known to kidnap innocent travelers, bystanders, and passersby, plying them with alcohol or drugs, then dragging them to polling station after polling station to repeatedly vote for a chosen candidate. Between excursions as repeat voters, these unfortunate individuals were held captive in tiny rooms referred to as pens or coops. Thus the practice became known as cooping.

John Reuben Thompson, the *Southern Literary Messenger* editor given a copy of "Annabel Lee" by Poe during the last days in Richmond, took to the lecture circuit with presentations about the writer's life and, at some point, started offering the cooping theory as an explanation of his death. Although an intriguing and viable possibility, it is a deduction based on coincidence rather than proof. Poe did, in fact, arrive in Baltimore during the high-hooligan days before an October 3 election for congressional representatives and the House of Delegates. If he had taken the train to Philadelphia and returned to Baltimore on October 2 or 3, he would have been an ideal target for cooping once he left the station and hit the streets. The case for cooping is entirely based on circumstantial

evidence, but enough evidence of that variety can persuade a jury. And Poe
was discovered by a printer named Joseph W. Walker outside of Gunner's
Hall, a public house being used as a polling place. Operated by Corne-
lius Ryan inside the Fourth Ward Hotel, the tavern was located at 44 East
Lombard Street. The semiconscious Poe was found sitting or stretched
out on a broad plank placed across barrels on the sidewalk. He was able
to identify himself and tell Walker that he was friends with Dr. Joseph
Evans Snodgrass, one of the editors who published "Ligeia" in Baltimore's
The American Museum. Walker was acquainted with Snodgrass, having
worked for him as a typesetter. He dashed off a message to Snodgrass:

> There is a gentleman, rather the worse for wear, at Ryan's 4th
> ward polls, who goes under the cognomen of Edgar A. Poe, and
> who appears in great distress, & he says he is acquainted with
> you, and I assure you, he is in need of immediate assistance.

Snodgrass answered the summons and headed for Gunner's Hall. He
found Poe, his head drooped forward, still in possession of Dr. Carter's
distinctive Malacca cane. He was sitting in an armchair, surrounded by
tavern patrons:

> When I entered the bar-room of the house, I instantly recognized
> the face of one whom I had often seen and knew well, although
> it wore an aspect of vacant stupidity which made me shudder.
> The intellectual flash of his eye had vanished, or rather had been
> quenched in the bowl; but the broad capacious forehead of the
> author of "The Raven," as you have appropriately designated him,
> was still there, with a width, in the region of ideality, such as
> few men have ever possessed. But perhaps I would not have so
> readily recognized him had I not been notified of his apparel.
> His hat—or rather the hat of somebody else, for he had evidently
> been robbed of clothing, or cheated in an exchange—was a cheap,
> palm-leaf one, without a band, and soiled; his coat, of commonest

alpaca, and evidently 'second-hand;' and his pants of gray-mixed cassimere, dingy and badly fitting. He wore neither vest or neck-cloth, if I remember aright, while his shirt was sadly crumpled and soiled. He was so utterly stupefied with liquor that I thought it best not to seek recognition or conversation, especially as he was surrounded by a crowd of drinking men, actuated by idle curiosity rather than sympathy.

The fact that Poe was found wearing cheap, thin, shabby clothes that were not his own possibly supports the cooping theory. Between visits to polling stations, the kidnapped repeat voters sometimes were forced to change clothes. Snodgrass jumped to the not altogether unfair conclusion that Poe had been drinking. It should be pointed out, however, that, although a physician, his diagnosis was not based on any examination of the sufferer beyond this observation at Gunner's Hall. His pronouncement of extreme intoxication was largely assumption, and given Poe's well-known periods of debilitation due to drink, perhaps an understandable one. He had not witnessed Poe drinking, however, or spoken to anyone who had seen Poe drinking. Moreover, Snodgrass was a temperance crusader who later would use Poe's "final binge" as the basis of articles and lectures warning against the perils of alcohol. The good doctor had an obvious motive for sticking with his original assumption. This along with the errors and contradictions in his accounts also place him in that crowded field of unreliable witnesses.

In an 1867 article titled "The Facts of Poe's Death and Burial," Snodgrass emphatically asserted that Poe died of "a drunken debauch." He began making his case by stating, "The facts of the case are simply these: On Tuesday, November 1, 1849 . . . I received a note bearing a signature which I recognized as that of a printer named Walker." The fact is he got his first simple fact dead wrong. Poe was discovered by Walker on October 3. By November 1, Poe had been dead and buried for more than three weeks. Snodgrass then claimed that Walker's note described Poe as being "in a state of beastly intoxication." There is no such description in Walker's note. The errors keep piling up, making it difficult to speculate on how much of the Snodgrass account is reliable.

Of course, if it had occurred to Snodgrass that Poe had been cooped, he might have assumed that he had been given liquor by his kidnappers, then dumped in a state of stupefaction outside Gunner's Hall. The state Snodgrass attributed to inebriation, however, could have been caused by any number of other conditions.

Was Poe cooped? It's certainly a theory that has found favor with a number of academics who have studied Poe's life and death. Biographer James M. Hutchisson and scholar Dennis Eddings are among those who believe the cooping explanation is the one that makes the most sense.

"Cooping is such a Baltimore explanation, and it conveniently fits the circumstances," Jang said.

Maybe too conveniently, it has been suggested. "No question, the cooping theory is compelling," said Poe Studies Association past president Amy Branam Armiento. "It explains a lot of the mysterious circumstances. But it's so tidy, you almost question it."

For Daniel Stashower, novelist and author of nonfiction works about Poe and Arthur Conan Doyle, one clue stands out: "The detail that always fascinates me is that he was found wearing another man's clothes, because that so much sounds like something that might be found in one of his stories or one of the Sherlock Holmes stories. It's the Dupin line about circumstances that rise above the plain of normal—the irregularities. It supports the theory of cooping and voter fraud."

But even if it could be conclusively determined that Poe had been cooped, that still wouldn't clear up the question of how he died. At best, it could explain some of the missing time.

"Being cooped wouldn't have caused his death, but it could have been another contributing factor to hastening his death from something else," Richmond curator Chris Semtner said.

Jerome agrees with Semtner on this point: "He was sick when he left Richmond, and sick enough that Elmira was concerned enough to go looking for him the next morning, which means she saw something, and it wasn't good. And then I think he was cooped when he got to Baltimore, possibly feverish and delirious."

One theory put forward is that Poe became suicidal after he left Richmond. He had made dark and melodramatic hints about suicide in some of his adult letters, and there was a supposed suicide attempt by swallowing laudanum in November 1848. But a 2020 study by a team of researchers at England's Lancaster University concluded that, even though Poe struggled with depression, his death was not at all likely to have been suicide. Their findings were published in the *Journal of Affective Disorders*. The researchers studied Poe's life and writings. Psychologists Dr. Ryan Boyd of Lancaster University and Hannah Dean of the University of Texas at Austin concluded that Poe's psychological markers of depression were not consistent with suicide. Computerized language analysis was used to search 309 of Poe's letters, 49 poems, and 63 short stories for linguistic clues consistent with suicide cognition. They focused on five language measures "established as diagnostic of depression and/or suicide" and reported: "Significant, consistent patterns of depression were not found and do not support suicide as a cause of death."

So, while he may well have been dying when he got to Baltimore, he probably was not suicidal. By the time Snodgrass saw him at Gunner's Place, haggard, insensible, and unwashed, he was beyond the hope of recovery. Snodgrass saw what he took to be the signs of drunkenness, not recognizing the shadow of death on the figure slumped in an armchair. He may have assumed that Poe would sober up and live to write another day. But the writer who had constantly probed the mysteries and boundaries of death had unquestionably arrived at the point where all was in vain "because Death, in approaching him had stalked with his black shadow before him, and enveloped the victim."

"BY HORROR HAUNTED"

MARCH 5, 1842–JANUARY 30, 1847

The twenty-first century has placed Edgar Allan Poe and Charles Dickens on equal footing as literary giants of the nineteenth century. They've been widely read and celebrated in each other's country, as well as around the world. But this was hardly the case when Charles Dickens first visited America in 1842. Dickens was already a superstar, wildly popular in Great Britain and America as the author of *The Pickwick Papers, Oliver Twist, Nicholas Nickleby, The Old Curiosity Shop,* and *Barnaby Rudge*. Poe, three years older, despite his success with the horror story, was still primarily known in America as a critic and was unknown in Great Britain.

Just as we think of Poe as he appeared in the last few years of his life, we might tend to think of Dickens in his grizzled maturity—door-knocker beard, receding hairline, remaining hair brushed out at the sides. Get that image out of your head. Just recently turned thirty when he arrived in Philadelphia on March 5, Dickens was beardless and still looking remarkably boyish with his long brown hair. Indeed, both men were without facial hair. The presence of such a famous writer in his city was too intriguing for Poe to ignore. With Dickens and his wife, Kate, staying at the United States Hotel on Chestnut Street, Poe sent a letter requesting an interview. He also sent along a copy of his two-volume *Tales of the Grotesque and Arabesque* and, perhaps more enticingly, his May 1, 1841, review of *Barnaby Rudge*.

Published in the *Philadelphia Saturday Evening Post*, it correctly forecasted the plot of Dickens's historical novel set during the Gordon Riots of 1780. What makes the feat all the more amazing is that the review was based only on the first quarter of *Barnaby Rudge*. As Norrie Epstein wrote in *The Friendly Dickens*, "the master of mystery deduced the identity of the murderer from just the clues given in the first chapter—and Poe had no compunction about giving away the mystery." Eight months later, in a second review of *Barnaby Rudge*, Poe made certain to boast about his deductive powers, as his forecast was proving to be all too accurate.

Dickens had already visited Boston, Hartford, and New York. He had already met many of the nation's best-known writers and poets, including Henry Wadsworth Longfellow, Richard Henry Dana, Washington Irving, and William Cullen Bryant. Why agree to meet with a critic whose name he wouldn't have recognized? Clearly, he was impressed and not at all put off by Poe's letter, which included a reference to the similarity between the manhunt in the Gordon Riots at the end of *Barnaby Rudge* and a scene in English novelist William Godwin's 1794 novel, *Things as They Are; or, The Adventures of Caleb Williams*. In a letter dated March 6, Dickens wrote to Poe from the United States Hotel:

> *My Dear Sir—I shall be very glad to see you whenever you will do me the favor to call. I think I am more likely to be in the way between half past eleven and twelve than at any other time. I have glanced over the books you have been so kind as to send me, and more particularly at the papers to which you called my attention. I have the greater pleasure in expressing my desire to see you on this account. Apropos of the 'construction' of* Caleb Williams, *do you know that Godwin wrote it backwards, the last volume first,—and then when he had produced the hunting dream of Caleb and the catastrophe, he waited for months, casting about for a means of accounting for what he had done?*
>
> *Faithfully yours always, Charles Dickens*

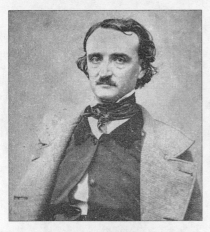

This daguerreotype portrait of Edgar Allan Poe, believed to be the only image of him that he personally commissioned, was taken in Providence, Rhode Island, in November 1848, eleven months before his death in Baltimore at the age of forty. *(Courtesy of the John Hay Library, Brown University, call number HM07)*

The only known image of Edgar Allan Poe's mother, actress Eliza Arnold Poe, to whom he owed "every good gift of his intellect, & his heart." *(Courtesy of the Poe Museum, Richmond)*

Richmond, Virginia, not the city of Poe's birth but the one that was closest to what he considered a hometown. *(Courtesy of the Poe Museum, Richmond)*

John Allan, the Richmond merchant who took young Edgar into his home as a foster child but never formally adopted him and eventually cut him off entirely. *(Courtesy of the Poe Museum, Richmond)*

The nervous and often indisposed Frances Valentine Allan was nonetheless a loving foster mother to the orphaned Edgar. *(Courtesy of the Poe Museum, Richmond)*

Moldavia, the Richmond brick mansion purchased by John Allan after a fabulously wealthy uncle died and left him an immense fortune. *(Courtesy of the Poe Museum, Richmond)*

It was in this small Baltimore house on Amity Street that Poe's aunt Maria Clemm provided the devoted motherly presence he so badly needed. *(Public domain)*

Poet and novelist Thomas Dunn English became Poe's friend in Philadelphia, but they would later become bitter enemies in New York, their clashes resulting in headlines, gossip, and a lawsuit.

(Courtesy of the Poe Museum, Richmond)

Poe's replacement as an editor at *Graham's Magazine* in Philadelphia was Rufus W. Griswold, the influential anthologist who nursed grudges, working up the great hatred that erupted as soon as he learned of Poe's death.

(Courtesy of the Poe Museum, Richmond)

The title character in Poe's 1839 doppelganger story "William Wilson" seems to have taken on some resemblance to the story's author in this illustration by Albert Edward Sterner (1863–1946).

(Public domain)

Artist Harry Clarke (1889–1931) provided this nightmarish image for Poe's "A Descent into the Maelström," first published in 1841. *(Public domain)*

Harry Clarke's striking illustration for Poe's 1842 story "The Masque of the Red Death," written during Poe's productive period in Philadelphia, which saw the writing of many of his macabre masterpieces, including "The Tell-Tale Heart," "The Pit and the Pendulum," and "The Black Cat." *(Public domain)*

The earliest known image of Poe, this daguerreotype was taken before 1843, when Poe was still sporting sideburns and had not yet grown the familiar mustache. *(Courtesy of the Poe Museum, Richmond)*

A stipple and line engraving of Poe based on the watercolor portrait of him by artist A. C. Smith in 1843 or 1844. *(National Portrait Gallery)*

One of several stirring images done by French artist Gustave Dore (1832–83) to illustrate Poe's "The Raven," the 1845 poem that momentarily brought the writer a taste of the acclaim and recognition so often denied him. *(Public domain)*

A miniature portrait by artist John A. Mc-Dougall showing Poe about 1846, a period of great turmoil for the writer, who was rocked by scandal, literary skirmishes, illness, and the tragic realization that his wife, Virginia, was dying of tuberculosis.

(Henry E. Huntington Library)

The cottage in Fordham where Poe moved with his wife, Virginia, and mother-in-law, Maria "Muddy" Clemm, in May 1846. *(Library of Congress, Prints and Photographs)*

Poe's wife, Virginia, died at the Fordham cottage of tuberculosis at age twenty-four on January 30, 1847, leaving him overwhelmed by a "sorrow so poignant as to deprive me for several weeks of all power of thought or action."

(Courtesy of the Poe Museum, Richmond)

Edgar Allan Poe, still looking relatively fit and healthy in a daguerreotype probably taken in New York in 1847, a few months after Virginia's death.

(Courtesy of the Harvard Art Museums)

A dramatic lithograph by Bernard Jacob Rosenmeyer depicting Poe walking the High Bridge, part of the Croton Aqueduct system opened in 1848 *(New York Public Library)*

Sarah Helen Whitman, the Providence, Rhode Island, poet courted by Poe and briefly engaged to him.

(Courtesy of the Poe Museum, Richmond)

An older Annie Richmond, who, as a married woman in her twenties, befriended an infatuated Poe.

(Courtesy of the Poe Museum, Richmond)

Poe looks doomed and haunted in what's known as the "Ultima Thule" daguerreotype, taken in early November 1848 in Providence, Rhode Island, four days after he swallowed laudanum in what he claimed was a suicide attempt.

(Library of Congress, Prints and Photographs)

Poe's physical deterioration is evident in this daguerreotype portrait probably taken in 1849.

(Courtesy of the J. Paul Getty Museum)

Elmira Royster Shelton, to whom Poe proposed marriage when they were teenagers, was a Richmond widow when they again contemplated marriage in 1849.

(Courtesy of the Poe Museum, Richmond)

One of Poe's two final portraits, taken during the same sitting in Richmond, about three weeks before his death in Baltimore.

(Courtesy of the Poe Museum, Richmond)

Poe's beloved aunt and mother-in-law, Maria "Muddy" Clemm, left alone when her darling Eddy died on October 7, 1849.

(Courtesy of the Poe Museum, Richmond)

The Westminster Presbyterian cemetery monument, dedicated in November 1875, marking the new gravesite for Edgar Allan Poe in the city where he died, Baltimore.

(Library of Congress, Prints and Photographs)

Hervey Allen noted in his sometimes-fanciful *Israfel: The Life and Times of Edgar Allan Poe* that it "was characteristic of Poe that he could always find 'the similarity'—that was annoying—but it always secured attention. Even Charles Dickens seated before his coal fire at the United States Hotel, eating his Philadelphia scrapple, which he called 'a kind of black pudding,' blinked at the 'similarity' as he opened his morning mail and read the beautiful, clear handwriting of 'your obedient servant, Edgar Allan Poe.' Here was a young Yankee it might be well to meet." Still, Poe had been extravagant in his praise of Dickens. To Poe, a review correctly guessing the ending of *Barnaby Rudge* was not an indication of anything lacking in the book. It was only evidence of his own genius. Yet he also recognized the genius of Dickens in reviews of *The Pickwick Papers* and *The Old Curiosity Shop*, of which he wrote: "This conception is indeed most beautiful. It is simply and severely grand. The more fully we survey it, the more thoroughly are we convinced of the lofty character of that genius which gave it birth . . . Mr. Dickens, through genius, has perfected a standard from which Art itself will derive its essence."

So Poe most likely came calling at the United States Hotel on March 7. His knock at the door was answered by Dickens, wearing a bright green tie and, over a velvet vest with gold chain, a dressing gown with quilted violet facings. Dickens would have seen a thirty-three-year-old writer wearing mended gloves and an oiled beaver hat.

There were two meetings. Dickens apparently enjoyed his talk with Poe enough to invite him back for a second visit. No record was made of the conversations, although it seems they discussed the need for better copyright protections. Poe asked Dickens to arrange for a London edition of his tales, and Dickens was impressed enough with Poe to promise to sound out some publishers—a promise he kept, even though no British publisher could be persuaded. When Poe returned to the United States Hotel for his second chat with Dickens, talk turned to the writings of Tennyson and Emerson. Poe read a poem by Emerson, and Dickens was impressed both by the poem and the reading.

These meetings, which took place less than two months after Virginia's hemorrhage, were not the end of the relationship. Letters were exchanged, Poe asking at one point if he could become the American correspondent for the *Daily News*. The request was made after Dickens had given up his editor's position with the London newspaper. And a bit of a rift occurred when Poe became upset by John Forster's article on "American Poetry" in the *London Foreign Quarterly*. Forster and Dickens were close friends. Poe resented being described as an imitator of Tennyson, and he was certain that Dickens not only had a hand in the article but may actually have written it. "I have private and personal reasons for knowing this," he wrote at the time; presumably these reasons were that the article contained pieces of information Poe had shared with Dickens in letters and during the meetings in Philadelphia. While Poe, like Dickens, could fly into a fit of temper over a slight real or imagined, his suspicions may have had some merit. The ill feelings all seemed to be on Poe's side, however, and when Dickens made his second tour of America in 1867, he made a point of calling on Maria Clemm and leaving her some money.

But Dickens did greatly benefit Poe, even if he couldn't find him an English publisher or a correspondent's position. Reading and reviewing *Barnaby Rudge,* Poe was taken with Grip, a talkative raven that's the constant companion of the title character. Being Poe, he did, of course, have some suggestions about how the gabby bird could have been put to better use: "The raven, too, intensely amusing as it is, might have been made, more than we now see it, a portion of the conception of the fantastic Barnaby. Its croakings might have been *prophetically* heard in the course of the drama." Poe filed this idea away, and Grip, of course, helped to inspire his most famous poem.

There had been a real Grip, a pet raven Dickens acquired around 1840. A talkative and rambunctious bird, the real Grip alarmed the children and visiting women by pecking at their ankles. He survived only about a year, and when he died on March 12, 1841, Dickens promptly had the bird stuffed and got another raven for a pet. And the stuffed Grip ended up in, of all places, the very city where Dickens and Poe met. He is on permanent display at the Free Library of Philadelphia.

Another work by Dickens, his 1845 Christmas book, *The Chimes*, may have inspired Poe's "The Bells." Poe supposedly told Frederick W. Thomas this was the case, but documentation for this has never been found. *The Chimes* gets very dark, though, and you can imagine it firing Poe's imagination for:

> *Hear the loud alarum bells—*
> *Brazen bells!*
> *What a tale of terror, now, their turbulency tells!*
> *In the startled ear of night*
> *How they scream out their affright!*
> *Too much horrified to speak*
> *They can only shriek, shriek . . .*

It's intriguing, therefore, that the Poe and Dickens biographers who make mention of the meeting come to radically different conclusions. Una Pope-Hennessy, a biographer of Poe and Dickens, offered the astonishing observation that, even if Dickens had read Poe's stories, "the morbidity of the theme" would not have "predisposed him in Poe's favour." Allen wrote in his biography of Poe, "Since the realms of imagination and interest were worlds apart, it seems a strange quirk of fate that Charles Dickens should have suggested 'The Raven' to Edgar Allan Poe." Other biographers say it's far too easy to stereotype Dickens as the merry optimist and Poe as the gloomy lost soul. They were, in fact, closer in spirit than the popular images suggest. Dickens biographer Edgar Johnson wasn't at all surprised that Dickens would have responded favorably to Poe's tales. His landmark 1952 biography corrected the Pope-Hennessy statements of six years earlier, stating, "The strain in Dickens that gave rise to the eerie delusions of Barnaby Rudge and the 'Madman's Manuscript' in *Pickwick* was not alien to the lunar, demon-ridden imagination of Poe, and Dickens had in him too which responded to the melancholy spell of Poe's lost maidens."

Dickens, Johnson maintained, demonstrated an "impish insight into the grotesque . . . Save for the healing sunlight of laughter, the bitter vapors hidden within this region of his soul might well have spread and made him a fellow wanderer with Edgar Allan Poe through regions of haunted and phantasmal dread." Peter Ackroyd, also a biographer of both Poe and Dickens, agreed with Johnson: "It ought always to be remembered that, in all the later accounts of Dickens's high spirits and vivacity, there was a lurking morbidity, a fascination with death and disaster, which he barely managed to keep in check." Ackroyd described Dickens as "a novelist who delighted in creating mysteries within his fiction, who used all the panoply of Gothic effects when he considered them to be appropriate and who, in a much more general sense, is filled with the morbid poetry of fantasy and death. Alexander Blok, the Russian poet, said that 'in reading Dickens I have felt horror, the equal of which Poe himself does not inspire.'"

Like Poe, Dickens was highly strung. Like Poe, Dickens could be hypersensitive. In his biography of Poe, critic and author Julian Symons astutely pointed out that Dickens and Poe responded to the same qualities: "the horrific, the sentimental and the detectival." The same things resonated in each writer's consciousness, but they made far different use of those intriguing corners of life that so attracted them. "It could be said that Dickens presented in his art the manic and Poe the depressive side of a personality," Symons observed, wisely confining the observation to their writing and not extending it to the simplistic images of them.

Dickens certainly encountered Poe when he had good reason to be depressed. Virginia's condition fluctuated until June, when she suffered another hemorrhage. She would be an invalid for much of the five years she had left to live. Filled with despair, Poe grew anxious and irritable. The possibility that Virginia might be dying, which he admitted to himself, could not be voiced by anyone else. A neighbor recalled that "the mention of it drove him wild."

The April 1842 edition of *Graham's Magazine* included Poe's story "Life in Death" (later retitled "The Oval Portrait"). Again, he gives us a beautiful young woman wasting away and dying. An artist paints a portrait of his wife, "a young girl just ripening into womanhood," determined to give his work the semblance of life. The more lifelike the painting becomes, the more life is drained away from the subject. So obsessed has he become with his art, he has permitted his beloved wife to drift nearer and nearer to death.

"People have suggested that Poe's life was a sort of an ironic twist on 'The Oval Portrait,' with Poe as the iconic archetype of the artist who pours his life out into his works and kind of fades because of it," said Jeffrey A. Savoye of the Edgar Allan Poe Society of Baltimore. "For the most part, that notion is completely bogus, and teaching Poe's works as essentially autobiographical is the cheap, easy way to interpret the stories and poems. But it is an example of how the stereotypes have fueled the public's imagination about Poe."

Also in that April issue of *Graham's Magazine* was the first of two articles praising Nathaniel Hawthorne's collection of short stories, *Twice-Told Tales*. These reviews gave Poe the chance not only to extol Hawthorne "as one of the few men of indisputable genius to whom our country has yet given birth" but also to present some ideas on the short story. For Poe, poetry is the highest expression, followed by the short story. Ideally, he argued, to preserve unity of effect and impression, each should be read in one sitting. Otherwise, the all-important "unity cannot be thoroughly preserved," because all "high excitements are necessarily transient" and an "exaltation of the soul . . . cannot be long sustained." That rules out novels and epic poems. Therefore, "The tale proper, in our opinion, affords unquestionably the fairest field for the exercise of the loftiest talent, which can be afforded by the wide domains of mere prose."

He would write more admiring assessments of Hawthorne, who would write Poe a letter with his own perceptive critical insights. The second paragraph probably reflects the feelings of many readers in the decades ahead:

I have read your occasional notices of my productions with great interest—not so much because your judgment was, upon the whole, favorable, as because it seemed to be given in earnest. I care for nothing but the truth; and shall always much more readily accept a harsh truth, in regard to my writings, than a sugared falsehood.

I confess, however, that I admire you rather as a writer of tales than as a critic upon them. I might often—and often do—dissent from your opinions in the latter capacity, but could never fail to recognize your force and originality in the former.

That April, Poe resigned from his editor's position at *Graham's*. "My reason for resigning was disgust with the namby-pamby character of the magazine—a character which it was impossible to eradicate," he wrote to his friend, writer Frederick W. Thomas. "The salary, moreover, did not pay me for the labor which I was forced to bestow. With Graham, who is really a very gentlemanly, although an exceedingly weak man, I had no misunderstanding." He added that, "I am rejoiced to say that my dear little wife is much better, and I have strong hope of her ultimate recovery."

The gentlemanly Graham, like most visitors to one of the family's residences, was struck by Poe's solicitousness toward Virginia and Muddy. All of his efforts, Graham said, "seemed to be to procure the comfort and welfare of his home." He remembered that Virginia's slightest cough caused "in him a shudder, a heart chill, that was visible." To the publisher, Poe's "love for his wife was a sort of rapturous worship of the spirit of beauty which he felt was fading before his eyes."

Poe's replacement at *Graham's* was Rufus Griswold, six years younger and editor of the just-published *Poets and Poetry of America*. They had met the previous May, and, although not by any means friends, they did not yet feel any antagonism toward each other. Certainly Griswold had not yet worked up the great hostility that he would unleash after Poe's death. Griswold's anthology included three poems by Poe: "The Coliseum," "The Haunted Palace," and "The Sleeper." They were accompanied by the highly unreliable biographical sketch that Poe had prepared. All told, Poe occupied two pages in the survey of America's poets. He would have been pleased to be included, of course, and outraged if excluded. But if Poe was keeping count, and he undoubtedly was, how must he have responded to seeing Longfellow get four pages, Charles Fenno Hoffman twelve, Whittier nineteen? While Poe first praised the anthology as "the best collection of American Poets that has yet been made," he later belittled the work in lectures and a review. He also took some mocking shots at Griswold in stories. On other occasions, however, he praised the editor and anthologist's great knowledge of American literature. Poe clearly had no idea what a bitter enemy he was making, and Griswold was content to hold his cards, as well as his anger, all the while nursing a smoldering grudge.

Again without any kind of regular income, circumstances for the Poe family became increasingly desperate. Just how desperate is described in a June letter Poe wrote to civil engineer and inventor James Herron: "The renewed and hopeless illness of my wife, ill health on my own part, and pecuniary embarrassments, have nearly driven me to distraction . . . Mrs. Poe is again dangerously ill with hemorrhage of the lungs."

As he would when overwhelmed by professional and personal woes, Poe turned to drink. He went missing for several days in late June, showing up drunk at the New Jersey home of his onetime Baltimore love, the now-married Mary Starr.

Realizing how effective Poe had been as an editor, Graham tried luring him back to the magazine in September. That same month, the family moved again, this time to a small row house on Coates Street in the Fairmount District (their landlord was cabinetmaker and importer Michel Bouvier, great-great-grandfather of Jacqueline Bouvier Kennedy Onassis). Despite his financial hardships, Poe turned down Graham's offer, still hoping that his magazine dream, *The Penn*, would become a reality. A few days later, the admiring and eager-to-help writer-editor Frederick William Thomas made the trip from Washington for a visit. He later provided a description of the house (small, neat, orderly, and comfortable) and of Virginia: "Her manners were agreeable and graceful. She had well formed, regular features, with the most expressive and intelligent eyes I ever beheld. Her pale complexion, the deep lines in her face, and a consumptive cough made me regard her as the victim for an early grave . . . [Poe's] pathetic tenderness and loving manners toward his wife greatly impressed me."

To Thomas, who was hoping to help him find a customhouse position, Poe admitted that he had been drinking. Neither efforts to finance *The Penn* nor interviews for a customhouse job led to anything that year. Then came a letter from Dickens, telling him that the London publisher Edward Moxon had passed on publishing *Tales of the Grotesque and Arabesque*. Dickens wrote that he had mentioned the collection to every publisher "with whom I have influence," and "they have, one and all, declined the venture." By way of consolation, he added that these publishers said such a collection from an "unknown writer, even though he were an Englishman," would be rejected. It probably wasn't much consolation.

Another literary friend who tried to help during this time was poet, essayist, and editor James Russell Lowell. He had published his first volume of poetry in 1841, and Poe had complained that Lowell's work deserved more space in Griswold's anthology. Lowell was launching his own magazine, *The Pioneer*, in Boston, and, that December, he agreed to publish Poe's "The Tell-Tale Heart," which had just been rejected by *The Boston Miscellany*. The correspondence between them is full of praise and affection, with Poe saying that "there is no one in America whom I would rather hold by the hand than yourself." In a few years, they would be at each other's throats, the friendship and mutual admiration collapsing in spectacular fashion.

By early 1843, Poe was talking to Philadelphia publisher Thomas C. Clarke about his proposed monthly magazine, which he now was calling *The Stylus*. Meanwhile, Thomas still was trying to aid Poe by using his influence in Washington. His efforts yielded an attractive and promising possibility: there was a customhouse opening. It paid $1,500 a year. The duties would require him to be in the office from about nine in the morning to about two in the afternoon, leaving plenty of time for writing projects. Thomas was providing Poe with a letter of introduction to Robert Tyler, son of President John Tyler. What could possibly go wrong?

On the verge of at last catching a lucky break, Poe insured a miserable outcome by drinking when he hit Washington on March 8. By the time for his appointment with the president, it seemed wise to call it off. Poe was starting arguments. He was insisting on wearing his coat inside out. He was making less than a favorable impression on the people in position to do him favors. Poe was sent home on a train, and Muddy met him at the station in Philadelphia. Mortified by his behavior, Poe sent apologetic letters, hoping he hadn't extinguished his chances. He had. He also worried about how the D.C. disaster would sit with Clarke, a temperance champion who avoided alcohol and tobacco. He may have given Clarke cause for concern, but it was probably financial concerns that ultimately caused the publisher to withdraw his support for *The Stylus.*

In April, the family moved yet again, this time to a house on Seventh Street in the Spring Garden District. North of the city, the new home came with a garden and a wealthy landlord who didn't press too rigorously when the rent was late. Poe was overdue for some good news, and, in June, he got it. A family publication, *The Dollar Newspaper,* announced the winner of its short story contest: "THE GOLD BUG . . . written by Edgar Allan Poe, Esq., of this city—and a capital story the committee pronounce it to be." The prize was a hundred dollars. But with its search of Captain Kidd's buried treasure wrapped around a mysterious code to be deciphered, "The Gold-Bug" was just the career jolt he needed at that low ebb. The story about pirate booty was a runaway success, meaning it was constantly pirated. Poe estimated that there were three hundred thousand copies printed, adding to his fame but not his income. A stage version quickly was mounted at a Philadelphia theater.

Poe followed "The Gold-Bug" with "The Black Cat." He followed that by delivering his first lecture, "Poetry in America," on November 21, 1843, at the Julianna Street Church. That brought in another hundred dollars. Capitalizing on the success of his biggest hit to date, the organizer of the William Wirt Literary Institute lecture series billed him as the "author of the Gold-Bug." It was another smashing success. Not only did his lecture sell out, but hundreds more were left outside the church, trying to gain admission. The packed crowd inside rewarded his efforts with waves of enthusiastic applause. The son of actors with his own dramatic flair had found an outlet where his theatrical nature could thrive.

He repeated the lecture a week later for members of the Franklin Lyceum in Wilmington, Delaware. On December 23, he was delivering it at a boys' preparatory school in Newark, Delaware. And when popular demand resulted in a January encore presentation in Philadelphia, Robert Morris of *The Pennsylvania Inquirer* wrote that Poe's "Poetry in America" lecture was "one of the most brilliant and successful of the season" and that Poe's delivery was "finished and effective." Then there was a home-coming of sorts at the end of the month when he took the lecture to the Odd Fellows' Hall in Baltimore. It was followed in March by a booking in Reading, Pennsylvania.

In early April, Poe decided to leave the Seventh Street house and Phil-adelphia. He and Virginia traveled by train to Perth Amboy, New Jersey, taking the steamer to New York. It was raining hard when they got to the city, so Poe left Virginia and their trunks on the boat while he went looking for an umbrella and a room to rent. He found an umbrella for sixty-two cents. He found a room in a Lower Manhattan boardinghouse at 130 Greenwich Street. Although old and looking a bit "buggy," it had brownstone steps, a porch with brown pillars, and an agreeable landlady. He hired one of the ubiquitous city horse carts called hacks and went back to collect Virginia, who was astonished that he located lodgings so quickly. The next day, he wrote to Muddy, still in Philadelphia:

Last night, for supper, we had the nicest tea you ever drank, strong & hot—wheat bread and rye bread—cheese—tea-cakes (elegant) a great dish (2 dishes) of elegant ham, and 2 of cold veal, piled up like a mountain and large slices—3 dishes of the cakes, and everything of the greatest profusion. No fear of starv-ing here. The landlady seemed as if she could'nt press us enough, and we were at home directly. Her husband is living with her—a fat good-natured old soul. There are 8 or 10 boarders . . . I ate the first hearty breakfast I have eaten since I left our little home. Sis is delighted, and we are both in excellent spirits. She has coughed hardly any and had no night sweat. She is now busy mending my pants which I tore against a nail. . . . You ca'nt imagine how much we both do miss you. Sissy had a hearty cry last night, because you and [their cat] Catterina weren't here. . . . Give our best loves to Catter[ina].

The first twenty-four hours in Manhattan couldn't have gone better. The bountiful table and chatty landlady, however, were not typical of what the next years would bring. Muddy and Catterina soon joined them, and the reunited family returned to the struggle of finding sufficient funds for food and rent. New York would be home for the turbulent last five years of his life.

"His six years in Philadelphia marked the summit of his achievement as a man of letters," Arthur Hobson Quinn wrote in his biography of Poe. "For part of his stay in Philadelphia he was even happy, and when he left it, it is not too much to say that he left happiness behind him."

Poe enjoyed long walks, and, during one of these, he discovered the two-story home of Patrick and Mary Brennan. The house was located in an area far enough uptown to still be rural in the mid-1840s. The Brennan farm covered 216 acres. Quinn placed the house at what today would be 84th Street between Amsterdam Avenue and Broadway. The Brennans agreed to let Poe, Virginia, and Muddy board with them and their children. It proved another rare respite during the stormy New York days. Mary Brennan took a great liking to them. And Poe, always fond of children, took a great liking to young Thomas and Martha. Martha was even allowed to watch him write, arranging his manuscripts according to her whims. It was here that Poe set to work on revising and finishing a poem he'd started in Philadelphia, "The Raven."

In a reflective mood that summer, he sent fellow poet James Russell Lowell a long letter about his beliefs, along with an estimation of his best work. "I have no faith in human perfectibility," he wrote. "I think that human exertion will have no appreciable effect upon humanity. Man is now only more active—not more happy—nor more wise, than he was 6000 years ago." As for spirituality, he considered "the word a *mere* word." No one, he contended, "has really a conception of spirit." His own life had been "*whim*—impulse—passion—a longing for solitude—a scorn of all things present, in an earnest desire for the future."

> I am profoundly excited by music, and by some poems—those of Tennyson especially—whom, with Keats, Shelley, Coleridge (occasionally), and a few others of like thought and expression, I regard as the *sole* poets. Music is the perfection of the soul, or idea, of Poetry. The *vagueness* of exaltation aroused by a sweet air (which should be strictly indefinite and never too strongly suggestive) is precisely what we should aim at in poetry.

As for his own work, he counted "The Haunted Palace," "The Conqueror Worm," "Dream-Land," "Lenore," "The Sleeper," and "The Coliseum" among his best poems. He thought his best stories were "Ligeia," "The Tell-Tale Heart," "The Black Cat," "The Fall of the House of Usher," "William Wilson," "A Descent into the Maelström," "The Murders in the Rue Morgue," "The Gold-Bug," and the recently completed Dupin mystery, "The Purloined Letter," which he regarded as the best of his tales of ratiocination. Writers can be notoriously lousy judges of their own writing, but, all in all, Poe didn't do too badly with this exercise in self-evaluation.

A steady procession of short stories—mystery, horror, humor, and hoax—saw print throughout 1844: "The Purloined Letter," "The Spectacles," "A Tale of the Rugged Mountains," "The Balloon-Hoax," "The Premature Burial," "The Oblong Box," "The Angel of the Odd," "Thou Art the Man." As usual, productivity and versatility did nothing to alleviate the family's great financial need, so, in early October, Poe took a depressingly unattractive job for the badly needed salary of fifteen dollars a week. He became the assistant editor at the *New York Evening Mirror*. The work was drudgery. It required Poe to show up at the office every day at nine in the

morning and sit at a desk in a corner of the editorial room until the daily
evening newspaper went to press. The unrewarding duties encompassed
a myriad of workaday editorial tasks, including responding to correspon-
dents. He also contributed some criticism but consented to requests not
to state opinions too forcefully. The paper's editor, author-poet Nathaniel
Parker Willis, conceded that such work was "rather a step downward"
for Poe, "having been the chief editor" at such monthlies as the *Southern
Literary Messenger* and *Graham's Magazine*. Willis also confessed that,
given Poe's acknowledged brilliance and his fierce reputation as a critic, he
was resigned and ready for some difficult scenes. He was in for a pleasant
surprise there. Indeed, Willis never failed to be impressed with his assistant editor's professionalism and work ethic—"how absolutely and how
good-humoredly ready he was for any suggestion, how punctually and
industriously reliable, in the following out of the wish once expressed, how
cheerful and present-minded in his work, when he might excusably been
so listless and abstracted." Willis described Poe as "a quiet, patient, industrious, and most gentlemanly person, commanding the utmost respect
and good feeling by his unvarying deportment and ability."

In early 1845, poet and schoolteacher Anne Charlotte Lynch started
inviting Poe to her literary salons, where she always found him to be
polite, unpretentious, and engaging. "It's these kinds of descriptions of
Poe, which are not uncommon, that put the lie to the stereotype," Poe
biographer James M. Hutchisson said. "He actually was quite courtly and,
in many ways, quite conventional."

Around the same time, he started contributing lengthy reviews to
the *Broadway Journal,* a weekly just started by editor Charles F. Briggs
and publisher John Bisco. But the big news that January was captured in
a conversation he had with a young friend from Lexington, Kentucky,
poet William Ross Wallace. Encountering Wallace on a New York street,
he told him, "Wallace, I have just written the greatest poem that ever was
written."

"Have you?" Wallace replied. "That is a fine achievement."

"Would you like to hear it?" Poe asked him.

"Most certainly."

Poe read the poem, giving it the dramatic delivery and emphasis that both the poem and his theatrical nature required. When he was finished, Wallace judged it "fine, uncommonly fine."

"Fine?" Poe fired back. "Is that all you can say for this poem? I tell you it's the greatest poem that ever was written."

"The Raven" was first published in the February 1845 issue of *The American Review*, which probably came out in the last half of January. It then appeared in the January 29 edition of the *Evening Mirror*, ten days after its author's thirty-sixth birthday. It was more than a hit. It was a phenomenon. Overnight, everyone seemed to be quoting the Raven's "Nevermore." The poem was constantly published in newspapers and magazines across the country. And Poe had finally achieved a level of fame and recognition that must have been beyond gratifying.

"He certainly wrote the poem that broke all records for fame," Boston College professor Paul Lewis said. "And you can see that he's really enjoying the renown."

Spotted in his coat and customary black, he was hailed on the streets as "the Raven Man" or simply "the Raven." Children would follow him and toss rocks at his heels. Playing along, he'd wheel around and shout, "Nevermore!" at them. They'd run off, every bit as delighted as Poe. His new fame also boosted his star quality at the literary salons and soirees, where he was often asked to recite "The Raven." If the lighting wasn't right, he would have the lamps turned down to establish the proper mood for his poem about "this Home by horror haunted." Even those who cared little for his lectures on poets and poetry were fully engaged and completely impressed when he began a recitation that proved he was, indeed, the son of actors: "Once upon a midnight dreary, while I pondered weak and weary."

"Poe is still writing humorous pieces, and he understands what a great coping mechanism humor can be," Lewis said. "But in 'The Raven,' Poe effectively intensifies fear by showing that humor can't cope with the horror. The narrator tries to laugh off the raven the first time it says the word, and it just doesn't work. The horror is going to overwhelm him."

The triumph of "The Raven" gave Poe the opportunity to further expound on his philosophy of composition and the all-important unity of effect. When constructing a story or poem, he explained: "I prefer commencing with the consideration of an *effect*. Keeping originality *always* in view . . . I say to myself, in the first place, 'Of the innumerable effects, or impressions, of which the heart, the intellect, or (more generally) the soul is susceptible, what one shall I, on the present occasion, select?' Having chosen a novel, first and secondly a vivid effect, I consider whether it can best be wrought by incident or tone . . ."

The example Poe used was "The Raven," and nothing about its composition, he maintained, was the result of "accident or intuition." Instead, "the work proceeded, step by step, to its completion with the precision and rigid consequence of a mathematical problem." He was impressing on readers that such work wasn't dashed off between lightning flashes of inspiration. They required vision, perseverance, dedication, and understanding. And he takes great delight and several pages to detail how "The Raven" was written and why it worked so well. This analytical approach will be echoed later in the century by Emile Zola and Anton Chekhov, who both compared the writing of novels to scientific observation. To steadfast friend Frederick William Thomas, however, Poe wrote that the poem was written to garner him a degree of fame—to be both a popular and critical success: "'The Raven' has had a great 'run,' Thomas—but I wrote it for the express purpose of running—just as I did the 'Gold-Bug', you know. The bird beat the bug, though, all hollow."

And yet, with that penchant for being his own worst enemy, Poe was about to undo and undermine this new status with a combination of ill-advised literary feuds, poor judgment, a hint of scandal, and drink. Toss in the usual doses of bad luck and the ongoing battle with poverty, and the next couple of years were guaranteed to be rocky ones. Perhaps it is somewhat fitting that the story he published in July 1845 was "The Imp of the Perverse." Poe begins the tale by describing familiar patterns of human behavior that are pursued, even though it is intellectually acknowledged that they will lead to self-destructive or morally objectionable ends. It can be something as common as putting off a task that must be accomplished, even though we "know that it will be ruinous to delay." We are eager to complete the task, "and yet we put it off until tomorrow." And when tomorrow arrives, the desire to complete the task is greater, but so is the "craving for delay." The clock strikes, signaling that the deadline has arrived, and it is "the knell of our welfare . . . Alas, it is *too* late!" Why have we followed a course that guarantees disaster? "There is no answer, except that we feel *perverse* . . . Examine these similar actions as we will, we shall find them resulting solely from the spirit of the *Perverse*. We perpetuate them merely because we feel that we should not."

But soaring high on the success of "The Raven," Poe had good reason to feel optimistic when, in late February, he resigned from the *Evening Mirror* and arranged for a one-third interest in *The Broadway Journal*. "And yet, Thomas, I have made no money," he wrote his friend. "I am as poor now as ever I was I my life—except in hope, which is by no means bankable."

Throughout the year, he used *The Broadway Journal* as a New York platform for renewing his attacks on the beloved, widely admired Henry Wadsworth Longfellow. Poe had gone from calling Longfellow "unquestionably the best poet in America" to accusing him of being a "determined imitator," a "dexterous adapter of the ideas of other people," and a plagiarist. In February 1840, he had charged the Cambridge poet of plagiarizing Tennyson's "The Death of the Old Year" for his poem "Midnight Mass for the Dying Year." "We have no idea of commenting, at any length, upon this plagiarism, which is too palpable to be mistaken, and which belongs to the most barbarous class of literary robbery," Poe had written. While "the words of the wronged author are avoided," he continued, the theme, concept, and manner of Longfellow's "Midnight Mass" were borrowed goods. Now he was keeping up the assault in *The Broadway Journal* and on the lecture stage. It may have been partially motivated by his desire to kick up some publicity for the journal. It also may have been fueled by Poe's resentment of every enviable thing that had come Longfellow's way in terms of station, social circle, position, and financial security.

"All that animosity toward Longfellow is at least partly because he saw in Longfellow what he thought he himself should have been," Hutchisson said. "Longfellow was a well-liked professor at Harvard. He married an heiress. He had a private income. He lived in a comfortable and historic house in Cambridge. It was everything Poe aspired to. We have this image of Poe wanting to haunt cemeteries and gloomy old mansions. He didn't want to live in the House of Usher. He wanted to live in the house of Longfellow."

The incident became known as the Longfellow War, but, as literary feuds go, it was a one-sided affair. Longfellow refused to engage. He kept a dignified silence on the matter, never returning fire. And after Poe's death, Longfellow comes off as a total mensch, calling Poe "a man so richly endowed with genius." Without a hint of resentment for the accusations Poe made against him and with a remarkable degree of insight, Longfellow said, "The harshness of his criticisms, I have never attributed to anything but the irritation of a sensitive nature, chafed by some indefinite sense of wrong." He also visited Muddy, invited her to Cambridge, and left behind some money.

"No question, Longfellow is a prince of a guy," Poe scholar Paul Lewis said. "Everyone liked and admired him, and with good reason. And there are obvious elements of personal jealousy in what Poe wrote about him. But it's possible to like Longfellow for what he does and for who he was and still think Poe had valid points to make about him. Poe wasn't wrong about Longfellow. He certainly was absolutely right when he predicted that Longfellow's popularity and standing as a poet wouldn't survive."

Whether done for publicity or out of resentment or because of high critical standards, Poe's scorching articles about Longfellow alienated the Boston literary establishment. Longfellow's many friends and colleagues were not as magnanimous as the fireside poet.

"He stupidly attacks Longfellow for plagiarism, and it only hurts his career," Poe scholar Edward G. Pettit said. "And by plagiarism, Poe meant that Longfellow was aping the traditions and styles of European poets, and therefore was not a truly original poet. Poe's right. And nobody reads Longfellow today. But people read 'The Raven' and 'Annabel Lee' and 'The Bells.' Poe knows he's a genius. He knows he's better than most of the writers and poets around him. He's not deluding himself. His judgments are incredibly spot on."

By August, Poe had turned a valuable Boston friend into another enemy by accusing James Russell Lowell of plagiarizing Wordsworth. Arguing that the charge was unjust, Lowell was stung by the criticism, especially since he had done Poe some good turns and paid him some high compliments. Also friends with Longfellow, he decided that Poe lacked character. Lowell would take satirical aim at Poe with his 1848 poem "A Fable for Critics":

> There comes Poe, with his raven, like Barnaby Rudge,
> Three-fifths of him genius and two-fifths sheer fudge

The battle with the city of his birth intensified in October when Poe read his early poem "Al Aaraaf" at the Boston Lyceum. The New England press no more viewed him as one of their own than he viewed Boston as a hometown. And the city's newspapers, resenting his treatment of a poet they did consider one of their own, Longfellow, were hardly in a welcoming mood. They undoubtedly agreed with the verdict expressed by Longfellow's wife, Fanny—that the upstart Poe was guilty of "insolence." By this time, however, Poe's regional assault was by no means confined to Longfellow. He had taken his share of wickedly phrased shots at several New England writers in particular and the Boston literary scene as a whole. Quick to mock the transcendentalists and their spiritual view of nature and people, he had written in 1842 that "Mr. Ralph Waldo Emerson belongs to a class of gentlemen with whom we have no patience whatever—the mystics for mysticism's sake." He also believed, fairly or not, that the Boston writers viewed their literary citadel as a lofty perch from which they could look down upon authors and poets from other areas of the country. Ever the outsider, he sneeringly referred to the transcendentalists as the Frogpondians, using the Frog Pond on Boston Common as the watery geographic origin for a designation dripping with contempt. "I wish you would come down on the Frogpondians," he would write to Thomas. "They are getting worse and worse, and pretend not to be aware that there *are* any literary people out of Boston. The worst and most disgusting part of the matter is . . . They are decidedly the most servile imitators of the English it is possible to conceive. I always get into a passion when I think about it."

So, not surprisingly, the Boston newspapers pounced after his Lyceum recitation, heaping abuse on his poem, his recitation, and him. He didn't help the situation. Poe was supposed to read a new poem, but, having nothing on hand, chose the 1829 work, which he called "The Messenger Star" that evening. It first perplexed and then alienated the audience. A good many of them walked out. At the supper afterward, Poe contemptuously claimed he had perpetrated a grand hoax on Boston by presenting a poem he had composed at the age of ten. He had been eighteen when "Al Aaraaf" made its first appearance.

"Poe saw himself as an outcast," said J. Gerald Kennedy, editor of *A Historical Guide to Poe* and *The Portable Edgar Allan Poe*. "He tried to work his way up and position himself as a force, but he always was undoing his own success by shooting himself in the foot—true perverse decisions that haunted him. He had a profoundly oppositional personality. Even though he craved popularity, he loved to set himself against people of his own time and place. You can't emphasize too much the importance of his being an orphan, always being on probation, ultimately rejected and repudiated by a foster father, and pushed into the world, trying to make his way while constantly fighting against the wealth and privilege and entitlement of the literary cliques, particularly the Brahmins of Boston."

Poe gave his own account of the Boston Lyceum reading in a November article for *The Broadway Journal*. "It could scarcely be supposed that we would put ourselves to the trouble of composing for the Bostonians anything in the shape of an original poem," he wrote. "We did not." He conceded that his selection was "not sufficiently transcendental," adding that he didn't care "a fig for their wrath."

The snarky comments about the Frogpondians would continue into the last year of his life. And yet his history with Boston can't be viewed strictly through a transcendental lens. He did, after all, head for the city his mother so loved when John Allan banished him from his Richmond home in 1827. It was there that he published his first volume of poetry and billed himself as a Bostonian.

"So it's very clear at that point that he doesn't hate the city," Lewis said. "And then, near the end of his life, he wrote the letter to his mother-in-law about wanting to move near Annie Richmond in Lowell, Massachusetts, which says to me that he did not harbor any fundamental animosity toward Boston. If you look at the whole context, it's pretty clear that it's primarily a literary dispute. Boston represents to him a kind of literary mindset and establishment that he disapproved of for various reasons. He certainly disapproved of the notion that Boston was the only part of the country producing worthwhile writing."

Poe further undermined the popularity won by "The Raven" and his lectures by drinking. By April 1845, six months before the Boston disaster, Poe had been sober for about a year and a half, as Willis and others stressed in remembrances. He was scheduled to deliver a lecture in New York on April 17. A stormy mix of rain, hail, and sleet kept people at home, and only about twelve people showed up to hear him. The talk was canceled. Those who saw Poe that night described him as disappointed and upset. The next morning, Poe showed up at *The Broadway Journal* looking disheveled, leaning on the arm of a friend for support, and smelling of wine. In May, the family moved to a boardinghouse at 195 East Broadway. That same month, *Broadway Journal* coeditor Briggs had grown alarmed by Poe's drinking. When Lowell visited him in May, he found Poe "a little tipsy, as if he were recovering from a fit of drunkenness." Muddy tried to assure Lowell that her "darling" Eddy *was not himself.*

But there were reasons for the occasional smile to cross his face. One of these was the increasingly warm friendship with poet Frances "Fanny" Sargent Osgood, whom he met in March. She and her husband, artist Samuel Osgood, had separated, and the two poets carried on a playful flirtation with published poems. Poe's interest in her sounds passionate but platonic, and Virginia certainly encouraged the relationship. He may have had romantic feelings for her. She may have been another idealized figure to adore. The exact nature of the relationship remains unclear, especially with Virginia writing Osgood and imploring her to show an interest in Eddy. Could she have felt her own death must be imminent and wished to see her husband in the company of a kindred spirit?

In June, editor Evert Duyckinck collected twelve of Poe's stories and published them through Wiley & Putnam as *Tales.* The book included "The Gold-Bug," "The Tell-Tale Heart," "The Fall of the House of Usher," "A Descent into the Maelström," "The Man of the Crowd," and the three Dupin mysteries. In November, Wiley & Putnam published *The Raven and Other Poems,* which included "Dream-Land," "The Conqueror Worm," "The Haunted Palace," "The Sleeper," "The Coliseum," "Lenore," and "Israfel." Poe dedicated the volume to English poet Elizabeth Barrett (who, the next year, married poet Robert Browning). He was still producing the occasional story, like the humorous "The System of Doctor Tarr and Professor Fether" and his chiller about mesmerism carried to a macabre extreme, "The Facts in the Case of M. Valdemar," but much of his effort in the last half of 1845 was focused on keeping *The Broadway Journal* operating. A few weeks after moving the family into a three-story house at 85 Amity Street, he bought out Bisco in late October and finally realized his dream of owning and editing his own magazine. The dream didn't last two months, and Poe realized in December that he lacked the financial resources to keep the publication going. The year that had started with the triumph of "The Raven" closed with the collapse of the *Journal.*

Amity, meaning friendship, had also been the name of the street the family had lived on in Baltimore. If this was any kind of omen, it was a dark one. Poe was reeling into a year that would cost him several friendships. The dark period was about to get a lot darker. The failure of *The Broadway Journal* was such a devastating blow that it put him emotionally, physically, economically, socially, and, yes, creatively on the skids.

"Everything seems to be going from bad to worse," Hutchisson said. "He's depressed. Virginia is getting worse. He's drinking. He's sick. And, not surprisingly, he's entering the least productive period of his career."

So, the bad fortune not only carried over into 1846, it also increased when Poe was touched by a scandal that would prompt Anne Lynch and others to cut him off from the salon scene. Fanny Osgood had visited the family and befriended Virginia. Meanwhile, poet Elizabeth Ellet, married with four children, had become smitten with Poe. She sent him passionate letters, which he showed to Virginia. Flattered though he may have been by her attentions, Poe rebuffed her advances. During her own visit to the Poes, Ellet was infuriated to find Osgood and Virginia sharing a hearty laugh over one of her letters. By some accounts, they were sharing the laughter with Poe. Ellet was going to make trouble, and her opening came when she saw letters Osgood had sent to Poe at the Amity Street house. Jealous of Osgood, Ellet suggested to her that the letters were indiscreet and that, for her own protection, she should ask to have them returned. The request was made by friends, Lynch and journalist Margaret Fuller, and an outraged Poe suggested Ellet would be advised to "look after her *own* letters." It was an ill-fated, ill-advised remark. When Lynch and Fuller left with Osgood's letters, Poe made a bundle of Ellet's letters and left them at her home. Enter William M. Lummis, Ellet's bruiser of a brother, who showed up at the Amity Street house demanding the letters that had already been returned. Understandably, Poe couldn't produce letters he no longer had, so Lummis, glaring down at him in grand soap opera fashion, threatened to kill him unless he complied.

Just when you think things can't get any wackier, Poe heads to the home of onetime close friend Thomas Dunn English. The two writers had been on warm terms in Philadelphia, but the relationship started to fray when Poe made some disparaging remarks about English's poetry. English, who was no slouch when it came to prickly responses, took classic literary revenge by making Poe the model of unattractive characters in no less than three novels. Despite the fraying friendship, Poe still thought enough of English to ask him for a loan of thirty dollars to help fund his purchase of *The Broadway Journal*. And English still thought enough of Poe to give it to him. Now he had another request for English. He wanted to borrow a pistol for self-defense, presumably against a certain bruiser brother. English didn't give him the firearm, but he did give him plenty of ammunition for flying into a rage. First English told him that he didn't believe Ellet had ever sent him any letters (letters, remember, that had already been returned to her). And then he told Poe he should apologize and retract any statements made about her. Punches were exchanged, and both men claimed to have won whatever passed for a fight. Thomas Lane of *The Broadway Journal* separated the two literary brawlers and later reported that Poe was drunk and got the worst of it. His pride had also taken a beating, so Poe reworked the details and claimed he had given English "a flogging which he will remember to the day of his death."

Socially, Poe had put himself in a bad spot. In his anger toward Ellet, he had said something that was true but terribly unwise. Ellet, after all, had sent him suggestive and seductive letters, far more compromising than Osgood's letters. He no longer had the letters, however, and the Southern gentleman had put himself in the position of seeming less than chivalrous. He had also put himself at a strategic disadvantage. Ellet had access to the inner circles of New York gossip, and, by most accounts, she knew how to use them. Taking to his bed, possibly because of illness and possibly to avoid malicious whispering, Poe made things worse for himself by asking his doctor to take an apology to Ellet. He denied having said her letters to him were improper, and, well, if he had said such a thing, it was due to temporary insanity. It was just the type of admission his enemies could and would seize upon with wicked glee. An admission of insanity could be cruelly fashioned to run wildly through the rumor mill, and that's precisely what it did. It took an enormous toll on Poe's reputation and equilibrium.

Anne Lynch moved quickly and banned him from her salons. The bluestocking Manhattan crowd that was lionizing him a year ago now brutally ostracized him. What had remained of his friendship with English was obliterated. And his relationship with Fanny Osgood was at an end. Samuel Osgood, though, took aim at the real troublemaker in the scandal. He had a list of demands for Ellet: immediately stop the gossiping about his wife, retract every ugly implication, apologize, or else. The "or else" was get ready to face a charge of libel. Ellet buckled and wrote the apologetic letter to Fanny Osgood. But while absolving Osgood of any improper behavior, she insisted on putting all responsibility for the trouble on two people: Edgar and Virginia Poe.

For his part, Poe remained bitter and wary of Ellet. Two years later, when he was wooing poet Sarah Helen Whitman, he warned her that she should expect ugly letters from Ellet, "the most malignant and pertinacious of all fiends—a woman whose loathsome love I could nothing but repel with scorn [who] slanders me, in private society, without my knowledge and thus with impunity." He goes so far as to blame Ellet for hastening Virginia's death. Perhaps seeking an escape from a suddenly inhospitable Manhattan, Virginia composed an acrostic Valentine's Day poem for her husband. The first letter of each line spells out the name Edgar Allan Poe. Presented on what would be her last Valentine's Day, it is her only known piece of creative writing:

> *Ever with thee I wish to roam—*
> *Dearest my life is thine.*
> *Give me a cottage for my home*
> *And a rich old cypress vine,*
> *Removed from the world with its sin and care*

And the tattling of many tongues.
Love alone shall guide us when we are there—
Love shall heal my weakened lungs;
And Oh, the tranquil hours we'll spend,
Never wishing that others may see!
Perfect ease we'll enjoy, without thinking to lend
Ourselves to the world and its glee—
Ever peaceful and blissful we'll be

Her weakened lungs were beyond healing, but she did get that cottage removed, if not from the world, from Manhattan. In May, they moved to a small house owned by John Valentine in the village of Fordham (in what is now the New York borough of the Bronx). The rent was modest, and Virginia found the setting charming. The cottage sat at the top of a hill, shaded by the surrounding cherry trees. There was a sitting room on the first floor, along with the kitchen and a small bedroom. Muddy's bedroom was on the second floor, next to a small study for Poe. It was a cozy residence for the family, which included the beloved Catterina. The hope was that the country would improve Virginia's health and her husband's battered psyche. That sometimes proved the case for Poe, who enjoyed taking guests on walks that often included leaping contests, which Poe regularly won. He also enjoyed the company of President August J. Thébaud, Father Edward Doucet, and the Jesuit priests at nearby St. John's College (now Fordham University). The Canadian Doucet, only twenty-three and a dormitory prefect at the time, became something of a confidant for Poe. It was no more than a twenty-minute walk to the college, where he was granted use of the library and invited to sit in on card games. "They were highly cultivated gentlemen and scholars," Poe wrote of the Jesuits. "[They] smoked, drank, and played cards like gentlemen, and never said a word about religion."

Notary public Augustine O'Neil recalled seeing Poe on a train platform around this time. He left behind a description that is straightforward yet haunting in its imagery:

I once went down to the City in the same train and waited a considerable time for the car on the same platform. I had ample opportunity to observe him. I regret that I did not speak to him. . . . He was entirely alone. He was very neatly dressed in black. He was rather small, slender, pale and had the air of a finished gentleman. . . . I once saw him and his wife on the Piazza of their little cottage at Fordham. There was much quiet dignity in his manner. In my opinion neither Shakespeare nor Byron could have been handsomer. . . . There was nothing forbidding in his manner. He simply looked like one who had a decent self-respect.

Health reformer Mary Gove visited the family that summer. "The cottage had an air of taste and gentility that must have been lent to it by the presence of its inmates," she recalled. "So neat, so poor, so unfurnished, and yet so charming a dwelling I never saw." Her description of Virginia was telling: "Mrs. Poe looked very young; she had large black eyes, and a pearly whiteness of complexion which was a perfect pallor. Her pale face, her brilliant eyes, and her raven hair, gave her an unearthly look. One felt that she was almost a dissolved spirit, and when she coughed it was made certain that she was rapidly passing away."

Indeed, Virginia was now an invalid, and the gradual wasting away drove Poe deeper into despair and depression. He wasn't lecturing. He wasn't doing much writing of stories or poems. And he had no regular employment. He did, however, have a growing list of enemies. He helped to insure this with "The Literati of New York City," a series of profiles published from May to October in *Godey's Magazine and Lady Book*. He had been working on the "Literati" before all of the trouble erupted over the Ellet and Osgood letters. And not all of the sketches were by any means negative. But several of them got quite nasty, impugning a writer's intelligence and making disparaging comments about physical appearances. One of the first targets was his former *Broadway Journal* coeditor Charles F. Briggs. In the third installment, he went after Thomas Dunn

English. These were not the types who, like Longfellow, could let such ill treatment roll off their backs. Poe had gone to war at the worst possible time and from an incredibly weak strategic position. Some of the pieces were so spiteful, he couldn't even claim the intellectual high ground. He was also outgunned and outnumbered.

Briggs launched his counterassault in the *Evening Mirror*, claiming that Poe had been confined in an insane asylum and mocking his broad forehead as balloonish. It was a vicious and vindictive exercise that made Poe's profile seem positively restrained in comparison. Then English attacked. This led to an exchange of increasingly mean-spirited and vitriolic articles between the authors. In a serialized September installment of his novel *1844, or, The Power of the "S.F."*, English satirized Poe as the writer Marmaduke Hammerhead, who dresses in black and is identified as the author of a poem called the "Black Crow": "he never gets drunk more than five days out of the seven; tells the truth sometimes by mistake; has moral courage sufficient to flog his wife, when he thinks she deserves it." English finally went too far, accusing Poe of fraud and forgery. He also dared Poe to take the matter to court. Poe accepted the challenge, eventually being awarded $225.06 in damages and $101.42 for costs. The war, though, had cost him on several fronts. It was a drain and distraction that kept him from any work of genuine substance or merit. It was a needless battle that further damaged his reputation. And it was an emotionally disturbing procession of clashes at a time when he needed all his reserves to deal with Virginia's deteriorating condition.

The only positive to come out of the skirmishes with English was that they probably helped to shape one of his best horror tales, "The Cask of Amontillado," published in the November 1846 issue of *Godey's Magazine*. "The thousand injuries of Fortunato I had borne as I best could," the narrator, Montresor, tells us, "but when he ventured upon insult, I vowed revenge." Poe undoubtedly indulged in flights of revenge fantasy, imagining what it would be like to lure an unwitting English, who had ventured upon insult, to a horrific fate. For this one brief moment, Poe marshaled his creative forces and summoned the brilliance that otherwise had gone missing for many months. It was stirring proof that the reports of his creative demise had been an exaggeration. He was not done yet.

He was, however, entering one of the blackest periods of a life with no shortage of maelströms. It was clear that Virginia could not last much longer, and, as the weather grew colder, the family's poverty became more alarming. Ministering angels appeared, including Gove and the kind-hearted Marie Louise "Loui" Shew, who became Virginia's nurse in those final days. A doctor's only daughter, Shew had received medical training and was known for her mighty efforts to help the poor and destitute.

Gove captured the pitiful conditions in the Fordham cottage as the inevitable approached in November:

> The autumn came, and Mrs. Poe sank rapidly in consumption. I saw her in her bed-chamber. Everything here was so neat, so purely clean, so scant and poverty-stricken, that saw the poor sufferer with such a heart-ache. . . . There was no clothing on the bed, which was only straw, but a snow-white counterpane and sheets. The weather was cold, and the sick lady had the dreadful chills that accompany the hectic fever of consumption. She lay on the straw-bed, wrapped in her husband's great-coat, with a large tortoise-shell cat in her bosom. The wonderful cat seemed conscious of her great usefulness. The coat and the cat were the sufferer's only means of warmth; except as her husband held her hands, and her mother her feet.

Muddy, she said, "was passionately fond of her daughter, and her distress on account of her illness and poverty and misery, was dreadful to see." Greatly moved, Gove headed for the city and reported what she'd seen to Shew, "whose heart and hand were ever open to the poor and miserable." Shew secured a feather bed for Virginia, as well as sheets, blankets, and pillows. She also raised a private subscription of sixty dollars. She then, in Gove's words "watched over them . . . and ministered to the comfort of the dying and the living."

Word of Virginia's condition spread throughout New York in December, as did the false report that Poe, too, was desperately ill with consumption. Poet Mary Elizabeth Hewitt began a collection for them, and Walt Whitman reported in *The Daily Eagle*, "It is stated that Mr. Poe, the poet and author, now lies dangerously ill with the brain fever, and that his wife is in the last stages of consumption.—They are said to be 'without money and without friends, actually suffering from the disease and destitution in New York.'" Poe was obliged to write Nathaniel Willis and assure him that, while Virginia's case remained serious and he had been ill, he was not dying.

Shew prescribed sips of wine for Virginia, which Muddy called "a great blessing." It had a "cheering and tonic influence," which allowed for moments of cherished communication with her husband and mother. "The little darling always took it smiling, even when difficult to get down," Muddy wrote to Shew. "But for your timely aid, my dear Mrs. S., we should have had no last words—no loving messages no *sweet farewells*, for she ceased to speak (from weakness) but with her beautiful eyes!"

On January 29, 1847, Poe wrote Loui Shew, "My poor Virginia still lives, although failing fast and now suffering much pain. May God grant her life until she sees you and thanks you once again! Her bosom is full to overflowing—like my own—with a boundless—inexpressible gratitude to you." About the same time Poe was setting down these words, Mary Starr visited the cottage. Placed in an armchair, the dying Virginia sat with Poe on one side and Starr on the other. When Muddy went into the kitchen, Virginia implored Starr to remain a steadfast friend to Eddy and never forsake him, because "he always loved you."

Loui Shew did respond to Poe's summons and also made it to the cottage that day. Virginia called her to the bedside, took a picture of her husband from under the pillow, kissed it, and gave it to the nurse who had done her best to help the family in this bleak time. She then, according to Shew, pulled a letter from a portfolio and showed it to Poe. He read it. Weeping, he handed it to Shew. The letter had been written by John Allan's second wife, Louisa, who expressed the wish to see him. Louisa was acknowledging to Poe that, out of jealousy, she had, indeed, persuaded her husband to make a final break with him. She further stated that Poe had always acted as a gentleman toward her. Poe believed the letter had been destroyed, but Virginia wanted it preserved as proof of his proper conduct. Arthur Hobson Quinn and other biographers have cast doubt on the reliability of Shew's memory regarding the letter, which was never located. That night, Virginia was in a great deal of pain and growing even more feeble.

She died on January 30. Like Poe's mother and brother, she died of tuberculosis at the age of twenty-four. Not surprisingly, he fell apart. A year later, in a letter to now-regular Maine correspondent George W. Eveleth, he was able to find words to approximate what he had been through and what he had lost:

This "evil" was the greatest which can befall a man. Six years ago, a wife, whom I loved as no man ever loved before, ruptured a blood-vessel in singing. Her life was despaired of. I took leave of her forever & underwent all the agonies of her death. She recovered partially and I again hoped. At the end of a year the vessel broke again—I went through precisely the same scene. Again in about a year afterward. Then again—again—again & even once again at varying intervals. Each time I felt all the agonies of her death—and at each accession of the disorder I loved her more dearly & clung to her life with more desperate pertinacity. But I am constitutionally sensitive—nervous in a very unusual degree. I became insane, with long intervals of horrible sanity. During these fits of absolute unconsciousness I drank, God only knows how often or how much. As a matter of course, my enemies referred the insanity to the drink rather than the drink to the insanity. I had indeed, nearly abandoned all hope of a permanent cure when I found one in the *death* of my wife. This I can & do endure as becomes a man—it was the horrible never-ending oscillation between hope & despair which I could *not* longer have endured without the total loss of reason. In the death of what was my life, then, I receive a new but—oh God! how melancholy an existence.

"AS IF A CORPSE"

OCTOBER 3–6, 1849

Back at the Baltimore public house and hotel Gunner's Hall, doctor and editor Joseph E. Snodgrass ordered a room for Poe until some local relatives could be notified. Just then, one of those relatives arrived. A lumber dealer in his late fifties, Henry Herring had married Muddy's sister, Elizabeth, in 1814. Snodgrass had accompanied a waiter upstairs to select "a sufficiently retired apartment." He was returning to the bar when he encountered Herring at the stairway. Herring immediately shot down the idea of taking Poe home and caring for him. Also assuming his nephew by marriage was inebriated, he told Snodgrass that Poe had been "very abusive and ungrateful on former occasions, when drunk." Herring suggested Poe be taken to a hospital. While momentarily resentful that Herring was refusing to care for a relation so obviously in need of help, Snodgrass agreed. A carriage was summoned, but Poe was unable to manage the few steps from the tavern to the sidewalk. Snodgrass remembered, "The muscles of articulation seemed paralyzed to speechlessness." So, "mere incoherent mutterings were all that were heard" as Poe was carried "to the carriage, as if a corpse."

They managed to get him into the coach, which was directed to take the insensible Poe to the five-story hospital on Broadway. Situated on high ground east of the city, it was alternately known as the Washington University Hospital of Baltimore, the hospital of Washington Medical College, and Washington College Hospital, even though, in July 1849, it had been given a name to reflect its run of patients, the Baltimore City and Marine Hospital. An advertisement printed in *The Baltimore Sun* informed the public that the "establishment formerly known as the Washington College Hospital, has been reorganized and undergone a complete renovation in every comfort and convenience, and now presents one of the best retreats for the sick and invalid." The advertisement took the form of a letter, and the letter was signed by the resident physician, John J. Moran. By 1857, the establishment was known as Church Hospital and Infirmary. Decades later, that became Church Home and Hospital, or, simply, Church Home. It seems somehow fitting that even the place where Poe died had a muddle of names.

Driven through the wet and slick streets on that chilly October day, Poe was heading for a final destination where doubt would be piled upon doubt, uncertainty upon uncertainty. He was admitted around five o'clock in the afternoon, and almost everything that follows is up for debate, including what kind of care he received and in what room he received it. Yes, even the precise location of his death is in dispute. Were you expecting anything else?

Tradition has it that Poe was taken to a private room on the second floor of the hospital. Maybe he was; maybe he wasn't. Tradition also has it that his room was in an area set aside for patients overcome by drink. Maybe it was; maybe it wasn't. Tradition has it that he was immediately recognized by Moran, the other doctors, the medical students, and the nurses, who viewed Poe as a "*great* man" and "an object of unusual regard." Again and ever again, maybe. The problem isn't that we lack witnesses, it's that the witnesses, Snodgrass and Moran included, must be viewed with a fair degree of skepticism. Moran, in his mid-twenties and four years removed from earning his medical degree from the University of Maryland, sent Maria Clemm an account of the last days in a November 15, 1849, letter. It was the first of three essential accounts given by the primary witness to Poe's deathbed days. The second was an article, "Official Memoranda of the Death of Edgar A. Poe," published in the *New York Herald* on October 28, 1875. The third was his eighty-seven-page book, *A Defense of Edgar Allan Poe,* published in 1885. Even allowing for the number of years separating these accounts, the distortions and discrepancies are staggering.

Is the letter to Muddy the most reliable version because it was written about a month after Poe's death? Or do we take into account that Moran was writing to a grieving mother-in-law whose losses had been heart-rending and staggering? The later accounts, however, can also be called into question because of embellishments, increasingly heightened details, and massive contradictions—and because Moran had since taken to the lecture platform, profiting from his "memories" of Poe's final hours. He repeatedly claimed that he wrote to Muddy because Poe requested he do so. It was a lie. He only wrote to her after she sent him a letter requesting details about Eddy's death. The inescapable conclusion is that Moran was doctoring the truth all along.

In the letter to a devastated Muddy, he wrote, "When brought to the Hospital he was unconscious of his Condition. . . . He remained in this condition from five o'clock in the afternoon—the hour of his admission—until three o'clock next morning [October 4] . . . To this state succeeded tremor of the limbs, and at first a busy, but not violent or active delirium—constant talking—and vacant converse with spectral and imaginary objects on the wall. His face was pale and his whole person drenched in perspiration—We were unable to induce tranquility before the second day after his admission." Moran recorded that he had left orders for the nurses to inform him if it seemed Poe was at all capable of rational conversation:

> I was summoned to his bedside so soon as consciousness supervened, and questioned him in reference to his family, place of residence, relatives, etc. But his answers were incoherent and unsatisfactory. He told me, however, he had a wife in Richmond (which I have since learned was not the fact), that he did not know when he left that city, or what had become of his trunk of clothing. Wishing to rally and sustain his now fast sinking hopes,

I told him I hoped that in a few days he would be able to enjoy the society of his friends here, and I would be most happy to contribute in every possible way to his ease and comfort. At this he broke out with much energy, and said the best thing his best friend could do would be to blow out his brains with a pistol— that when he beheld his degradation, he was ready to sink into the earth, etc. Shortly after giving expression to these words, Mr. Poe seemed to doze, and I left him for a short time.

The doctor's wife, Mary, also left an account, writing that Poe "was brought into the hospital in a stupor," supposedly "overcome by drink":

We soon saw he was a gentleman; and as our family lived in a wing of the college building, the doctor had him taken to a room easily reached by a passage from our wing. I helped to nurse him here, and during an interval of consciousness he asked if there was any hope for him. Thinking he referred to his physical condition, I said, "My husband thinks you are very ill, and if you have any directions to give regarding your affairs I will write them down." He replied, "I meant, hope for a wretch like me, beyond this life." I assured him that the Great Physician said there was. I then read him the fourteenth chapter of St. John's Gospel, gave him a quieting draught, wiped the beads of perspiration from his face, smoothed his pillow, and left him.

While Snodgrass was adamant about Poe's condition being the result of alcohol, Moran was just as adamant that Poe was not suffering from intoxication. In the 1875 account, he wrote that, upon being admitted to the hospital, Poe "was immediately placed in a private room, carefully undressed and critically examined."

There was no smell of liquor upon his person or breath. There was no delirium or tremor. His skin was pallid, with slight nausea at the stomach and a strong disposition to sleep. His condition was more of a stupor. He was sponged with lukewarm water, sinapisms [mustard plasters] applied to the feet, thighs and abdomen, and cold applied to the head.

I had the room darkened and he was otherwise made as comfortable as he could have been in his own room. I placed an experienced nurse at the threshold of his room door, with orders to watch him closely and prevent the slightest noise from without . . .

Can any of the details offered by Moran be trusted? As with the accounts left by Snodgrass, there are obvious exaggerations and blatant errors. It's tantalizing to think that the following conversation between Moran and Poe actually took place. Moran's memoranda, composed a quarter of a century after Poe was his patient, states that he was summoned in time to see Poe throw back the covers, open his eyes, and ask, "Where am I?" Moran said he drew a chair close to the bedside and asked how he felt.

"Miserable."

"Do you suffer any pain?"

"Yes."

"Are you thirsty?"

"No."

"Does your head suffer—have you pain there?" Moran asked, placing his hand on Poe's head.

"Yes."

"Does it feel heavy or dull?"

"Heavy; mind cloudy."

"How long have you been sick?"

"Can't say."

"Where have you been stopping?"

"In a hotel on Pratt Street, opposite the depot."

"Have you a trunk, or valise, or anything there which you would like to have with you?"

"Yes, a trunk with my papers and manuscripts."

"If you order it I will send for it."

"Do so at once. You are very kind. Where am I, Doctor?"

"You are in the care of your friends."

It is at this point that Moran placed the line he had attributed to Poe in his letter to Muddy, although, this time, he put it in quotes and made the wording more exact: "My best friend would be the man who would blow my brains out with a pistol." Even if we accept that Poe said something like this to Moran, a side-by-side-by-side comparison of the doctor's three accounts casts all of his testimony in doubt. The 1875 account is much more specific, to be sure, but it not only lacks details he provided to Muddy in November 1849, it also recounts a very different conversation in tone and content. His "Official Memoranda" has Poe answering "all my questions calmly and rationally" rather than giving "incoherent and unsatisfactory" ones. This is no minor contradiction. It's a complete reversal. There is no mention of having a wife in Richmond. There is no mention of not remembering when he left Richmond. Indeed, there is no mention of Richmond at all in the "Memoranda."

Moran's credibility takes another major hit with the next melodramatic whopper he puts in Poe's mouth. Continuing his "record" of the conversation with Poe, Moran quotes himself giving his patient assurances that they would do everything in their power to make him comfortable and to relieve his distress. To this, Poe is supposed to have replied, "Oh, wretch that I am! Sir, when I behold my degradation and ruin, what I have suffered and lost, and the sorrow and misery I have brought upon others, I feel that I could sink through this bed into the lowermost abyss below, forsaken by God and man, an outcast from society. Oh, God, the terrible strait I am in! Is there no ransom for the deathless spirit?"

With a curtain speech that flowery and grandiloquent, it's a wonder that Moran didn't record the nursing staff bursting into spontaneous applause. There is nothing remotely incoherent about this ornate decla-mation, and there is also nothing that sounds like Poe. One can imagine him cringing over the notion that, even on his deathbed, he indulged in such playing-it-to-the-balcony bombast.

"Moran goes on the lecture circuit, redirecting himself from medi-cine to a literary career," said Poe scholar, English professor, and regis-tered nurse Carole Shaffer-Koros. "He publishes articles about Poe's final days, embroidering the tale as he told it. He becomes a kind of Poe-esque unreliable narrator. He says one thing, then says another. He was coun-tering the Griswold and Snodgrass accusations of Poe being drunk, but he gives us all those lines that sound like they're from a Victorian melo-drama. On top of that, Moran only graduated from medical school a few years prior to treating Poe as a patient. So the facts of that hospitalization are fuzzy, to say the least."

Moran's improbable 1875 version reads like a work of fiction—a bad work of fiction. How to separate the truthful recollections from the obvi-ous and embarrassing embellishments? When asked if he would accept a toddy to calm him, Moran's Poe replies, "Sir, if its potency would trans-port me to the Elysian bowers of the undiscovered spirit world I would not taste it—I would not taste it. Of its horrors who can tell?"

When told that his chances aren't good, Moran's Poe references "The Raven," proclaiming, "How long, oh, how long, before I see my dear Vir-ginia? My dear Lenore! I would like to see my love, my dear love!" When asked if he has a family, Moran's Poe bursts forth with, "No, my wife is dead, my dear Virginia; my mother-in-law lives. Oh, how my heart bleeds for her! Death's dark angel has done his work. I am so rudely clashed upon the storm with compass or helm. Language cannot tell the gushing wave that swells, sways and sweeps, tempest-like over me. . . . I must lift the pall and open to you the secret that sears the heart, and, dagger-like, pierces the soul. I was to have been married in ten days."

Here, Moran tells us, he stopped to weep. While the tears are flowing, consider that the wife in Richmond from the 1849 letter has been trans-formed into a fiancée, and she has a name: Mrs. Shelton.

As hard as all of this is to swallow, Moran may yet have offered a crucial bit of testimony, and it concerns swallowing. Poe apparently had no problem swallowing and drinking during these last days at Washington University Hospital. If so, this knocks down at least one theory regarding his death.

"One thing it almost certainly wasn't was rabies," said Poe scholar Jeffrey Savoye.

Someone dying of rabies cannot swallow water, and even the suggestion of drinking can cause excruciating spasms.

"There's no record of an animal bite," Shaffer-Koros said. "And Poe was given water, which he had no trouble swallowing. That rules out rabies."

Moran claimed that, at one point, he gave Poe water specifically "to ascertain what difficulty, if any, he had in swallowing." He drank half a glass. He was also given beef tea. And in none of his accounts does Moran mention an inability to swallow water. What evidence we have shoves rabies way down that long list of possibilities.

Further reducing the pool of likely suspects are the two tests done on samples of Poe's hair. Neither test could tell us how Poe died, but each proved incredibly valuable in telling us how Poe didn't die—and, in some surprising ways, how he lived. The first of these, in 2002, tested three strands of hair from both Virginia and Edgar Poe. Supplied by the Edgar Allan Poe Society of Baltimore, the strands were from locks cut following Virginia's death in 1847 and Poe's death in 1849. Albert Donnay, the Baltimore environmental health engineer who designed the test funded by the Toronto production company Alliance Atlantis, had put forth the theory that Poe had died of carbon monoxide poisoning from inhaling the coal gas fumes produced by the indoor lighting of the time. Donnay has noted that Poe suffered from many of the physical and mental symptoms associated with carbon monoxide poisoning, including headache, fatigue, muscle ache, nausea, bloating, confusion. He also believed that an 1849 picture of Poe (the "Annie" daguerreotype) displayed a tell-tale sign of carbon monoxide poisoning: an abnormality with one eye lower than the other while the mouth slants the other way.

Testing Poe's hair was a way of testing the theory. Inductively coupled plasma mass spectrometry could measure the levels of toxic heavy metals in the hair samples. It was one of the only forensic tests that could be conducted regarding Poe's death. Federal department of environmental and toxicologic pathology researchers analyzed both ends of the strands of Poe's hair, determining the levels of arsenic, lead, mercury, nickel, uranium, and vanadium. Given the diet and environmental factors of their time, Virginia and Edgar could have been exposed to heavy metals in everything from medicine and drinking water to cosmetics and, yes, illuminating gas.

The tests on Poe's hair revealed that no heavy metal reached a toxic level. Although the analysis could not completely disprove Donnay's theory, it was a blow to what was an intriguing possibility. But if inconclusive on the matter of how Poe died, the tests did reveal that he had fifteen times the normal level of arsenic in his system—short of the level where symptoms of arsenic poisoning start to appear and probably present in the drinking water. The tests also showed that mercury increased during the last months of his life, probably from the calomel prescribed in Philadelphia during the cholera epidemic. And they showed that his lead level fell over 33 percent, which may have been an indication that he had, indeed, honored the temperance pledge in the last months.

The test for uranium was particularly revealing since the leading reason for the presence of that heavy metal would have been illuminating gas. For Poe, the level was below the detection limit. But Virginia's hair sample was considerably longer and allowed for testing on three sections, covering a much greater length of time. For the pre-Fordham period when she was exposed to gas lighting in Manhattan, she had the same level found in uranium miners. It dropped below the detection limit when they moved to the Fordham cottage.

"Edgar lived another two and a half years, and the testing showed that the levels for illuminating gas were insignificant," said Chris Semtner, curator of the Edgar Allan Poe Museum in Richmond. "Even if they could have tested for the period when the family was in Manhattan, Poe got out all the time. He took long walks. He wasn't cooped up the way Virginia was. He was getting a lot of fresh air. Illuminating gas would work better as a theory if the stereotype of Poe was correct—hunched over a lamp, writing his stories, and never seeing the outdoors. But the stereotype is wrong."

The 2017 test on Poe's hair was conducted by University of Virginia professor of isotope and organic chemistry Stephen Macko, who was working with strands supplied by the Enoch Pratt Free Library in Baltimore. "The Hair Doctor" measures the amounts of carbon, nitrogen, and sulfur isotopes to find signatures for certain foods and environmental factors. The entire hair sample is burned at one thousand degrees Celsius, converting it into gas that can be analyzed with a mass spectrometer. It was Donnay who led Macko to Poe, and Semtner featured the findings of both tests in a 2017 exhibit at the Poe Museum.

"Hair is the long-term record, so whatever killed him probably was not the kind of long-term exposure that would show up in hair analysis," Macko said. "Nothing I found would support a particular cause of death. My objective was to find a signal that showed he was exposed to dangerous levels of coal gas, and that not only contributed to his death but affected his writing and accounted for the hallucinations and brain fever. But I found no evidence of that signal in his hair."

There were traces of heavy metals, but, as with the earlier tests, they didn't reach levels that would cause significant symptoms.

"There was no evidence of organic pollutants that were significantly higher than for most people of that time," Macko said. "There was no evidence of significant levels of coal gas. I found nothing that suggested that breathing or being exposed to coal gas in any way contributed to his death."

Yet Macko's tests did reveal some surprises about Poe's diet, which, turns out, was pretty good.

"There are all of those romantic accounts of him surviving off of water and molasses for weeks at a time," Semtner said. "And the tests showed, no, he was eating grains, beans, potatoes, poultry, beef, pork. It looked like 30 percent of his diet was seafood, and if you're in Richmond for the last months of your life, they had daily oyster boats coming here bringing oysters and seafood."

In examining the overall mystery of Poe's death, Macko's testing becomes addition by subtraction. The investigation gets slightly clearer because we can get rid of a couple more suspects.

"You can't solve it using these tests, but you can get rid of some of the speculation," Macko said. "And I think our tests do dismiss the idea that illuminating gas or malnutrition were causes of his death."

Moran could have helped a great deal, of course, had he been a reliable witness offering consistent testimony. The one doctor observing Poe as he was dying, he could have provided key clues to strengthen some theories and dismiss others. Mostly, he left us a pile of uncertainty.

One person who surely didn't observe Poe in these final days was Neilson Poe, who had been informed that his cousin was gravely ill and been taken to Washington University Hospital. Born the same year as Poe, Neilson had married Virginia's half sister, Josephine Emily Clemm, in 1831. "As soon as I heard that he was at the college, I went over," he wrote to Muddy, "but his physicians did not think it advisable that I should see him, as he was very excitable." If he had been able to recognize Neilson Poe, the patient might have grown even more excitable. Although a lawyer, publisher, and journalist who shared the writer's Whig leanings, Neilson was the cousin who caused Poe great distress in 1835 by suggesting to Muddy that he take Virginia into his home and see to her welfare. Already not what you'd call a Neilson fan, Poe put him on the enemies list when a letter requesting a favor went unanswered. That prompted Poe to pour his anti-Neilson feelings into an October 1839 letter to Snodgrass: "I believe him to be the bitterest enemy I have in the world. He is more despicable in this, since he makes loud professions of friendship." There is no evidence that Neilson returned this anger in any way, or that he was aware of Poe's dark view of him.

Neilson returned the next day, presumably October 5, with changes of linen. "And was gratified to learn that he was much better," he wrote

Muddy six days later. "Much better" probably meant that he had grown quiet and seemed to be resting. This tranquil state did not last. Moran recorded that, again checking on Poe, he discovered a drastic change in his condition. "When I returned, I found him in a violent delirium resisting the efforts of two nurses to keep him in bed. This state continued until Saturday evening [October 6] (he was admitted on Wednesday) . . ."

Moran's various timelines are difficult to reconcile. If the violent delirium lasted until Saturday evening, it most certainly was intermittent. There must have been periods of unconsciousness accompanied by growing weakness and infirmity. Moran described visiting Poe's bedside and finding his pulse feeble and irregular. The pupils of his eyes were dilating and contracting. Moran believed that death "was rapidly approaching." The opinion seems to have been seconded by Moran's friend and mentor, Professor John Cavendish Smith Monkur, a professor of the theory and practice of medicine. One of the oldest and most experienced physicians on the faculty, Monkur examined Poe and said, "He will die; he is dying now." Monkur, who was forty-nine, had joined Washington College in 1831. He told Moran that Poe "would die from excessive nervous prostration and loss of nerve power, resulting from exposure, affecting the encephalon, a sensitive and delicate membrane of the brain."

Soon after, if Moran is to be believed, Poe opened his eyes and stared at the window for more than a minute. The doctor couldn't help wondering (or couldn't resist adding the wonder as a fanciful fabrication in later years) if the stricken author of "The Raven" heard a "gentle tapping at the window lattice." How, one wonders, did Moran miss quoting the passage about death in "William Wilson"? "Death approaches; and the shadow which foreruns him has thrown a softening influence over my spirit. . . . And am I not now dying a victim to the horror and the mystery of the wildest of all sublunary visions?"

"I SHALL HARDLY LAST A YEAR"

FEBRUARY 1847–JUNE 1849

Marie Louise "Loui" Shew continued to be a tender and comforting presence in the Poe household after Virginia's death. She took the lead in making funeral arrangements, purchasing Virginia's coffin and beautiful white linen burial clothes. With a little financial assistance from Mary Starr, she also bought Poe's mourning clothes. The only known portrait of Virginia, a watercolor, was painted a couple of hours after her death. John Valentine, the owner of the Fordham cottage, was so moved by the family's loss that he offered a place for Virginia in his family crypt, about a half mile away, at the Old Dutch Reformed Church. The funeral was held on the brutally cold afternoon of February 2.

Not long after Virginia's death, Poe took up a pencil and wrote the following words on a copy of his 1845 poem "Eulalie—A Song":

Deep in earth my love is lying
And I must weep alone.

"Eulalie" is a husband's tribute to a marriage that has been the saving of him. It begins:

I dwelt alone
In a world of moan,
And my soul was a stagnant tide,
Till the fair and gentle Eulalie became my blushing bride—

Eulalie's love has made the poem's narrator confident enough to tell doubt and pain to "Come never again." Both came crashing upon Poe with the loss of Virginia, and there would be reports of neighbors finding him in the churchyard on wintry nights, covered in snow, mourning outside the crypt. He was overwhelmed by a "sorrow so poignant as to deprive me for several weeks of all power of thought or action."

Poe talked about being ill before and after the loss of his adored Sissy, and at least one visitor to the Fordham cottage believed that he, too, was dying of consumption. Shew and Muddy nursed him through the dark days after the funeral, keeping a close watch on his alarming condition. His exhausted system had been overtaxed by constant stress and worry. He was shattered by grief. He was, obviously and understandably, an emotional wreck. All of this may explain some of his sorry state in the weeks following Virginia's death, but, clearly, something more was going on—something beyond the toll of great loss on a sensitive nature. He managed to tackle some correspondence in February. He was physically and emotionally capable of little else. Not even the February 17 jury verdict that delivered him a very public legal victory over Thomas Dunn English did much to revive his spirits. He completely collapsed, and, for a while, it was thought he might die.

Shew and Muddy took turns on the watch, alternating nights at his bedside. When Shew returned to the city and Muddy took over, she provided updates by letter: "I write to say that the medicines arrived the next train after you left today, and a kind friend brought them up to us that same hour . . . I very much fear this illness is to be a serious one. The fever came on at the *same time* today (as you said it would)." Shew, with her medical training and nursing experience, became convinced that something was attacking Poe's brain and nervous system. She took notes and kept a diary, recording her observations:

I made my diagnosis, and went to the great Doctor [Valentine] Mott with it: I told him that at best, when Mr. Poe was well, his pulse beat only, ten regular beats, after which is suspended, or intermitted (as doctors say). I decided that in his best health he had lesion of one side of the brain, and as he could not bear stimulants or tonics, without producing insanity, I did not feel much hope that he could be raised up from brain fever brought on by extreme suffering of mind and body—actual wan, and hunger, and cold having been borne by this heroic husband in order to supply food, medicine, and comforts to his dying wife—until exhaustion and lifelessness were so near at every reaction of the fever, that even sedatives had to be administered with extreme caution.

Shew was determined to get Poe back on his feet. In her own great grief, Muddy was eager to help. She would do anything in her power not to lose her Eddy, especially so soon after losing her Virginia. Shew ordered a new diet, with an emphasis on seafood. He was "still quite sick and overwhelmed with business," as he reported in a March 11 letter to George W. Eveleth, but Shew's regimen began to show results. Although he was gradually recovering, any improvement seemed a precarious proposition to Shew: "I knew that organic disease had been gaining upon his physical frame through the many trials and privations of his eventful life. I told him in all candour that nothing could or would save him from sudden death but a prudent life of calm, with a woman fond enough and strong enough to manage his affairs for him." Poe probably saw some wisdom in this. As erratic as his behavior could be, marriage—and the unconditional love he found at home—had provided him with the emotional anchor that kept him focused and incredibly productive for long stretches. It's entirely possible Virginia recognized the great need for this as well. Had they both, on some level, viewed Fanny Osgood as an ideal candidate to fill that role?

Whatever his feelings might have been for Osgood, Poe spent much of the next two years lurching from one ill-fated relationship to another, always with marriage in mind. His own neediness and uncertainty in this peripatetic search resulted in a great deal of personal turmoil and confusion, all compounded by the ongoing torment over the loss of Virginia. It did not result in a great many new poems and short stories. In these two areas where his creative powers had found their most profound and enduring outlet, he was struggling through one of the most fallow periods of his career. Over the fifteen-month stretch that began in December 1846, the only new published works that appeared were two poems: "To M.L.S—" and "Ulalume," a lament for a beloved who died a year before:

> And we passed to the end of the vista,
>> But were stopped by the door of a tomb—
>> By the door of a legended tomb;
> And I said—"What is written, sweet sister,
>> On the door of this legended tomb?"
>> She replied, "Ulalume—Ulalume!—
>> 'T is the vault of thy lost Ulalume!"

Which isn't to say Poe was not writing, and thinking about writing, in 1847. Sticking close to Fordham, he was channeling his energies into contemplation of the work he was convinced would be his masterpiece, the cosmological essay that would tackle nothing less than an explanation of God and the universe, "Eureka." He resumed the long walks, which probably aided his spiritual and physical recovery. He'd stroll among the pines in back of the cottage and into the surrounding woods. He'd head east for a visit with the Jesuits at St. John's College. He'd push farther east and amble along the banks of the Bronx River. And, starting in 1848, he'd head west to a new favorite spot, the just-opened High Bridge, with its pedestrian walkway 145 feet above the Harlem River. Part of the Croton Aqueduct, the bridge and its sixteen stone arches connected the Bronx and Manhattan. It became a pacing and thinking place for Poe, who, day or night, might be spotted on the grass causeway at the top of the lofty structure.

Visitors to the cottage that year were greeted warmly and hospitably. In June, Episcopal minister and elocutionist Cotesworth P. Bronson came calling with his young daughter, Mary. Thirteen years later, Mary, then Mrs. William G. LeDuc, recalled this first encounter with the writer. Her expectations were the same as those that many Poe enthusiasts today would have—that this surely must be one grim, gloomy, and morose fellow. What happened to the stereotype she took along to Fordham?

> [I]t was quite early in the forenoon when we reached the depot, from which we walked up a pleasant winding road with branching trees on either side, to Mr. Poe's cottage. I silently recalled "The Raven," by way of sobering my spirits to enter the presence of a grave and melancholy poet, as I imagined Mr. Poe to be. We saw Mr. Poe walking in his yard, and most agreeably was I surprised to see a very handsome and elegant-appearing gentleman, who welcomed us with a quiet, cordial, and graceful politeness that ill accorded with my imaginary sombre poet. I dare say I looked the surprise I felt, for I saw an amused look on his face as I raised my eyes a second time . . .

She noted that Muddy always called him Eddy and, in her voice and manner, showed "a mother's love." When settled in the parlor, someone remarked on the French print of a young girl. Poe smiled and told them, "No, it's not the lost Lenore." Then, perhaps still amused by Mary's initial surprise upon meeting him, he playfully added, "Some of my friends look above the door, as if in search of 'The Raven.'" Here we find Poe well aware of the gloomy "Raven Man" image that public perception had crafted for him—a caricature that would take stronger hold and grow through the centuries. Perhaps there's also an acknowledgment that he had done much to create the image. But, like the later horror writers he would so profoundly influence, including Stephen King and Robert Bloch, he not only acknowledges his fright merchant standing, he has some good-natured fun with it.

Similarly, a visitor in the fall was enchanted by Poe's attention to his flower garden, with its rare dahlias and colorful array of autumn blooms, and the care he gave his pet birds kept on the cottage's porch. It all "seemed quite inconsistent with the gloomy and grotesque character of his writings." And perched upon his shoulder as he wrote? Not a stately raven of the saintly days of yore, but the well-loved tortoiseshell Catterina: "A favourite cat, too, enjoyed his friendly patronage, and often when he was engaged in composition it seated itself on his shoulder, purring as in complacent approval of the work proceeding under its supervision."

Another frequent visitor to the Fordham cottage in 1847 was Sarah Anna Lewis, an amateur poet who called herself Stella. Her husband, Brooklyn lawyer Sylvanus D. Lewis, paid Poe one hundred dollars for a positive review of her work. Poe surrendered his principles regarding criticism, probably because the money was badly needed and because the couple did him many kindnesses. Stella had started making the trip from Brooklyn to Fordham in January, when Virginia was still alive. Sylvanus Lewis gave Poe legal advice and loaned him money, and the Lewises often invited Poe and Muddy to dinner at their handsome three-story brick home. Poe not only puffed her poems in extravagant terms, he also revised her work and offered literary advice. To Stella, Poe was "always the refined gentleman—the scholar—the Poet." But Poe could grow weary of her company, and, on at least one occasion, he escaped to the woods when the gaudily dressed Stella came calling. Muddy found him "sitting on a favorite rock, muttering his desire to die and get rid of literary bores."

Poe occasionally would venture into Manhattan throughout the year. In May, he visited Shew's house near Washington Square. In June, he paid a return visit to Bronson and his daughter. In July, he felt confident enough to travel as far as Washington and Philadelphia, but ill health forced a retreat back to Fordham and Muddy's care. On Christmas Eve, he accepted Loui Shew's invitation to attend a midnight service conducted by Reverend William Augustus Muhlenberg at the Church of the Holy Communion. She recalled that he followed the service like a "churchman," singing the psalms in a fine tenor to her soprano. But when the phrase "He was a man of sorrows and acquainted with grief" was repeated during a sermon, he rushed out of the church telling Shew he would wait outside. He returned to her side, however, when the congregation rose for the hymn "Jesus Savior of My Soul." He joined in the singing, without looking at the book.

It has been argued that, prodded by Shew, Poe had found a measure of traditional belief during this time. This is by no means certain, yet it also can't be rejected out of hand. Like so many other aspects of his life, his religious views are a matter of considerable debate. The Allans had a pew at the Monumental Episcopal Church, and, as a boy, he frequently attended services with Frances Allan. He and Virginia were married by a Presbyterian minister. And in 1845, he had written the poem "Catholic Hymn," a prayer to the Virgin Mary:

> In joy and wo—in good and ill—
> Mother of God, be with me still!

He was not a regular churchgoer as an adult, however, and, perhaps seeking to shock a coworker at *The Broadway Journal,* he described the Bible as "all rigmarole." But he also wrote, "A strong argument for the religion of Christ is this—that offenses against *Charity* are about the only ones which men on their death-beds can be made—not to understand—but to *feel*—as *crime*." And he related to Shew that she had "renewed my hopes and faith in God." Then, too, the theories he detailed in "Eureka" were by no means conventional, and he realized that they opened him to charges of being a pantheist, a polytheist, "a Pagan, or a God knows what." He argued that his work was not impious, and, indeed, passages certainly contradicted those who jumped to the conclusion that Poe was an atheist:

> That Nature and the God of Nature are distinct, no thinking being can long doubt. By the former we imply merely the laws of the latter. But with the very idea of God, omnipotent, omniscient, we entertain also, the idea of the *infallibility* of his laws. With

Him there being neither Past nor Future—with Him all being *now*—do we not insult him in supposing his laws so contrived as not to provide for every possible contingency?—or, rather, what idea *can* we have of *any* possible contingency, except that it is at once a result and a manifestation of his laws?

Poe was not a scientist, yet he believed that "Eureka" was a work of profound scientific significance. He began writing in earnest in the fall of 1847, often with the devoted Muddy sitting up with him until four in the morning, dozing in a chair while he wrote. They would walk around the garden, his arm around hers as he explained what he was attempting with "Eureka." He'd stop every few minutes and ask if she understood him.

Not many did understand "Eureka," which he subtitled "An Essay on the Material and Spiritual Universe" and "A Prose Poem." He introduced the basic principles of the piece in a sparsely attended lecture on February 3, 1848, at Manhattan's Society Library. Tickets were fifty cents. It was a stormy night, however, and only about sixty people heard Poe's remarks on "The Cosmogony of the Universe." He spoke for two and a half hours, sticking largely to the manuscript for "Eureka." John Henry Hopkins Jr., a divinity student at the General Theological Seminary, was one of those few to brave the elements and make it to the lecture room. He wrote a glowing review, calling it the most elaborate and profound lecture he'd ever heard. While hardly the only positive account, it was not indicative of what would be the general response. Most seemed confused, mystified, and exasperated by Poe's ruminations on, among other things, nature, matter, gravitation, the creation and end of the universe, death, unity, and the soul's connection to God. It was a treatise based on his reading of cosmological works, mathematics, his stated poetic principles, and a grandly confident trust in his own analytical acumen, intuition, and imaginative powers. Among the works that most influenced his thinking were the 1796 nebular hypothesis of French scholar, mathematician, and astronomer Pierre-Simon Laplace and *Cosmos* (1845) by German scientist Alexander von Humboldt, to whom the book version of "Eureka" was dedicated. Laplace's work on the formation of the solar system was itself a refinement of Immanuel Kant's *Universal Natural History and Theory of the Heavens* (1755). Poe believed: "What I have proposed will (in good time) revolutionize the world of Physical and Metaphysical Science. I say this calmly—but I say it."

One critic dismissed his lecture as "hyperbolic nonsense." Even his friend, editor Evert Duyckinck, called it a "mountainous piece of absurdity." Poe had no doubt it was the supreme expression of his genius. He carried this conviction into a meeting with publisher George Putnam, explaining that the work was so monumental that it would require a printing of fifty thousand copies. That would do for a start. Putnam agreed to an edition of five hundred copies. The forty-thousand-word essay was published in July, with a sale price of seventy-five cents. In his preface, Poe insisted that it was, indeed, a prose poem, and "it is as a Poem that I wish this work to be judged after I am dead." Few have honored his wish.

Not counting *The Conchologist's First Book*, it was the ninth and final book he saw published in his lifetime. Although very different from the volumes that had preceded it, "Eureka" suffered a familiar commercial fate. The sales were dismal. The reviews were mixed. And arguments over the merits of the work continue 175 years after its publication. The loftiest claim for "Eureka" is that it anticipates modern physics, from relativity to the big bang theory. No less than Albert Einstein praised it as "a beautiful achievement of an unusually independent mind." There is even a school of thought that holds "Eureka" was intended as a burlesque, despite Poe's many declarations of its serious intent.

"You can't dismiss 'Eureka' altogether, but the claims for it can be overstated," Poe scholar J. Gerald Kennedy said. "It is a magnificent failure. It is driven by the need to answer the questions that don't get answered in 'The Raven.' So, it is the search for the rational explanation, but it's also a search destined for failure. Poe is desperate to find some confirmation of that hope, that desire to believe. There's a huge amount of inconsistency in 'Eureka,' but the big argument about divine spirit and energy is pretty irresistible. He's still trying to persuade himself of an intellectual argument for a deity he could believe in."

Perhaps, then, "Eureka" does share thematic elements with the poems, short stories, and even the criticism. Perhaps it isn't as much of an outlier as commonly thought. The author of horror stories asks the questions, and fueling the horror is the realization that, maybe, there are no answers. The author of mystery stories believes that, with logic and ratiocination, the answers can be found. The poet, at least in Poe's mind, should ever be in pursuit of unity and oneness. And the critic is always weighing, evaluating, searching—looking to embrace the highest and grandest possibilities. Each of these represents an approach that informs "Eureka."

"Poe gives us characters in the grip of the pursuit of some exciting knowledge, some never imparted secret whose attainment is destruction," Kennedy said. "It resonates so perfectly with the kind of striving that lies behind 'Eureka.'"

He also gives us characters like Dupin, who not only is in pursuit of truth but also finds it, captures it, and illuminates it.

"Poe always wanted to find the rational, whether it was in the solution to a murder or the meaning of the universe," said Harry Lee "Hal" Poe, author of *Evermore: Edgar Allan Poe and the Mystery of the Universe*. "Horror stories somewhat rejected the rational, but they sold well. There was an audience for them. But while it doesn't fit the stereotype, Poe was much more on the side of the rational, the logical, the analytical."

Even Poe enthusiasts who greatly admire the effort stop short of sharing its author's boundless admiration for "Eureka." Yet Poe must have seen it as a culmination and a confluence, merging all of the primary forms that had most attracted him. He also viewed "Eureka" as a way of attracting support for his long-nurtured dream of running his own literary magazine. Yes, through it all, he had not given up on *The Stylus*. He again was trying to kick up interest in the publication, circulating a new prospectus he had printed in January. Poe believed that *The Stylus* and "Eureka" would not only restore his battered literary reputation but also stand as his monumental accomplishments.

"If I succeed, I put myself (within 2 years) in possession of a fortune and infinitely more . . . but at all events succeed I *will*," he wrote to Maine correspondent Eveleth.

"This is yet another way that the stereotype is wrong," Hal Poe said. "Most people think of Poe as a gloomy pessimist, but, in reality, he was the eternal optimist. No matter what life threw at Poe, he always was kind of like Mr. Micawber in *David Copperfield*, sure that something was going to turn up. He always believed that. He never gives up."

Poe certainly didn't give up looking for love, but here confusion would reign as he moved awkwardly from one romance to another. What was behind the uncertainty? While biographer Arthur Hobson Quinn rightly warned that it is dangerous "to read much of a poet's personal life into his verse," it is possible he gave us a clue in "Ulalume." His poem reveals the struggle of a man torn between earthly love and memories of his lost love. It was in this uncertain state of mind that Poe began to contemplate relationships that could lead to marriage. The first of these might have been the divorced Loui Shew. He definitely used passionate terms to express his gratitude toward her, but it's hardly certain that this turned into any kind of romantic attraction for either of them. Unlike the married Fanny Osgood, Shew did not fancy herself an intellectual or a poet. She was also a devout Christian and regular churchgoer. Despite their differences, they shared what was undoubtedly a warm friendship. If Poe was not in love with Loui, he had come to trust her and emotionally rely on her.

During one of his visits to Shew's house in 1848, Poe told her, "Marie Louise, I have to write a poem. I have no feeling, no sentiment, no inspiration." She promised to help. Sitting in the conservatory with the windows open after supper, they were having tea when bells started ringing at a nearby church (likely Grace Church at the corner of East Tenth Street and Broadway). "I so dislike the noise of bells tonight," he said. "I cannot write. I have no subject. I am exhausted." Taking his pen in hand, she wrote "The Bells. By E.A. Poe" on a piece of paper. Then she added, "the

Bells, little silver bells." Poe was off and rhyming, building on ideas for what would become one of his greatest poems. Ever the exacting artist, he continued tinkering with his tinkling, mellow, jangling, and groaning bells, rewriting the poem at least three times. The four stanzas of "The Bells" dwell on seasons of a life, with the last tolling anticipating the melancholy approach of death. Whether he sensed it or not, this was the "muffled monotone" surrounding this season of his life. Indeed, "The Bells" would not see print until a month after Poe's death.

Shortly before the May evening when Shew suggested "The Bells," she might have been hearing an alarm bell regarding her friendship with Poe. The previous month, he had fallen to drinking after dining with Rufus Griswold, who had traded barbs with Poe yet successfully kept hidden the extreme and bitter depths of his feelings toward him. Poe had the wherewithal to send to Shew's home for help. Shew dispatched her friend Hopkins, who had attended and reviewed Poe's "Eureka" lecture, and the man she would marry in 1850, clergyman Roland Stebbins Houghton. They found Poe intoxicated and being detained by the police. He was delivered into their custody. They guided him home to Fordham, where a worried Muddy was waiting. He had been gone for three days. It seemed that Poe had gone into the city to collect payment for an article, but once he had collected the money, he started drinking. The money was all gone, and Hopkins and Houghton were moved to give Muddy five dollars for necessities.

Yet it wasn't Poe's drinking that frightened Shew away. It was the concern voiced by Hopkins after the publication of "Eureka." Although he had written admiringly of Poe's February lecture, Hopkins had grown increasingly troubled by the pantheism sent into the world in book form. Poe suspected him of writing the *Literary World* critique that attacked "Eureka" as "mere bald assertion, without a particle of evidence." The reviewer then added, "In other words, we should term it *arrant fudge*." Poe penned an attack on the attack, repeatedly referring to the author of the anti-"Eureka" piece as "the Student of Theology." He probably correctly deduced the critic's identity, but he couldn't have guessed how strongly Hopkins was suggesting Shew should drop a literary friend espousing what he found to be dangerous and controversial views about God and creation. The son of an Episcopal bishop, Hopkins cautioned her that an association with Poe could damage her work, her reputation, and, yes, her faith. He told her that Poe, at least on the subject of pantheism, was either insane or a hopeless infidel. He also would repeatedly recount the story of taking an intoxicated Poe back to Fordham. His campaign was successful. Shew, the champion of lost souls, decided that Poe was, indeed, lost.

Poe had already detected a cooling attitude toward him when her letter arrived. She no longer wished to associate with him. He was badly hurt, and his anguish was evident in the letter he sent in reply that June:

> Can it be true Louise that you have the idea [fixed] in your mind to desert your unhappy and unfortunate friend and patient . . . must this follow as a sequel to all the benefits and blessings you have so generously bestowed?, are you to vanish like all I love, or desire, from my darkened and "lost Soul"—I have read over your letter again, and again, and can not make it possible with any degree of certainty, that you wrote it in your right mind (I *know you did not without tears of anguish and regret*), Is it possible your influence is lost to me? . . . and for me alas! unless some true and tender and pure womanly love save me, I shall hardly last a year longer, alone! . . . you must know *and be assured,* of my *regret,* my *sorrow,* if aught I have ever written has hurt you! My *heart* never *wronged you. I* place you in *my esteem* in all *solemnity* beside the friend of my boyhood, the mother of my school fellow, of whom I told you . . . in life or death, I am ever yours gratefully & devotedly . . .

Poe correctly gauged her true nature. Shew would tell biographer John Ingram in 1875 that she realized how much her letter hurt his feelings. She deeply regretted writing it. As Loui Shew fell out of his life, two New England women were being drawn into it: Sarah Helen Power Whitman of Providence, Rhode Island, and Nancy Locke Heywood Richmond of Lowell, Massachusetts. To Poe, Whitman would be, at least for the rest of 1848, "Helen," and Richmond would forever be "Annie."

Poe and Whitman had seen each other at a party after his 1845 lecture in Providence, but they were not formally introduced on that occasion. Three years later, Manhattan salon hostess Anne Lynch asked Whitman to send her a contribution for her Valentine's Day party. She replied with several poems, one addressed to Poe. Whitman clearly was intrigued by Poe, who had written admiringly of her poetry. So she also asked Lynch to tell her something about the author of "The Raven." Lynch's response should have been enough to scare off Whitman. She told the Providence poet that she hadn't seen Poe for more than a year, that he had not acted honorably during the scandal involving the letters of Fanny Osgood and Elizabeth Ellet, that he possessed no moral sense, and that there were many things about him "very abominable." Nevertheless, Whitman's playfully romantic poem "To Edgar A. Poe" was well received at the February 14 party. Even Lynch admitted that she "admired exceedingly" this exercise in fanciful flirtation that referred to Poe as the Raven:

> *Oh, thou grim and ancient Raven,*
> *From the Night's Plutonian shore,*
> *Oft in dreams, thy ghastly pinions*
> *Wave and flutter round my door.*
> *Oft thy shadow dims the moonlight*
> *Sleeping on my chamber floor!*

She regularly echoed phrasings from "The Raven," hoping and fearing while pondering "On thy loved and lost Lenore." She also worked in a mention of "The Gold-Bug," building to a request that he "Be a Raven true as ever." If so, then:

> *Not a bird that roams the forest*
> *Shall our lofty eyrie share!*

Lynch wrote Whitman that she would like to have published "To Edgar A. Poe" with her consent, but "he is in such bad odour with most persons who visit me that if I were to receive him, I should lose the company of many whom I value more." Lynch did forward the manuscript of the poem to Poe through Fanny Osgood. Poe immediately responded by tearing a copy of his 1831 poem "To Helen" from one of his books, sending it anonymously to Whitman. Meanwhile, Lynch advised Whitman not to pursue having it published, "not because it is not beautiful in itself but there is a deeply rooted prejudice against him." Undeterred, Whitman saw the valentine to Poe published on March 18 in the *Home Journal*. Fanny Osgood decided Whitman could use some advice regarding the subject of her poem. She did so with her own plays on words: "I see by the Home Journal that your beautiful invocation has reached the Raven in his eyrie and I suppose, ere this, he has *swooped* upon your little *dove cote* in Providence. May Providence protect you if he has!—for his croak the most eloquent imaginable. He is in truth 'A glorious devil, with large heart & brain.'" This was, at least, a voice of experience.

On June 1, Poe sent his actual response to the valentine. It was a new poem bearing the same title as an early poem, "To Helen":

> *I saw thee once—once only—years ago;*
> *I must not say how many—but not many.*
> *It was a July midnight; and from out*
> *A full-orbed moon, that, like thine own soul, soaring,*

He then described his first vision of her on that July night. It was in a rose garden during the reception after his lecture:

> *Clad all in white, upon a violet bank*
> *I saw thee half reclining; while the moon*
> *Fell on upturn'd faces of the roses,*
> *And on thine own, upturn'd—alas, in sorrow!*
> *Was it not Fate that, on this July midnight—*

Was it not Fate (whose name is also Sorrow)
That bade me pause before that garden-gate,
To breathe the incense of those slumbering roses?

Now, he was intrigued. They still had not met, however, and he was about to be intrigued by another woman. In July, he traveled to Lowell, Massachusetts to lecture on "The Poets and Poetry of America" at Wentworth Hall. It was announced that he would also be reading "The Raven." The appearance had been arranged by Jane Ermina Locke, an amateur poet and Fanny Osgood's sister-in-law. She had sent him a poem in December 1846 and may have suggested to Poe that she was a widow. He wasn't sure. He delicately inquired in letters about her marital status. She managed to evade giving a direct answer. But Locke invited him to stay with her in Lowell, where evasion was no longer possible. He discovered she was forty-three, had five children, and that her husband, lawyer John G. Locke, was very much alive. She introduced Poe to her friends and neighbors, the Richmonds, and was more than a little put out when he started ignoring her to spend time at the Richmond home. She was positively miffed when he started showing an intense interest in twenty-eight-year-old Nancy Richmond. He thought her the perfection of natural grace. He was entranced by her deep-set "spiritual gray" eyes and light chestnut hair. She, too, was married, and she had a three-year-old daughter. Yet her husband, wealthy paper manufacturer Charles Richmond, didn't seem to mind a relationship that neither his wife nor Poe would consider carrying too far. Poe fell to calling her Annie, believing it suited her better than Nancy. She eventually agreed, encouraging her relatives to call her Annie. Like Loui Shew, the sweet-natured Annie Richmond had no literary ambitions and was drawn to charitable work. And she was intrigued by Poe. She found him "incomparable," unlike any other person she had met. But Poe was unwittingly making a bitter enemy of Locke, who, like Ellet, would find an ugly outlet for her jealousy.

Later that summer, Poe traveled to Virginia with hopes of gathering subscriptions for *The Stylus*. The plan was, if things went well in Richmond, he would continue on and tour the Southern states. Things did not go well. He was drinking, and this was when he challenged *Semi-Weekly Examiner* editor John M. Daniel to a duel. The duel never happened. To his credit, Daniel was among those journalists praising Poe's Richmond lecture the following year. When Poe died, he wrote, with an admirable measure of understanding, "His taste for drink was a simple disease—no source of pleasure or excitement."

In early September, Poe received a letter Muddy had forwarded to Richmond. It had been sent to Fordham by Whitman, and it contained a verse using a phrase from a poem he had sent her: "Beauty which is Hope." Poe took this as a message of encouragement. He was just about to embark on the tour in support of *The Stylus*. The dream of love trumped the dream of having his own magazine. He reversed course and headed north. His destination was Providence, which he reached on September 21, calling at Whitman's 76 Benefit Street home. Poe showed up at the door with a gift. He presented her with the 1845 Wiley & Putnam editions of his *The Raven and Other Poems* and *Tales,* bound in one volume and inscribed, "To Mrs. Sarah Helen Whitman—from the most devoted of her friends, Edgar A. Poe." The next day they visited the Athenaeum library, and she asked him if he'd ever read a poem called "Ulalume," an unsigned work published the previous December. Whitman was astonished when he informed her that she was in the presence of the author.

Given the theme of this poem, Poe must have taken this as another encouraging sign. He also had reasons for thinking that here was a kindred spirit. She not only had what Poe called a "poet-nature" but also was viewed by some as slightly eccentric. She, too, dressed in a manner that suggested a theatrical poet's pose, favoring silky dresses and scarves. The blue-eyed Helen Whitman, with her pale face framed by brown curls, certainly was a more ethereal presence than the down-to-earth Loui Shew and Annie Richmond.

As they got to know each other, the forty-five-year-old Whitman also entertained the belief they were kindred spirits. She viewed this as an actual psychic bond, however, for, adding to her otherworldly demeanor, she was something of a mystic. They shared a birthday, January 19, although she was six years older. Married at twenty-five to lawyer John Winslow Whitman, she was a widow at thirty. She had moved in with her domineering, controlling mother and her temperamental, emotionally unstable sister. There were suitors during the fifteen years between her husband's death and Poe's first visit to the Benefit Street house, but her mother and sister were not likely to approve of them. Quick to make moral judgments, her mother enforced them through a tight hold on the family finances. Further increasing the odds against remarriage were Whitman's strong feelings of responsibility for her sister. And then there was her own precarious health. She suffered from a heart condition, usually carrying a handkerchief soaked in ether to ease her through attacks.

Poe used his time in Providence to tell Whitman about himself. He stressed to her that Virginia had been more of a sister and that the marriage had been primarily for her care, education, and happiness. Although he probably was trying to lessen obstacles to the altar, this was about his most execrable rewriting of his history. It was a betrayal he must have realized with a sharp stab of guilt, because, as Whitman recorded, he immediately recriminated himself for expressing such a thought. Still, the woman from his past he compared her to was the mother of a Richmond classmate who befriended him as a teenager, Jane Stanard. He had invoked Stanard's memory when Shew dropped him cold. Now he was using it to warm Whitman's affections and float his own psychic link. Hadn't Stanard inspired the first poem titled "To Helen"? Before he left Rhode Island on September 24, he impetuously proposed to her. Unsettled by the intensity and suddenness of it all, she asked for time to sort out her feelings. Returning to Fordham, he set about winning her over with passionate letters.

Poe knew there were formidable impediments hindering his cause. In addition to her mother's influence, there would be no shortage of warnings about his character. Ellet was one of Whitman's friends, and that was a perturbing thought. "My heart is heavy, Helen," he told her, "for I see that *your* friends are not my own." She wrote to him on September 30, giving her precarious health as the main reason for not accepting his proposal. If younger and in better health, "I would live for you and die with you." Poe's first letter after their meeting, dated October 1, dismisses her concerns about health, age, and nervous disposition. He also strikes a mystical note that he knew would resonate with her. He recalled their first meeting:

> As you entered the room, pale, timid, hesitating, and evidently oppressed at heart; as your eyes rested appealingly, for one brief moment, upon mine, I felt, for the first time in my life, and tremblingly acknowledged, the existence of spiritual influences altogether out of the reach of the reason. I saw that you were *Helen*—*my* Helen—the Helen of a thousand dreams—she whose visionary lips had so often lingered upon my own in the divine trance of passion—she whom the great Giver of all Good had preordained to be mine—mine only . . .

On October 10, she replied with a letter listing more reasons against their marriage, among them, on the entirely practical side, financial dependence on her mother and responsibilities toward her sister. She also wondered why so many had a bad opinion of him. He defended his reputation as best he could, fairly certain where the bad opinions had originated. If he didn't know for certain, we surely do, since her query included the precise "no moral sense" phrase that Lynch had used in assessing Poe's character to Whitman. And Lynch, of course, had already admitted to Whitman that the Manhattan society of Ellet and the bluestocking circle was more important to her than that of the Fordham exile. Whitman's question was sure to touch his sensitive nature like the glowing tip of a red-hot poker. He admitted to the sensitivity, devastated that she would not only give credence to such attacks on his character but also repeat them to him.

> I have no resource—no hope:—Pride itself fails me now . . . I *have been* loved, and a relentless Memory contrasts what *you* say with

the unheeded, unvalued language of others.—But ah,—again, and most especially—you do *not* love me, or you would have felt too thoroughly a sympathy with the sensitiveness of my nature, to have so wounded me as you have with this terrible passage of your letter:—"How often I have heard men and even women say of you—'He has great intellectual power, but *no* principle—*no* moral sense.'" Is it possible that such expressions as these could have been *repeated* to me—to me—by one whom I loved—ah, whom I *love* . . . ?

He sensed Ellet's influence in it all, and said so, without using her name. He tried to reassure her by writing, "I swear to you that my soul is incapable of dishonor—that, with the exception of occasional follies and excesses which I bitterly lament, but to which I have been driven by intolerable sorrow, and which are hourly committed by others without attracting any notice whatever—I can call to mind no act of my life which would bring a blush to my cheek—or to yours." Although he was overstating his case in a familiarly melodramatic fashion, it was not a case without merit. Ellet was free to run him down on the salon circuit, and he was powerless to stop it or even to respond. But Whitman was also in a tough spot, and Poe was pushing her to move toward the altar at a dizzying speed. Behind the otherworldly pose was a rather cautious and conservative nature. "The excesses of Shelly, Byron, and Goethe that she defended in her writings, charmed her little in a potential suitor," observed Poe biographer Kenneth Silverman.

She didn't get a chance to answer his letter. Soon after writing, Poe again showed up at her door. He was in Providence on his way to Lowell, where he had been asked to repeat his "Poets and Poetry of America" lecture. He again pressed her to accept his proposal. She agreed to write him in Lowell after taking a few days to make a decision. It was during this time that ill feelings with Jane and John Locke broke into an open quarrel. He later wrote Annie Richmond that it was over insulting things they said about her. Jane Locke set her vindictive sights on destroying

Poe's bond with Richmond. Her letters attacking Poe did nothing to alter Richmond's affectionate view of him, but they did make her consider the risks of continuing the friendship.

Poe's lecture in Lowell was canceled, and Whitman's letter, when it arrived, offered neither acceptance nor rejection. She hadn't yet made up her mind. She believed that her response had left him agitated and perplexed. Richmond knew he was in a deep state of depression and did her best to comfort him. She told him that marriage to Whitman would be the best thing. His personal and professional prospects stymied at every turn, he was troubled by Whitman's reluctance and, at the same time, in Richmond's presence, tortured by his own doubts. He made Richmond promise that, if he were near death, she would come to him. Poe returned to Providence on November 4, but, rather than call on her, he passed what he described to Richmond as "a long, long, hideous night of despair." The next morning, he took a brisk walk in the cold air, hoping it would clear and quiet his mind. He purchased two ounces of laudanum at a pharmacy, then boarded a train for Boston. Upon his arrival, he set about writing a note to Richmond—a suicide note.

> I opened my whole heart to you—to *you*—my Annie, who I so madly, so distractedly love—I told you how my struggles were more than I could bear . . . Having written this letter, I swallowed about half the luad[a]num & hurried to the Post-Office—intending not take the rest until I saw you—for, I did not doubt for a moment, that *my own* Annie would keep her sacred promise—But I had not calculated on the strength of the laudanum, for, before I reached the Post Office my reason was entirely gone, & the letter was never put in . . . It appears that, after the laudanum was rejected from the stomach, I became calm, & to a casual observer, sane—so that I was suffered to go back to Providence . . .

A reddish-brown tincture widely available in pharmacies, laudanum mixed powdered opium in an alcohol solution. It was used to treat a variety of ailments, including coughs, headaches, muscle pain, menstrual cramps, and insomnia. Death by laudanum overdose, both intentional and accidental, was common in the nineteenth century. It was part of that era's version of an opioid crisis. The amount Poe had purchased was enough to be fatal, but some Poe scholars question whether this was an actual attempt to take his own life.

"Poe knew what he was doing, and he would have known the proper dose to end it all, if that's what he truly wanted to do," said Baltimore dean of Poe studies Jeff Jerome. "He took just enough to get sick. And my belief is that he took it as a cry for pity."

Whatever his intention, his retching stomach had other ideas. Back in Providence, he did not tell Whitman about the laudanum. Instead, he told her he became confused after taking something at a druggist's, then fell ill and depressed. She suspected him of drinking. He again tried to convince her to marry him. She put him off. He renewed his efforts the next day. She parried with all the warnings and cautions sent by her friends. He was again angered that she would put any stock in such slander and gossip. When he took his leave of her, she asked, "We shall see you this evening?" His only answer was a bow. She believed he left the house deeply pained and wounded. He was.

Poe headed back to his hotel and spent the evening in that establishment's bar. In his despair, he wrote Whitman a note saying that the next time they met it would be as strangers. The next morning, November 9, with all of the angst of the previous days and years mirrored on his face, he sat for a daguerreotype at the Providence studio of Samuel Masury and S. W. Hartshorn. Why would Poe, in such emotional turmoil and recovering from both a suicide attempt and an alcoholic binge, agree to have his picture taken?

During his night at the bar, he had met a Mr. MacFarlane, who took a deep interest in him, treated him kindly, and persuaded him to go to Masury and Hartshorn's studio. MacFarlane's identity remains another mystery. The remarkable study of Poe, however, became known as the "Ultima Thule" daguerreotype, taken from a passage in his poem "Dream-Land":

By a route obscure and lonely,
Haunted by ill angels only,
Where an Eidolon, named NIGHT,
On a black throne reigns upright,
I have reached these lands but newly
From an ultimate dim Thule—

Whitman felt that this passage perfectly captured the emotional state Poe was in when the photographic image was taken. And, indeed, Poe looks haunted and doomed in what has become one of the most reproduced of those few daguerreotypes of him.

"He ages dramatically in the last three years of his life, and the daguerreotypes are a compelling record of that," said Michael Deas, the leading expert on portraits and images of Poe. "For the first few months after Virginia's death, he still looks pretty healthy, and you can see that in what's called the Daly daguerreotype, probably taken in the summer of 1847. After that, there is a dramatic physical decline. There is a physical deterioration that is obvious if you look at the pictures in proper order. He starts to lose the youthful slimness. He starts to look haggard, more bloated. It truly is a study of a man going downhill and in poor health. They're dramatic. They're beautiful. They're marvelous. But they're not truly representative of Poe throughout most of his life. They are a compelling record of the last three years. And in what's called the 'Ultima Thule' daguerreotype, he is the very image of the tragic and romantic poet."

It is also a portrait of Poe on the verge of a breakdown. Not long after this sitting, Poe headed back to Whitman's house in what she would call a wild and delirious state. He showed up pleading for her to save him from impending doom. Frightened by the appalling tone of his voice, she remained upstairs while her mother sat with him for more than two hours. When Whitman finally worked up the nerve to see him, she was alarmed by what was waiting her. Poe clung to her so desperately, he tore a piece of her muslin dress. Her mother sent for a physician, Dr. Abraham H. Okie, who said that Poe was suffering from "cerebral congestion." He sent the ailing writer to stay with William J. Pabodie, a lawyer with literary aspirations and, apparently, romantic hopes regarding Whitman. Poe recovered in the attorney's kind care and, amazingly, renewed his efforts to win Whitman. Even more amazingly, she had not given up on him. Poe had said she was the angel who could save him, and perhaps she believed this to be true. She also clung to the belief that they were destined for each other in a mystical sense. On November 13, she agreed to conditionally accept his proposal. The conditions, though, were daunting. He must give up drinking. And her mother must consent. Even as he was contemplating the possibility of marriage to Whitman, Poe was thinking of Richmond. He envisioned her, like Virginia, as an adored sister and soul mate who would be part of a family overseen by Muddy's care and devotion. Muddy, who had already met and bonded with Richmond, had grave doubts about Whitman. She gave voice to these doubts in a letter to Richmond, writing of Whitman, "I so much fear *she* is not calculated to make him happy." Muddy added, "I fear I will not love her." Then, more tellingly, "I *know* I shall never love her as I do *you,* my own darling." So, Muddy, too, saw Annie as the ideal replacement for Virginia.

In December, Whitman's mother made her move, drawing up a document stipulating that, should the marriage take place, the bride would be cut off from any claim on an inheritance. Although a substantial amount was at stake, Whitman agreed. Poe, however, was incensed. Later in December, Whitman watched him give a talk at the Franklin Lyceum at Howard's Hall in Providence. His presentation included recitations of "The Raven" and "The Bells," and Whitman sat right in front of him. It was a packed house, he reported, "and such applause!" She was impressed enough to agree to an immediate marriage. Her mother, sensing that she couldn't stop the union, now insisted that Poe sign documents relinquishing any claim to the estate. Galling as it was, on December 23, Poe wrote a note asking Reverend Nathan Bourne Crocker, minister of St. John's Episcopal Church, to publish the banns of matrimony. That same day, Whitman was handed a letter cautioning her that Poe had already violated the terms of the engagement. She didn't reveal the author of the letter, saying only that his or her testimony was beyond question. She also instructed the admiring lawyer, Pabodie, not to send Poe's note to Crocker. Exhausted and distressed, Whitman collapsed on a sofa. While he was trying to defend his reputation, her mother insisted he leave the house. Whitman's silence spoke volumes to him. He left, speaking of her family's intolerable insults. "I never saw him more," Whitman related a year after his death.

Whitman's mother wasn't the only one pleased to see the engagement fall apart so suddenly. Muddy, too, was delighted, and said so in a letter to Annie Richmond. Even Poe and Whitman, both rocked by doubts, separately confessed to others that the collapse of the engagement felt like the lifting of a great burden. But on January 21, two days after Poe's fortieth birthday, Richmond wrote him to say that family and friends had condemned his conduct during his "engagement" to Whitman. He was "deeply wounded" by her letter. Once again, the abandoned child in need of unconditional love saw a relationship imperiled by those eager to impugn his character. Yet, for his "own faithful Annie," he was ready to forgive all and trust that she wouldn't abandon him. "How shall I ever be grateful enough to God for giving me, in all my adversity, so true, so beautiful a friend!" he wrote to her. He and Richmond continued exchanging letters. In February, he was wondering if Charles Richmond had been "influenced against" him "by the malignant misrepresentations" of the Lockes. He was even more troubled by the possibility that her husband had become suspicious of their relationship: "I much fear that he has mistaken the nature—the purity of that affection which I feel for you." He went so far to suggest he stop the visits to Lowell and that they put an end to the letter correspondence. "[I]t only remains for me beloved Annie to consult *your* happiness—which under all circumstances, will be & must be mine . . . I cannot & *will* not have it on my conscience that I have interfered with the domestic happiness of the only being in the whole world, whom I have loved, at the same time with truth & with *purity*."

She showed her husband the letter, and Charles Richmond responded by not only dressing down the Lockes in no uncertain terms but also inviting Poe and Muddy to Lowell. Poe and his Annie continued exchanging letters as winter gave way to spring. In late May and early June, he spent about a week with the Richmonds in Lowell. She asked him to sit for a daguerreotype but was unhappy with the result, thinking it made his thin face look stout and heavy.

On the literary front, he was working on poems and short stories. The terror tale "Hop-Frog" was published in March. Like another of his later stories, "The Cask of Amontillado," it is a tale of revenge. Forced to play the fool as a court jester, the diminutive and deformed title character endures daily humiliation at the hands of the king and his ministers. Hop-Frog is close friends with the beautiful Trippetta, a wonderful dancer who is "very little less dwarfish than himself." During the planning for the grand masquerade, the king amuses himself by forcing Hop-Frog to drink wine, knowing his jester has little tolerance for alcohol. Indeed, it excites him "almost to madness." Trippetta intercedes on his behalf and is rewarded with a goblet of wine thrown in her face. The attack on such a pure and noble spirit is too much for Hop-Frog, who uses the masquerade as the stage for his horrific dose of payback. Given everything that had occurred in the last three years, it's tempting to speculate just which enemies Poe envisioned as the king and his ministers.

The poems "Eldorado" and "For Annie" appeared in April. He revised "The Bells." And in May, he composed "Annabel Lee." With the promise of financial support for *The Stylus* from investor Edward Howard Norton Patterson, the darkness and confusion that had enveloped him since late 1845 seemed to finally be lifting. Like the tortured man in "The Pit and the Pendulum," Poe endured and persevered through the darkness. Still, there had been many health scares, and the uncertainty of the future weighed on him, especially with a trip about to take him away from home and the care of the ever-attentive Muddy. He wanted to depart with the reassurance that his affairs were in order. On June 29, he gave Muddy two directives to follow in the event of his death. The first was that Rufus W. Griswold act as his literary executor and supervise the publication of his works. The second was that New York editor Nathaniel

P. Willis be charged with writing about his life and character. The next day, Poe embarked on the three-month journey that would take him to Philadelphia, Richmond, and, finally, Baltimore.

After his death, both Fanny Osgood and Helen Whitman would defend Poe's character, refuting the attacks made by his enemies, particularly Griswold (Whitman's book *Edgar Poe and His Critics* appeared in 1860). Loui Shew sent several letters, not always reliable on details but earnest in her admiration, to English biographer and editor John Henry Ingram. And, when her husband died in 1873, Nancy Locke Heywood Richmond had her first name legally changed to the one Poe had selected for her, Annie.

"DOUBLY DEAD"

OCTOBER 7, 1849

Most accounts of Poe's final hours have him calling out for someone named Reynolds on Saturday evening, October 6. It has become part of the lore and legend surrounding his death, yet this often-repeated detail is by no means certain and in no way verifiable. Once again, we have the magnificently unreliable resident physician at Washington College Hospital, John Joseph Moran, to thank or curse. In his November 15, 1849, letter to Muddy, the young doctor wrote that Poe was in state of delirium until Saturday evening,

> . . . when he Commenced Calling for one "Reynolds," which he did through the night up to *three* Sunday Morning. At this time a very decided change began to affect him. Having become en-feebled from exertion he became quiet and seemed to rest for a short time, then, gently moving his head he said *Lord help my poor Soul!* and expired.

Few believed that Moran would invent such details in a letter written so soon after Poe's death. Thus, another mystery was added to the pile. Who was the mysterious Reynolds? Had Poe been associating with a person bearing that name after he left Richmond? If so, no strong candidate emerged, and it wasn't for any lack of searching by biographers, scholars, amateur sleuths, and Poe enthusiasts. In 1902, James A. Harrison, editor of the seventeen-volume *Complete Works of Edgar Allan Poe*, put forth the theory that the dying Poe, about to embark on his final journey, was thinking of Jeremiah N. Reynolds (1799–1858), the American explorer, navigator, newspaper editor, and lecturer who advocated for an expedition to the South Pole. And, indeed, Poe had twice written admiringly of Reynolds in articles for the *Southern Literary Messenger*. He also used an 1836 address by Reynolds as a primary source when writing *The Narrative of Arthur Gordon Pym*. By the time Arthur Hobson Quinn published his still-indispensable biography of Poe in 1941, this all seemed to make logical and poetical sense:

> Perhaps to his dim and tortured brain, he seemed to be on the brink of a great descending circle sweeping down like the phantom ship in the "Manuscript Found in a Bottle" into "darkness and distance." In that first published story, Poe had written, "It is evident we are hurrying onward to some exciting knowledge— some never to be imparted secret, whose attainment is destruction. Perhaps this current leads to the South Pole itself."

The South Pole? It all seemed to make sense. By then, it was accepted as an ah-ha! deduction worthy of Dupin himself. But building on what Harrison had started, Quinn uncharacteristically was engaging in an unwise game of speculation that Poe described in "The Raven": "I betook myself to linking Fancy unto fancy." These were the fanciful links Quinn presented:

> It would have been natural enough for his favorite theme, the terror of the opening chasm, to lead his thoughts to that other story, *Arthur Gordon Pym*, and from that to Jeremiah Reynolds, projector of voyages to the South Seas, whose very language he

had used in that tale. He could easily have known Reynolds, but what led to his wild cries must still remain uncertain.

This thinking held sway for most of the twentieth century. There at least seemed to be a strong candidate for Poe's Reynolds and a strong reason for him calling his name. In his 1978 biography of Poe, Julian Symons repeats the assertion that Jeremiah Reynolds was "the most likely candidate." He had plenty of company until 1987 when Poe scholar William T. Bandy pushed back on the assumption with a dissection of what he called "the Poe-Reynolds myth." Bandy pointed out that Moran's first account has Poe shouting out the name Reynolds for anywhere from three to six hours—Saturday evening until three Sunday morning. It's not something a doctor would easily or likely forget, Bandy noted, yet, "in his 'Official Memoranda,' published in 1875, Moran does not say one word about Poe's nocturnal shouts." Moran also moved the time of death to around midnight in this second account, maybe because the aspiring writer felt this was a more dramatic time for departure. And when the name Reynolds does appear in the 1875 account, it now belongs to a family who lived near the hospital. The female members of this Reynolds family, Moran claimed, visited the hospital. Almost certainly, if there was such a visit, it was by Baltimore relatives, the female members of the Herring family. In the 1885 account, Moran did change the name of the visitors from Reynolds to Herring. In fact, the name Reynolds disappeared completely from the final hours, as did those agonizing hours of delirious shouting. Indeed, Moran, as he had in 1875, depicted Poe as capable of earnest conversation at the very end. He went so far as to change the final words . . . for a second time. This is the unbelievable exchange Moran presented, with Poe declaring:

"Doctor, it's all over."

"Mr. Poe, I must tell you that you are near your end. Have you any wish or word for friends?"

"Nevermore . . . O God! is there no ransom for the deathless spirit?"

"Yes, look to your Saviour; there is mercy for you and all mankind. God is love and the gift is free."

"He who arched the heavens and upholds the universe, has His decrees legibly written upon the frontlet of every human being, and upon demons incarnate."

He had given Poe equally melodramatic but different final words in 1849 and 1875. The time of death is also in doubt. After suggesting a short time after three o'clock and then midnight, Moran gave no specific time of death in 1885. Neilson Poe placed the time of death at five o'clock, Sunday morning, October 7. Biographical consensus seems to have settled on five in the morning.

Decades after Jeremiah Reynolds became a candidate for the person Poe supposedly was summoning on his deathbed, another contender emerged: Henry R. Reynolds, a carpenter who was an election judge at the Fourth Ward polls. But there's never been any proof that Poe knew Henry Reynolds, or Jeremiah, for that matter. Bandy concluded that, in searching for the identity of Reynolds, biographers had been chasing "a figment of Moran's imagination." Certainly the doctor's accounts differ so wildly, the question is not what name did Poe call out as he was dying but, rather, did he call out any name at all? Like the time of death and the last words, it is another seemingly unsolvable mystery. Symons argued that, despite Moran's later elaborations, "there seems no reason to question its general truth." But if you read the three accounts in order, it's an audacious assault on reason, and you're left with nothing but questions, including whether Moran actually was present when Poe breathed his last, whatever time that was.

The only certainty is that, by the time Neilson Poe received the news early Sunday morning, Edgar A. Poe had ended his tenure on this globe at the age of forty. Moran cited "inflammation of the brain" as the cause of death. He also noted to Muddy that many locks of the deceased writer's hair were snipped for remembrances and that those who had known him "pronounced his corpse the most natural they had ever seen."

Moran's account of Poe's death became grander and more elaborate with each telling. By 1875, he was claiming:

> After death he was washed and carefully laid out, dressed in a suit of black cloth, and placed in state in the large rotunda of the college building, where hundreds of friends and admirers came in crowds to pay their last tribute of respect to the deceased. Not less than fifty ladies were each furnished, at their earnest solicitations, with a small lock of his beautiful black hair. His body was kept in the rotunda for one whole day. On the morning of the 9th he was buried in the Westminster burying-ground. . . . A large number of our citizens, many of the most distinguished and prominent and literary and professional men, followed their remains to the sepulture.

Almost no part of this description is true. Moran, the writer wannabe, was furnishing Poe with the funeral he believed a literary genius deserved. It's close to complete fiction, though, with Moran getting all manner of details, large and small, wrong. How tall a tale was he spinning in 1875? Well, he even added two inches to Poe's height, stating that his patient was five foot ten. Poe's hair was brown, not black. What there was of a funeral was a pitiful procession attended by just a handful of people, not the distinguished and prominent multitudes Moran summoned more than twenty-five years later. And the journey to the cemetery took place on a cold and overcast Monday, October 8, the day after Poe died, not October 9.

Moran also claimed to have done much of the planning for the funeral. In his 1885 account, he wrote that he was the one who purchased the coffin. He described it as a plain one made of poplar, without a lining, a cushion for the head, handles, or a name plate. It was the best he could do with limited means, Moran told his readers. Yet Henry Herring, Poe's uncle, said it was he who provided the coffin, and that it was made of mahogany. And Neilson Poe, who paid for the hearse and the one carriage for the mourners, might have been the one to have procured the coffin. It seems more likely that relatives would have taken the lead on planning and paying for a funeral, although it certainly might have been done with Moran's assistance.

One carriage was all that was required on that raw and rainy Monday. The hearse made its way in a mournful afternoon drizzle to Baltimore's small Presbyterian cemetery (Westminster Presbyterian Church had not yet been constructed, and the completed edifice would stand over the north end of the cemetery). The Methodist-Episcopal ceremony was conducted by the Reverend William T. D. Clemm, Virginia's cousin, and lasted only three minutes. Poe was buried about four o'clock. Also in attendance were Herring, Neilson Poe, Dr. Joseph Snodgrass, Baltimore lawyer Z. Collins Lee (a Poe classmate at the University of Virginia), cousin Elizabeth Herring and her husband, Edmund Morton Smith, sexton George W. Spence, undertaker Charles Suter, and Joseph Clarke, the schoolmaster who had taught Poe in Richmond and recognized his student as a genuine poet. Snodgrass recalled:

> A grave had been dug among the crumbling mementos of mortality. Into this the plainly-coffined body was speedily lowered, and then the earth was shoveled directly upon the coffin-lid. This was so unusual even in the burials of the poor, that I could not help noticing the absence of not only the customary box, as an inclosure for the coffin itself, but of even the commonest boards to prevent the direct contact of the decomposing wet earth with it. I shall never forget the emotion of disappointment, mingled with disgust and something akin to resentment, that thrilled through my whole being as I heard the clods and stones resound from the coffin-lid and break the more ordinarily solemn stillness of the scene, as it impressed me. It seemed as if Heartlessness, too often found directing the funeral rites of the poor and forsaken ones of earth, had suddenly become personified into a malign goddess, and that she had ordered those awfully discordant sounds as best befitting her own unearthly mood.

One onlooker, J. Alden Weston, categorized the hasty ceremony as "cold-blooded and unchristianlike." He believed that if the funeral had been postponed even a day, many more who knew and admired Poe would have attended. As it was, neither Muddy in Fordham nor Elmira Royster Shelton in Richmond yet knew Poe was dead.

"Even though he made so little money off of 'The Raven,' he secured the reputation with it," Poe scholar Amy Branam Armiento said. "But then there was so little time left. He gets that glimpse of success and acclaim, and just when he gets it, he's gone."

Poe was buried near his grandparents. Neilson Poe did get around to arranging for a tombstone, but the writer's run of bad luck extended beyond the grave—and concerning the grave. The stone was destroyed before it reached the cemetery. A freight train jumped the track and smashed into the area of the mason's yard where it was being stored.

"The end is very Poe-esque, from the missing days to the funeral," said Enrica Jang, executive director of the Edgar Allan Poe House & Museum. "It is a plot he could have written."

The day after the funeral, Poe suffered that second death and burial when Rufus Griswold's infamous obituary appeared. Published under the pseudonym Ludwig, it described Poe as unamiable, envious, arrogant, irascible, and cynical. Poe was, as the phrase in his poem "Lenore" put it, "doubly dead." The assessment of Poe was so brutal, many rushed to his defense, including George Lippard, John Neal, Nathaniel Willis, George Rex Graham, and Lambert Wilmer. This alone put the lie to Griswold's depiction of Poe as friendless. The growing school of French admirers, led by Baudelaire, joined the chorus praising Poe and condemning Griswold. And, over the decades, Fanny Osgood and Helen Whitman would add their voices. Even as bitter an enemy as Thomas Dunn English emphatically denied the later persistent but groundless rumors that Poe had been an opium addict.

"Someone approached Thomas Dunn English and asked him about the supposed use of drugs, and he replied that, if Poe had been an opium addict, he would have noticed and that he considered the charge baseless slander," Poe scholar Jeff Jerome said. "Here's someone who had hard feelings toward Poe and plenty of unkind things to say about him, and he was adamant about there being nothing to it. There are several misconceptions about Poe, and one of the main ones is that he was addicted to drugs, that he used cocaine, LSD, and opium. Did Poe use opium for pain? Almost everyone back then did. He probably did use it for medicinal reasons, but that's all."

But as a couple of Poe's friends noted resignedly, the American public was more eager to hear the ugly slanders than to give the deceased a fair hearing.

"We haven't changed," Jerome said. "We hear these salacious stories about people, and the first thing we say is, 'Oh, that's awful, that's terrible.' We don't say, 'Hold on, there's two sides to every story.' It's human nature to gravitate toward the salacious stuff. But in a perverse sort of way, Griswold is partly responsible for the interest in Poe. His obituary and biography kind of jumpstarts the fascination with Poe with all of this sordid gossip and nonsense. It really captured the public's imagination. But that rascal really stuck it to Poe."

Or as Harry Lee Poe put it, "His biggest mistake was dying before his enemies."

Griswold's determined campaign to blacken Poe's reputation ultimately backfired in two ways. First, as Jerome points out, his falsehoods, as persistent as they proved to be, did end up making Poe more intriguing to one generation after another. Second, as the extent of his lies and forgeries came to light, Griswold was cast as the blackhearted villain driven by jealousy, resentment, and blind hatred.

"It certainly was not Griswold's intention to do Poe a favor, but that unquestionably was the result," literary historian Rob Velella said. "People are complicated, and it's easier to reduce a human being to one image than deal with all of the complexities and nuances and subtleties. If you look at how Poe has been depicted in the popular culture, it's either the dark, brooding, melancholy loner obsessed with the macabre or it's the aloof, hyper-analytical detective type. But it's never both. Griswold inadvertently elevated Poe's reputation by creating this character, and, ever since, casual readers of Poe want him to be insane, want him to be a loner, want him to be a humorless and friendless recluse, because it works with the stories he wrote."

Mark Twain's reputation similarly was reduced to caricature after his death, beloved as the rather tame, avuncular, and grandfatherly author of family literature and witty cracker-barrel observations. Twain became American literature's genial man in white to Poe's tortured man in black. Both achieved enduring fame, but Twain was granted the far kinder path. For one thing, in the 1960s, Twain's reputation expanded and grew as literary critics and biographers began to appreciate his social criticism and darker writings. Poe remained as popular, but the caricature view of him, if anything, grew stronger. For another, Samuel Clemens created the character of Mark Twain. He shaped the public persona that pop culture would embrace. Poe did not.

"Somebody else created Poe's persona, and it was somebody who didn't like him very much," Velella said. "The concept of the Renaissance man was very real in Poe's time. So Poe is many kinds of writer and many kinds of artist, and the twentieth century didn't give him credit for that."

The bitter irony for Griswold would have been the knowledge that, without Poe, nobody would be talking about him today. He also created a caricature for himself, that of the wretched literary assassin. In his ongoing efforts to reduce Poe, he reduced himself. In setting a snare constructed of falsehoods and forgeries, he got caught in his own trap.

"No one is the villain of his own story," Velella said. "And there was much more to Griswold, just as there was much more to Poe. My intent is not to fashion a defense of Griswold. I just think we should see his intent in the context of a bigger career. I'm not saying he was a good person, but he did see himself as an arbiter of literary tastes. He had an old-fashion religious background, so he praised works with messages he approved of—works of great morality. So he loved Longfellow. He didn't see any of this in Poe's writing. He feared that literature that was immoral or amoral could make readers immoral or amoral. The best Poe had to offer was in something like 'The Black Cat': don't drink too much or you might go insane and kill somebody. Griswold's real intent with Poe, I think, is that he doesn't want people reading him at all."

It is true that most Americans at the time of Poe's death were in complete agreement with Griswold's view of literature's role as an agent of uplift. His attacks on Poe certainly would have found many eager and willing listeners among the New England Frogpondians, who championed the presence of proper morals in prose and poetry.

"Poe didn't accept the pieties and the truisms of the culture and the time," Boston College English professor Paul Lewis said. "He disapproved of the notion that the purpose of literature was to inculcate truth. It wasn't a popular viewpoint, not just in Boston, but in all of America."

The works of Dickens were immensely popular in the United States before and after the Civil War, primarily because the author of *A Christmas Carol* and *David Copperfield* believed a good story should provide a good dose of that uplift so prized by fireside poets Whittier, Bryant, Lowell, and Longfellow. Poe and Dickens were drawn to similar macabre and mysterious settings and plot elements, but Poe rejected the didactic tendencies of Dickensian storytelling. This seemed to lend credence to Griswold's assault on Poe's character. The underhanded equation was a simplistic yet effective one: no moral in the tale, no morality in the author of the tale. Poe even mocked the story of uplift with one of his most successful humorous tales, the antimoral spoof "Never Bet the Devil Your Head."

"There's nothing Victorian, wholesome, convivial, or communal about Poe," said Poe scholar J. Gerald Kennedy. "He wasn't interested in that. He wrote about lonely characters in isolated situations confronting forces and effects that they couldn't understand. They felt threatened and horrified. That was so far out of keeping with the sensibility of most Americans at the time. It helps to explain why Poe was never very big in the Chautauqua movement of the later nineteenth century, which emphasized uplift and Christianity and moral goodness. A whole lot of cultural water has to flow under the bridge until the moment was right for Poe to be read and understood and appreciated."

When would the time be right for a proper appreciation of Poe? Try today, Kennedy suggested.

"Poe really anticipated the feel of our own time, even more than Twain did," he said. "Poe is alive to our culture today and to readers today in ways that he wasn't alive to readers in his lifetime. Poe was so far ahead of his own time in terms of intuiting changes that were already happening in the culture. And a lot of that has to do with the atrocities of the twentieth century: the Holocaust, the terrible wars, the inventions of mass destruction. We are now properly in a place where Poe resonates. A reader in the 2020s instantly understands 'The Masque of the Red Death' and gets the sense of entrapment and fatality and the claustrophobic effect that Poe creates. That's where the quarantine put us. We are trapped. And we have people bidding defiance to contagion."

The glow of the fireside poets failed to warm a world coping with the cold realities of a new century. Their light faded as we became less sure of comforting messages and more intrigued by Poe's troubling questions. "We recognize Poe's modern view of the dark side of humanity," said Jeffrey A. Savoye of the Edgar Allan Poe Society of Baltimore. "We don't expect sentimental moralizing. So we've embraced the very thing that made Poe distasteful in his own era."

The early prejudice against Poe extended to academia, where Poe's approach to writing, particularly poetry, also worked against him.

"Most scholars who write about and teach poetry are committed to thematic interpretations and approaches to poetry, and that is exactly what Poe opposed," said Jerome McGann, author of *The Poet Edgar Allan Poe: Alien Angel*. "Poe attacked what he called the didactic heresy. The academic approach may have very high-minded vocabularies to deliver their moral interpretations, but Poe opposed that. Poe believed that if the poet introduced ideas, it should be treated like themes in music. This is extremely difficult for most academics and scholars to deal with. How do you talk about or write about poetry that is as abstract and as intense and as powerful as Poe's when you are forbidden by the poet himself to deal with it in thematic terms?"

Henry James, T. S. Eliot, Ernest Hemingway, Ezra Pound, and Robert Frost were among those to write dismissively of Poe's work. Some acknowledged his talent but denigrated what he accomplished with it. Although he continued to be popular, there was still much dirt being shoveled his way—just of a slightly different variety from the type used by Griswold. During a 1948 lecture delivered at the Library of Congress, Eliot said that the best way to view Poe was "as a man who dabbled in verse and in kinds of prose, without settling down to make a thorough job of any one genre." He added that Poe had "the intellect of a highly gifted young person before puberty."

"That attitude remains prevalent at the universities, where Poe still is lightly regarded," Harry Lee Poe said. "I should emphasize that's American universities. That's not the case in foreign universities. It's foolish not to acknowledge that there is such a thing as literary politics, and Poe always has been a victim of literary politics in America. T. S. Eliot very much embodied the dismissive attitude toward Poe, to the point that, when he talked about how the French embraced Poe, he became fixated on the question, what's wrong with the French for liking Poe? That's the attitude. Eliot even claimed that a lot of Poe's work would be forgotten in ten years."

But Poe did have his champions, even among leading American poets, including Hart Crane and William Carlos Williams.

"One of the academic charges against Poe is that he is a popular writer, and that is no doubt true, but he himself said that he wanted to write poetry and prose fiction that would be simultaneously important for popular readers and more intellectual and specialized readers," McGann said. "And he achieved that. So Poe's standing as a poet is pretty high these days with the most interesting people writing about poetry today. The founders of high modernism—Baudelaire, Mallarmé, Valéry—were all complete enthusiasts of Poe. They regarded Poe as the founder of the modernist approach, which makes you completely understand why a person like Hart Crane or William Carlos Williams would have been enthusiastic about Poe."

It would take decades for Poe's reputation to gradually recover from these premature burials. And many in late 1849 would have been excused for thinking it might never recover.

On a personal level, no one was more grieved by Poe's death and the damage done to his reputation than the devoted Muddy. The news reached her on October 9, and she immediately wrote to Neilson Poe for the details: "If it is true God have mercy on me, for he was the last I had to cling to and love." That same day, her anguish found even more heartrending expression in a letter to Annie Richmond. "Annie my Eddy is dead," she wrote. "Annie my Annie pray for me your desolate friend. My senses *will leave me.*" To complete her devastation and desolation, Muddy was preparing to leave the Fordham cottage when she found that the adored pet, Catterina, had died.

"This poor woman has lost her daughter and a son-in-law she viewed as a son," Jang said. "She's the one who goes on. And then she gets overshadowed by Griswold's biography. It's heartbreaking."

Maria Clemm outlived her Eddy by more than twenty years, staying with friends in Richmond, Fordham, and Baltimore. She died on February 16, 1871, at Baltimore's Church Home and Infirmary. It was the new name for the hospital where Poe had died. Poe's sister, Rosalie, died in a home for indigents in 1874. The following year, Poe was buried yet again. His body was exhumed so it could be moved to a spot that could accommodate a more fitting monument to a writer increasingly embraced and celebrated by the city where he died. The cheap, rapidly buried coffin of twenty-six years earlier was discovered in ruinous shape. It had caved in and was falling apart. The sexton, George Spence, observed that a well-preserved skeleton was all that remained of Poe's, well, remains. Spence also said that he heard something like a lump of mud rattling around inside the skull. He believed it to be Poe's brain in a shriveled state of preservation. But since the brain quickly liquefies after death, this item caught the imagination of Matthew Pearl, author of *The Poe Shadow.* After consulting a coroner, he added another theory to the list of possible causes: a brain tumor, which can calcify into a hard mass after death. It did fit the observations made in 1847 by Loui Shew and Dr. Valentine Mott, who believed a brain lesion was the cause of Poe's intolerance to alcohol. Is that what Spence heard? It's not a theory than can be easily dismissed or proven. It's largely based on the newspaper reports quoting Spence, who was neither a doctor nor a criminologist. The coffin was also badly degraded, so it's not out of the question that mud, sediment, or a pebble could have fallen through the woodwork.

"That was most likely a rock," said Patrick Hansma, the full-time Michigan forensic pathologist, autopsy historian, and Poe scholar. "I approach the brain tumor theory with a great degree of skepticism. It's way down on the list of possibilities and not very high on the list of probabilities. Also, there are circumstances where parts of the brain will calcify. That's not unheard of."

It's yet another theory that can't be properly substantiated or definitively rejected.

"The brain tumor theory really came from research for the novel, but I have no dog in the fight," Pearl said. "I do think some of the theories are silly. The brain tumor theory makes sense to me, but I don't think it's a final catch-all. I'd never claim that. It remains a mystery, and that's incredibly useful. I think having this blank space that we can't solve helps us to understand Poe. It gives us a lens to understand who he was as a person and a writer."

Poe was reburied under a new monument in the cemetery's northwest corner. Recovering from a stroke, Walt Whitman loyally made the trip to Baltimore for the dedication ceremony honoring his fellow American poet on November 17, 1875. Whitman's famous evaluation of Poe was not entirely enthusiastic. He said that Poe "was among the electric lights of imaginative literatures, brilliant and dazzling, but with no heat." But the two poets had met once, in November 1845 in the *Broadway Journal* office. Whitman, then twenty-six, said of the then-thirty-six-year-old Poe, "I have a distinct and pleasing remembrance of his looks, voice, manner and matter; very kindly and human, but subdued, perhaps a little jaded."

Poe's family was reunited in death when the marble monument designed by Baltimore City Hall architect George A. Frederick also became the final resting place for the remains of Maria Clemm and Virginia. A cenotaph (a monument marking the initial site of burial or entombment) with the image of a raven marks the original burial spot.

"PENETRATE THE MYSTERIES"

> To conceive the horror of my sensations is, I presume, utterly impossible; yet to penetrate the mysteries of these awful regions, predominates even over my despair, and will reconcile me to the most hideous aspect of death.
>
> —"MS. FOUND IN A BOTTLE"

If this were your classic drawing-room mystery, the last chapter would begin with the master detective gathering all of the suspects for the big reveal. One by one the clues would be brilliantly dissected until, at last, the solution of the case was made known with a dazzling display of irrefutable logic and ingenious deduction. Just such a scene is wonderfully played out at the end of MGM's 1934 film version of Dashiell Hammett's *The Thin Man*. Super sleuth Nick Charles (William Powell) has put aside the martinis and Scotch long enough to sift through the evidence at a dinner party to which all the suspects have been invited. As Nick explains how the murderer schemed his way through three killings, his wife and partner-in-crime-detection, Nora (Myrna Loy), asks him sotto voce, "Is this true?" Nick replies, "I don't know." So, reasonably enough,

Nora wants to know, "Then why are you saying it?" Nick's answer is, "It's the only way that makes sense." And, of course, he's right. By putting together the puzzle one piece at a time, he demonstrates that there's only one way it all fits.

If only biography could work so neatly, offering the same level of assurance that we get from C. Auguste Dupin, Sherlock Holmes, Hercule Poirot, Lieutenant Columbo, and Jessica Fletcher. The problem with the mystery of Poe's death is that the evidence is so sketchy and undependable, it can be twisted so almost any answer makes some kind of sense. "Everyone has an opinion, and that opinion is the correct one, and everybody else is wrong," Baltimore Poe scholar Jeff Jerome said. "I think we now have more than twenty-two current theories, and a new one shows up every year."

We're also denied the satisfaction of a last drawing-room scene because, in this case, the leading suspects are not people. They have names like hypoglycemia, rabies, diabetes, tuberculosis, alcoholism, encephalitis, and heart disease. Poe's symptoms during the last three months of his life can be bent to fit a staggering number of causes. Hallucination, fever, delirium, stupor, and agitation can be caused by any number of ailments—or combinations of ailments. It also doesn't help matters that the witnesses make it difficult to determine how much stock to put in the widely ascribed symptoms. "As dubious as the record is, the best evidence tells us that Poe was delirious and feverish," said Patrick Hansma, the Michigan forensic pathologist whose fascination with Poe's life and works began in elementary school. "Those are what we call nonspecific symptoms because there are an incredible number of causes for those symptoms."

In addition to the possibilities already discussed, theories about Poe's death include diabetes, a drug overdose, influenza, hypoglycemia, epilepsy, apoplexy, an enzyme deficiency, liver disease, and meningeal inflammation due to a viral or bacterial infection. It becomes the bedeviling opposite of the "only way" mapped out by Powell's Nick. Hammett, though, had done his time as an actual Pinkerton detective, and, in his book, he has Nick strike a far more realistic investigative note. When he is explaining the murders to Nora, Nick uses the word *probably*, and it bothers her. She wants certainty in all the details. She doesn't like *probably*. "It's a word you've got to use a lot in this business," he tells her. When he's finished, having used a *probably* and a *maybe* here and there, Nora complains that "it's all pretty unsatisfactory."

While Poe, who died in Baltimore, is credited with creating the literary prototype of the erudite master detective, Hammett, who grew up in Baltimore, gave us the hard-boiled private investigator who gets to the answer through grit, rugged determination, and street smarts. They each turned a form of the mystery story into literature, one forever represented by a talking raven, the other by a Maltese falcon. But it was Hammett who knew the detective's trail will take its share of turns determined by that word so troubling to Nora. Such is the approach that must be taken with the mystery of Poe's death.

Still, that doesn't mean we haven't learned a great deal by probing the mystery. For one thing, we follow the path of *probably* and all but eliminate some of the suspects thought to be responsible for Poe's death. We can narrow the field a bit. For instance, if Poe did swallow liquids during his final days, and he probably did, that takes rabies off the list of candidates. John Evangelist Walsh's murder theory, as entertainingly as it was presented in his book *Midnight Dreary: The Mysterious Death of Edgar Allan Poe*, seems even more unlikely. The two tests done on samples of Poe's hair seem to rule out carbon monoxide poisoning from illuminating gas and malnutrition. It advances the case some, but even when you eliminate several of the theories because of improbability and the hair tests, you're still left with no shortage of suspects. You're also left with almost no forensic way to proceed. Former FBI agent John Douglas submitted his take on the near impossibility of unearthing anything new by applying modern behavioral analysis and profiling to the enduring mystery: "An ice-cold case from the middle of the nineteenth century would be difficult to profile under any circumstances, since the behaviors and social norms were likely quite different from our own. But it becomes wholly unsuitable for profiling or behavioral analysis in the absence of reliable witness statements, accounts from family or friends about the victim's state of mind in the days and weeks preceding death, accurate autopsy protocols, photographs, or any physical or forensic evidence."

"Essentially, all we have to go on is a situation in which a deceased individual is found," Douglas said, "with no way of knowing" for certain what caused him to be found in such a condition. Poe scholar Jeffrey A. Savoye describes the difficulty in a slightly different way: "Unless you dig up that body and find a hatchet sticking out of his back, I'm not really sure what additional information could be found. It's endlessly fascinating because it can't be solved. There is no definitive explanation, and there won't be unless there is some startling revelation. We just really don't have enough evidence."

Even if an autopsy had been conducted, it probably wouldn't have been much help to us today. "He died when there was no real compelling need to document his death with any of the scientific rigor we'd use today," said Hansma, also an author working on a history of autopsies. "The autopsy of that time had not yet gained a fair degree of scientific rigor. If he had died fifty years later, his death would have been very well handled, very meticulously recorded. Today, the vast majority of autopsies are done by forensic pathologists, a specialty that didn't exist back then."

Hansma has studied all of the accounts of Poe's final days, and, as a forensic pathologist, he shares the biographer's generally skeptical view of Moran's various versions. "After reading everything Moran wrote and said about Poe's death, we clearly have very little reason to believe the clinical accounts he gives us," he said. "If Moran had done an autopsy, quite frankly, I wouldn't have trusted it. The evidence speaks against his reliability. So much seems improbable and dubious." So he joins Douglas and Savoye in the belief that Poe's death remains in a realm beyond a final solution. The FBI agent, the Poe scholar, and the forensic pathologist are in agreement. This view might best be summarized by a line Poe wrote for "The Fall of the House of Usher": "It was a mystery all insoluble."

"It is unknowable because everything was carelessly handled from the beginning," Hansma said. "It is now so far removed from us, and the evidence that does exist is at best tenuous, dubious, and fragmentary. Many of the key witnesses are questionable and unreliable. The anatomic evidence that we'd work with doesn't exist. What's left? Some skeletal remains, and we don't even know the condition of those. The best we can do is weigh the available evidence and suggest the strongest possibilities. And I believe that, although it's not provable, there is one incredibly strong possibility."

Hansma has, indeed, reached the same thought now shared by some Poe scholars and medical experts who have examined his case. There is one possible cause of death that stalked and haunted Poe his entire life: tuberculosis. Did it cause his death? Well, we already know it shaped his life, since both of his parents, his foster mother, his brother, and his wife died of consumption. There's no doubt about it. As a prime suspect, tuberculosis had plenty of means and opportunity.

"No question in my mind that tuberculosis is at the top of the short list of strongest possibilities," Hansma said. "It is unquestionably prime suspect number one."

If this were an active criminal investigation, the suspect we'd keep calling back into the interrogation room as a person of interest would be tuberculosis. An infectious disease that usually affects the lungs, tuberculosis is an airborne infection spread when someone with an active case coughs, sneezes, spits, or just talks. Evidence for tuberculosis goes back at least seventeen thousand years in animal bones. The presence of TB has been found on the skeletal remains of prehistoric humans and in Egyptian mummies. The oldest known evidence for TB in humans was found in the nine-thousand-year-old bones of a Neolithic woman and an infant found submerged about six miles off the coast of Haifa, Israel, where the ancient village of Atlit-Yam stood.

One out of seven people died from tuberculosis in the nineteenth century; three out of four children were infected with tuberculosis by the age of five. As prevalent as it was throughout Poe's life, however, TB was not put forward as a leading candidate for his death in most of the biographies published in the nineteenth and twentieth centuries. Gretchen Worden, the esteemed director of the Mutter Museum at the College of Physicians of Philadelphia from 1988 until her death in 2004, might have been heading in this direction in the first years of the twenty-first century. Worden frequently lectured on Virginia's tuberculosis and Poe's mysterious death. Her notes for these lectures are now in the College of Physicians archives, and, while she summarized several of the leading theories, on one index card she listed the many Poe relations claimed by tuberculosis. So, back to Philadelphia we go with a logical enough question: How likely was it that Poe had tuberculosis?

"As a historian of medicine, retrospective diagnosis is very much frowned upon," said Dr. Steven J. Peitzman of the Drexel University College of Medicine. "But it's almost a complete certainty that Poe had tuberculosis."

W. Henry Boom, the director of the Tuberculosis Research Unit at Case Western Reserve University, agrees with Peitzman's diagnosis: "Given his family history and the time he lived, he undoubtedly was infected. The only thing you can say with near certainty is that he had TB."

It is something that many Poe scholars, including Semtner and Helen McKenna-Uff, do say with certainty. "We don't know what killed him, but there's no question Poe had tuberculosis," J. Gerald Kennedy said.

But is it logical to consider that Poe had something as serious as tuberculosis and didn't know it? Once again, the medical experts weigh in.

"It's entirely possible to have tuberculosis for much of your life and not know it," Peitzman said. "What can occur is trans-pulmonary exposure, leading to some inflammation of the lungs. Then it heals. People can go for decades with these healed granulomas, but there is living bacilli inside, and they tend to break down in periods of stress or malnutrition or just old age."

Boom again concurs: "If you're exposed and infected and you're otherwise healthy, you can do very well with microbacterium tuberculosis and not get sick. You may not show any symptoms, and, unless you have a positive TB test, either as a blood test or a skin test, you may not know you're infected. That's called latent TB, and we know that this can reactivate many years later, depending on general health and well-being."

McKenna-Uff had personal experience with this. Her grandmother had tuberculosis, and when her father was forty, he had to get an X-ray. "And they told him he had lesions and an undiagnosed case of tuberculosis," she said. "He had absolutely no idea."

It's possible, therefore, that Poe could have been infected in infancy. The cause of his death could have been his birthright. He could have been carrying it in his body for almost his entire time on this planet. Although it adds nothing in the way of hard evidence, there is something grimly poetic about that possibility. It is a scenario worthy of a Poe horror tale: the enemy TB that would rob him again and again lurking in his body, waiting to go active. But Eliza Poe's consumption would have been merely the first of many windows of opportunity for the infection to strike.

Studying what we know of Poe's symptoms and the last months of his life also raises the Hammett "probably" factor for Hansma: "Poe's symptomatology at death fits the dying tubercular really well. This is really well documented in the sanatoriums of the time that specialized in tuberculosis. There is an incredible record of patients dying from tuberculosis being artistically and intellectually flourishing for weeks and months at a time near the end. They could be whimsical, oddly optimistic, and profoundly productive, and then this disease that is killing them could resemble the narcotizing effect of opium or ethanol. How does that not sound like Edgar Allan Poe?"

The stereotyped Poe would not seem healthy enough to have kept a latent TB infection at bay for so many years. But that is the stereotype. How about Poe the gifted young athlete who excelled at swimming, boxing, and long jumping? How about Poe the good soldier with a brisk gait and erect posture? How about the Poe who took long rambling walks through woods and down city streets? He could be that healthy.

"There's a popular image of Poe, which isn't reality, but it is pervasive," said *Mindhunter* coauthor and filmmaker Mark Olshaker. "And that image demands that his death be caused by his personality or his obsessions or his supposed addictions. The cause may well have been something organic, and that doesn't fit the image."

If tuberculosis is the prime suspect, though, there are some accomplices to consider. Something must have suppressed the immune system and caused the tuberculosis to go active. Here, too, there are suspects with ample opportunity.

"I believe it was tuberculosis, and there are so many factors in Poe's adult life that could have weakened his system: poverty, stress, alcohol, poor housing, environmental pollutants," said Carole Shaffer-Koros, a Poe scholar, English professor, and registered nurse who worked with tuberculosis patients. "The amount of carbon monoxide wasn't lethal, but it could have been a contributing factor. I'm not ready to say Poe was a chronic alcoholic, but he clearly had an intolerance and an allergic reaction to alcohol, and it had a devastating effect on him. We really don't know how much Poe was drinking, but latent tuberculosis aggravated by the consumption of alcohol could have proved deadly for Edgar Allan Poe."

Semtner and McKenna-Uff go beyond TB as the likely cause, specifically suggesting tuberculosis meningitis, which attacks the central nervous system and the meninges, the membranes that envelop the brain. Symptoms of tuberculosis meningitis include confusion, fever, stupor, coma, headache, and behavioral changes. Tuberculosis meningitis "makes the most sense," Semtner said, "and it explains the ranting, the raving, the fever, and the head pain."

If Poe did have cholera in Philadelphia, it's one thing that was unlikely to have suppressed his immune system. "Cholera is an acute illness, but, as horrible as it is, it's something you get and are over it in a week," Boom said. "So, it's less likely that it would cause long-term immune suppression to the point where TB would reactivate." The mercury in the calomel "medicine" used to treat cholera, though, wouldn't have done his system good. Even without cholera, the suspects for compromising the immune system are all around him. If Poe was cooped, exposed to the cold, and given alcohol, the combination would have been horrific on someone with an active case of tuberculosis.

"It's certainly plausible," Peitzman said. "If you have latent tuberculosis and you live long enough, it's very likely going to break down and re-disseminate and be carried by the bloodstream, which is how it would get to the bones and the meninges."

Plausible, okay, but is it probable? Here's where the good doctors won't allow themselves to stray too far into speculation. The expert witnesses will go just far enough to make the possibility as promising as it is intriguing.

"It's feasible," Boom said. "TB meningitis is not something that develops overnight and kills you the next day. It's a chronic meningitis. It takes weeks, sometimes months, to fully manifest. If he had some confusion, fever, moments of paranoia and erratic behavior, disorientation, delusion, or hallucinations, that certainly could fit the pattern of TB meningitis. If he had TB meningitis, and then you add alcohol or exposure, that could be enough to tip him over. It's entirely possible, but there's nothing here that says it's definitely TB meningitis or anything else."

Even if Moran had been a completely reliable eyewitness, accurately chronicling every minute of Poe's final days, neither he nor any other doctor in 1849 would have known how to recognize, test for, and properly diagnose tuberculosis meningitis.

"Tuberculosis meningitis was aggressive, catastrophic, and always fatal back then," Hansma said. "He might have had spinal and meningeal involvement with tuberculosis, and it would explain his symptoms very well, particularly the fluctuating period of consciousness and rationality, and the fever. But delirium is not uncommon with all forms of tuberculosis. The most you can say is that tuberculosis has to remain a serious consideration for anyone who wants to tackle this problem and, given everything we know about Poe's life and death, it should always be near the top of anyone's list of suspects. So Poe's death remains a mystery, despite such a likely cause as tuberculosis."

Could any kind of forensic testing on Poe's remains definitely solve the mystery? Certainly tests on bones could reveal whether or not he had an active case of tuberculosis, but it wouldn't determine if he actually died from it. And even if such testing did prove he had tuberculosis, so what? We already know it's almost certain he was infected.

An exhumation is beyond unlikely in Poe's case, yet there is one other test that could settle the matter. The trick here is that word *could*.

"Right now, the case for tuberculosis meningitis is highly probable and certainly possible but largely circumstantial," said Linda B. Spurlock, a Kent State University anthropology professor whose specialties include forensic anthropology, biomedical science, and forensic art. "Still, a strong enough circumstantial case will stand up in court. If you're searching for that one piece of hard evidence, the bones could still tell us much. It is possible for tuberculosis meningitis to leave tell-tale granular impressions inside the skull. They are highly common in cases of tuberculosis meningitis."

According to the National Center for Biotechnology Information, "granular impressions (GIs) on the inner skull surface have been considered as pathognomonic features of tuberculosis meningitis (TBM)." These GIs may be created by "pressure atrophy of the tubercles formed on the outermost meningeal layer."

If there is such evidence for how Poe died, it will remain buried in a Baltimore cemetery under that monument dedicated in 1875. Nora wouldn't like it, but she and everybody else will have to settle for Nick's *probably*. That's the best we can do. The answer can't be conclusive or definitive. Not now. Perhaps not ever. And maybe that is how it should be.

"There is a part of me that doesn't want to know," author Daniel Stashower said.

And, as the maxim reminds us, some mysteries are not meant to be solved, and it must be acknowledged that anything beyond *probably* would surely rob us of the grand mystique surrounding Poe's death.

"By leaving us so young and leaving so many mysteries behind, he can be for us what we need him to be and what we want him to be," Poe scholar Amy Branam Armiento said.

Some want him and need him to be the master of the macabre, and he'll forever play that role, as he did sometimes in life. This was pretty much assured in the 1930s when Universal released its "Poe" movies: *Murders in the Rue Morgue*, *The Black Cat*, and *The Raven*.

"He was associated in the public's mind with Boris Karloff and Bela Lugosi," Semtner said. "And it's fine if the master of the macabre is what Poe means to you, but we do him a disservice if we don't recognize how good those stories and poems are that have kept him alive. Then you have to take those stories seriously and explore why what he's doing with those stories is so much better than Horace Walpole and all the other people who were writing horror stories at the time."

Even the horror actors most associated with Poe were quick to acknowledge how much more there was to his stories and poems. "Poor Poe," Karloff said in a mid-1960s interview. "The things we did to him when he wasn't there to defend himself. Some of those films weren't in the least like him."

Karloff's costar in the 1963 version of *The Raven*, Vincent Price, believed that the best of the Poe-inspired films captured the essence of Poe's haunting tales and poems: "They caught the spirit of Poe, if not the specifics. But you hope people will look beyond the death and dying stuff to see how much life he packed into such a short time. You hope they understand he was an original—a distinctive American voice. He had the soul of an artist and the voice of a poet, but it was an original voice, and that's what the Europeans responded to."

Yes, many European writers, and some Americans. Among those Poe admirers not already mentioned: William Butler Yeats, Franz Kafka, Jules Verne, Rudyard Kipling, Edith Wharton, Algernon Swinburne, Friedrich Nietzsche, Dorothy L. Sayers, F. Scott Fitzgerald, and Vladimir Nabokov.

"And we're all still reading Poe, in America and round the world," Jerome said. "Where are all the other geniuses who were going to live forever? But we're still not just reading Poe, we're obsessed with him."

Given how little success Poe experienced during his lifetime, you wish you could go back and tell him, don't worry, you're the one they're going to read and remember.

"I think he knew," McKenna-Uff said. "Poe knew that he was a writing genius and it would have legs."

He might be miffed about being overwhelmingly identified as a horror writer, but he surely would be pleased to see how it has carried his writing through the centuries and around the world. The young Poe may well have identified with the ambitious hero of his early poem "Tamerlane," who charges into battle with a philosophy of conquer or die in the attempt. Poe reversed that. He died, then conquered. And death, and the mystery of it, ended up working for him.

"There is a powerful universality in what Poe wrote about in those stories," Kennedy said, "and it sort of confirms his own determination to write for the world and not to write from a provincial perspective."

When Stephen King appeared at a Big Read event devoted to Poe, he brought along "The Old Dude's Ticker," his reworking of "The Tell-Tale Heart." "You really want to hear this story?" he asked the audience in North Carolina. "Everything in the story that I'm going to read to you is in Poe's story, so if you get grossed out or if you get scared or if you go 'Yuk!' or something like that, don't blame me. Blame it right on Poe. And you can't get at him, he's dead."

But is he? "The boundaries which divide Life from Death are at best shadowy and vague," Poe told us in "The Premature Burial." "Who shall say where the one ends, and where the other begins?" Who's to say in literature? "Fashions in dead authors come and go, but Poe is, I would wager, beyond fashion," author Neil Gaiman has said. It's a smart wager.

So the mystery of Poe's death becomes an enduring part of the wonder that he is the most alive writer in the world today. Never mind the clunky dying words attributed to him by Moran. The line that best suits his last moment in Baltimore is one he gave the title character of "Morella": "I am dying, yet shall I live."

ACKNOWLEDGMENTS

In the introduction to what remains, in my estimation, one of the best-written biographies of Edgar Allan Poe, *The Tell-Tale Heart*, crime writer and literary historian Julian Symons told his readers that he avoided talking to Poe scholars while working on his book. That suited his method, of course, but I took precisely the opposite approach. I eagerly sought out many of the leading authorities on various aspects of Poe's life and literary output. As mentioned in the opening chapter, this was my way of recognizing their indispensable work while also putting them to work as expert witnesses. I'll start with Chris Semtner, curator of the Edgar Allan Poe Museum in Richmond, because, well, I kind of started with him when the research began in earnest. Chris was unfailingly generous, patient, and helpful, spending hours in conversation, pointing out valuable directions to pursue, and promptly supplying needed files, documents, and pictures. It would be an understatement of extreme proportions to say I am in his debt.

I was gratified to learn that this willingness to give of one's time and knowledge was typical of the university professors, curators, and researchers who have consistently challenged and furthered our understanding of a writer whose life is so mired in myth and mystery. More complete identifications, titles, and credits for these magnanimous

Poe scholars can be found at the beginning of the following notes and sources section, but this is the place where thanks are in order. So, for illuminating everything from Poe's personality to his writing, these heartfelt thanks go to Amy Branam Armiento, Michael Deas, Dennis Eddings, James M. Hutchisson, Enrica Jang, Jeff Jerome, J. Gerald Kennedy, Paul Lewis, Jerome McGann, Helen McKenna-Uff, Steve Medeiros, Scott Peeples, Edward G. Pettit, Harry Lee "Hal" Poe, Jeffrey A. Savoye, Carole Shaffer-Koros, and Rob Velella. Many followed up on our conversations by sending useful articles, copies of documents, maps, and illustrations.

During my forty-plus years as a film and television critic, there were many opportunities to interview leading practitioners in the horror genre. Many of these led to lively conversations about Poe's tales of terror and his importance to the fright field. They included the late Robert Bloch, Ray Bradbury, Wes Craven, Vincent Price, and Anne Rice, as well as such reigning horror royalty as Stephen King.

For their perceptive takes on Poe as a working writer, with specific focus on his crime writing, major thanks to authors Mark Olshaker, Matthew Pearl, and Daniel Stashower. For their guidance and expertise on medical, scientific, and forensic matters regarding Poe's death, much appreciation to tuberculosis and infectious disease authority Dr. W. Henry Boom, former FBI agent John Douglas, forensic pathologist Patrick Hansma, Professor Stephen Macko ("the hair detective"), medical historian Dr. Steven J. Peitzman, and forensic anthropology professor Linda B. Spurlock.

I am also deeply grateful to the late Herb Moskovitz of Philadelphia for sending timely materials and suggestions. Thanks also go to Heather Cole, curator of the Harris Collection, John Hay Library, Brown University, for providing access to requested documents as well as a high-resolution copy of the "Whitman" daguerreotype of Poe. Among the many other institutions providing documents and images: the University of Virginia Library's special collections; the Philadelphia Free Library; the J. Paul Getty Museum; the Fine Arts Library's Special Collections at Harvard University;

the College of Physicians of Philadelphia; the National Park Service; the National Archives; and the Library of Congress.

The work of the Poe Studies Association and copies of *The Edgar Allan Poe Review* are key resources for anyone studying the writer's life and work. And special acknowledgment needs to be made of eapoe.org, the Edgar Allan Poe Society of Baltimore's endlessly useful online archive of material maintained by Jeffrey A. Savoye. When you go looking for a source or citation, again and again you're not disappointed to find it among the vast riches at eapoe.org. It was consulted constantly during the writing of this book.

Thanks for advice and feedback go to Stephen S. Power, who suggested I write this book, St. Martin's editor extraordinaire Sarah Grill, and ace agent Charlotte Gusay.

And there's no way to adequately recognize the patience and understanding and support provided by the home team, my wife, Sara, and our daughter, Becky. Sara never fails to bring Poe alive during our performances of his stories and poems, brilliantly interpreting "The Bells," "The Masque of the Red Death," and other pieces. That's a pretty wonderful dose of inspiration. She and Becky are the keepers of my tell-tale heart.

SELECTED BIBLIOGRAPHY

Poe Biographies, Studies, Reference Works, and Related Publications

Ackroyd, Peter. *Poe: A Life Cut Short*. New York: Nan A. Talese, Doubleday Publishing Group, 2008.

Allen, Hervey. *Israfel: The Life and Times of Edgar Allan Poe*. New York: Farrar & Rinehart, 1934.

Bittner, William. *Poe: A Biography*. Boston: Atlantic Monthly Press / Little, Brown and Company, 1962.

Bloom, Harold, ed. *Bloom's Modern Critical Views: Edgar Allan Poe*. Updated edition, New York: Chelsea House Publishers, 2006.

Bloomfield, Shelley Costa. *The Everything Guide to Edgar Allan Poe*. Avon, MA: Adams Publishing, 2007.

Bondurant, Agnes M. *Poe's Richmond*. Richmond, VA: Garrett & Massie, 1942.

Carlson, Eric. W. *Critical Essays on Edgar Allan Poe*. Boston: G. K. Hall & Co., 1987.

Case, Keshia A., and Christopher P. Semtner. *Edgar Allan Poe in Richmond*. Charleston, SC: Arcadia Publishing, 2009.

Collins, Paul. *Edgar Allan Poe: The Fever Called Living*. New York: Houghton Mifflin Harcourt, 2014.

Connelly, Michael, ed. *In the Shadow of the Master: Classic Tales and Essays by Jeffery Deaver, Nelson DeMille, Tess Gerritsen, Sue Grafton, Stephen King, Laura Lippman, Lisa Scottoline, and Thirteen Others*. New York: William Morrow, 2008.

Deas, Michael J. *The Portraits and Daguerreotypes of Edgar Allan Poe*. Charlottesville: University of Virginia Press, 1989.

Didier, Eugene L. *Life of Edgar A. Poe*. New York: W. J. Widdleton, 1877.

Foye, Raymond, ed. *The Unknown Poe*. San Francisco: City Lights Books, 1980.

Gaylin, David F. *Edgar Allan Poe's Baltimore*. Charleston, SC: Arcadia Publishing, 2015.

Haining, Peter, ed. *The Edgar Allan Poe Scrapbook*. New York: Schocken Books, 1978.

Hoffman, Daniel. *Poe Poe Poe Poe Poe Poe Poe*. Baton Rouge: Louisiana State University Press, 1998.

Hutchisson, James M. *Poe*. Jackson: University Press of Mississippi, 2005.

Ingram, John H. *Edgar Allan Poe: Life, Letters, and Opinions*. 2 vols. London: John Hogg, 1880.

Kennedy, J. Gerald. *Poe, Death, and the Life Writing*. New Haven, CT: Yale University Press, 1987.

Kennedy, J. Gerald, ed. *A Historical Guide to Edgar Allan Poe*. New York: Oxford University Press, 2001.

Kennedy, J. Gerald, and Scott Peeples, eds. *The Oxford Handbook of Edgar Allan Poe*. New York: Oxford University Press, 2019.

Meyers, Jeffrey. *Edgar Allan Poe: His Life and Legacy*. New York: Charles Scribner's Sons, 1992.

Miller, John C. *Building Poe Biography*. Baton Rouge: Louisiana State University Press, 1977.

Montague, Charlotte. *Edgar Allan Poe: The Strange Man Standing Deep in the Shadows*. New York: Chartwell Books, 2015.

Ocker, Matthew. *Poe-Land: The Hallowed Haunts of Edgar Allan Poe*. New York: The Countryman Press, 2015.

Pearl, Matthew. *The Poe Shadow*. New York: Random House, 2006.

Peeples, Scott. *The Afterlife of Edgar Allan Poe*. Rochester, NY: Boydell & Brewer, Camden House, 2004.

Peeples, Scott. *The Man of the Crowd: Edgar Allan Poe and the City*. Princeton, NJ: Princeton University Press, 2020.

Phillips, Mary E. *Edgar Allan Poe: The Man*. Chicago: The John C. Winston Co., 1926.

Pope-Hennessey, Una. *Edgar Allan Poe: A Critical Biography*. London: Macmillan, 1934.

Quinn, Arthur Hobson. *Edgar Allan Poe: A Critical Biography*. Baltimore: The Johns Hopkins University Press, 1998 reprint of 1941 biography.

Rein, David M. *Edgar A. Poe: The Inner Pattern*. New York: Philosophical Library, 1960.

Semtner, Christopher P. *Edgar Allan Poe's Richmond: The Raven in the River City*. Charleston, SC: History Press, 2012.

Silverman, Kenneth. *Edgar A. Poe: Mournful and Never-ending Remembrance*. New York: HarperCollins Publishers, 1991.

Sova, Dawn B. *Edgar Allan Poe A to Z*. New York: Facts On File, 2001.

Stashower, Daniel. *The Beautiful Cigar Girl: Mary Rogers, Edgar Allan Poe, and The Invention of Murder*. New York: Dutton, 2006.

Symons, Julian. *The Tell-Tale Heart: The Life and Works of Edgar Allan Poe.* New York: Penguin Books, 1981.

Thomas, Dwight, and David K. Jackson. *The Poe Log: A Documentary Life of Edgar Allan Poe, 1809–1849.* Boston: G. K. Hall & Company, 1987.

Wagenknecht, Edward. *Edgar Allan Poe: The Man Behind the Legend.* New York: Oxford University Press, 1963.

Walsh, John Evangelist. *Midnight Dreary: The Mysterious Death of Edgar Allan Poe.* New Brunswick, NJ: Rutgers University Press, 1998.

Weiss, Susan Archer. *Home Life of Poe.* New York: Broadway Publishing Company, 1907.

Whitman, Sarah Helen. *Edgar Poe and His Critics.* New York: Rudd & Carleton, 1860.

Woodberry, George. *The Life of Edgar Allan Poe.* Boston: Houghton Mifflin, 1909.

Other Works

Ackroyd, Peter. *Dickens.* New York: HarperCollins Publishers, 1990.

Bloom, Harold, ed. *Classic Horror Writers.* New York: Chelsea House Publishers, 1994.

Douglas, John, and Mark Olshaker. *Mindhunter: Inside the FBI's Elite Serial Unit.* New York: Gallery Books, 2017.

Epstein, Norrie. *The Friendly Dickens.* New York: Viking, 1998.

Johnson, Edgar. *Charles Dickens: His Tragedy and Triumph.* New York: Simon & Schuster, 1952.

King, Stephen. *Danse Macabre.* New York: Everest House, 1981.

King, Stephen. *On Writing.* New York: Scribner, 2000.

Pearson, Hesketh. *Dickens.* London: Methuen & Company, 1949.

Pope-Hennessy, Una. *Charles Dickens.* New York: Howell, Soskin, Publishers, 1946.

Price, Victoria. *Vincent Price: A Daughter's Memoir.* New York: St. Martin's Press, 1999.

Schroth, Raymond A. *Fordham: A History and Memoir.* New York: Fordham University Press, 2008 revised edition.

Stashower, Daniel. *Teller of Tales: The Life of Arthur Conan Doyle.* New York: Henry Holt and Company.

NOTES AND SOURCES

Citations are keyed to phrases in the text. Full citations are given for information or quotations from books, articles, and archival material. However, more than fifty interviews were conducted for this book with experts from several fields, including Poe studies and various forensic disciplines. The following last names are used for those interview subjects most frequently quoted:

ARMIENTO: Amy Branam Armiento, professor of English at Frostburg State University and past president of the Poe Studies Association, taped phone interview, September 23, 2020.

BLOCH: Robert Bloch, horror writer best known for the novel *Psycho,* in-person taped interview, Hyatt Regency Hotel, Crystal City, Virginia, May 29, 1993.

BOOM: W. Henry Boom, MD, Case Western Reserve University, School of Medicine; chief, Division of Infectious Diseases and HIV Medicine; director, Tuberculosis Research Unit; professor, Department of Molecular Biology and Microbiology, taped phone interview, October 1, 2020.

BRADBURY: Ray Bradbury, fantasy, science-fiction, and horror author, taped phone interview, Los Angeles, California, October 1, 1991.

CRAVEN: Wes Craven, screenwriter-director specializing in horror films, taped in-person interview, Ritz-Carlton Huntington Hotel, Pasadena, California, July 10, 2006.

DEAS: Michael Deas, painter, illustrator, and author of *The Portraits & Daguerreotypes of Edgar Allan Poe,* taped phone interview, December 8, 2020.

DOUGLAS: John Douglas, former FBI agent, the bureau's criminal profiling pioneer, one of the creators of the *Crime Classification Manual,* and coauthor of *Mindhunter: Inside the FBI's Elite Serial Crime Unit,* interview responses by email, July 19, 2021.

EDDINGS: Dennis Eddings, Poe and Mark Twain scholar, emeritus professor of Humanities at Western Oregon University, interview responses by email, November 25, 2019.

HANSMA: Patrick Hansma, full-time forensic pathologist, Poe scholar, and Michigan-based author of *The Grave Below*, taped phone interviews, April 17, 2021, and May 4, 2021.

HUTCHISSON: James M. Hutchisson, professor of American literature and southern studies at the Citadel and author of *Poe*, taped phone interview, September 28, 2020.

JANG: Enrica Jang, executive director, Poe Baltimore and the Edgar Allan Poe House & Museum, taped phone interview, November 24, 2020.

JEROME: Jeff Jerome, Baltimore Poe scholar and former curator of the Edgar Allan Poe House & Museum, taped phone interview, September 10, 2020.

KENNEDY: J. Gerald Kennedy, English professor at Louisiana State University, author of *Poe, Death, and the Life of Writing*, and the editor of *A Historical Guide to Poe* and *The Portable Edgar Allan Poe*, taped phone interview, August 12, 2020.

KING: Stephen King, horror writer, taped phone interview, May 7, 2004.

LEWIS: Paul Lewis, English professor at Boston College and past president of the Poe Studies Association, taped phone interview, September 8, 2020.

MACKO: Stephen Macko, professor at the University of Virginia, Charlottesville, whose areas of specialty include biogeochemistry, marine organic chemistry, stable isotope geochemistry, isotope geometry, and isotopic hair analysis (known as "the hair detective"), taped phone interview, November 25, 2019.

McGANN: Jerome McGann, professor emeritus, Department of English, University of Virginia, and author of *The Poet Edgar Allan Poe: Alien Angel*, taped phone interview, October 20, 2020.

McKENNA-UFF: Helen McKenna-Uff, retired National Park Service ranger, Edgar Allan Poe National Historic Site and Independence Park, Philadelphia, taped phone interview, April 24, 2020.

MEDEIROS: Steve Medeiros, Poe scholar and former National Park Service ranger regularly assigned to the Edgar Allan Poe National Historic Site in Philadelphia, taped phone interview, August 6, 2020.

OLSHAKER: Mark Olshaker, novelist, nonfiction author, Emmy-winning filmmaker, taped phone interview, September 18, 2020.

PEARL: Matthew Pearl, novelist whose works include *The Poe Shadow* and *The Dante Club*, taped phone interview, October 6, 2020.

PEEPLES: Scott Peeples, professor, College of Charleston, author of *The Man of the Crowd: Edgar Allan Poe and the City*, and coeditor of *The Oxford Handbook of Edgar Allan Poe*, taped phone interview, October 1, 2020.

PEITZMAN: Steven J. Peitzman, MD, FACP, professor of medicine and medical history, Drexel University College of Medicine, taped phone interview, September 6, 2020.

PETTIT: Edward G. Pettit, Poe scholar, manager of public programs, the Rosenbach Museum, Philadelphia, taped phone interview, July 31, 2020.

POE: Harry Lee "Hal" Poe, an Edgar A. Poe cousin, professor at Union University, author of *Edgar Allan Poe: An Illustrated Companion to His Tell-Tale Stories* and *Evermore: Edgar Allan Poe and the Mystery of the Universe,* taped phone interview, Thursday, July 23, 2020.

PRICE: Vincent Price, actor known for Poe readings and for appearing in horror films based on Poe's works, taped in-person interview, Beverly Hills Hotel, California, January 1985.

RICE: Anne Rice, novelist whose best-selling titles include *Interview with the Vampire, The Vampire Lestat,* and *The Queen of the Damned,* taped in-person interview, Ritz-Carlton Hotel, Cleveland, Ohio, November 8, 1993.

SAVOYE: Jeffrey A. Savoye, secretary, treasurer, and webmaster, Edgar Allan Poe Society of Baltimore, and editor of *The Collected Letters of Edgar Allan Poe,* taped phone interview, September 11, 2020.

SEMTNER: Chris Semtner, curator of the Edgar Allan Poe Museum in Richmond and author of *Edgar Allan Poe's Richmond: The Raven in the River City,* taped phone interviews, September 20, 2019, and September 18, 2020.

SHAFFER-KOROS: Carole Shaffer-Koros, Poe scholar, English professor, registered nurse, taped phone interview, October 12, 2020.

SPURLOCK: Linda B. Spurlock, professor of anthropology, Kent State University, whose specialties include forensic anthropology, biomedical science, and forensic art, August 31, 2021.

STASHOWER: Daniel Stashower, novelist and author of such nonfiction works as *The Beautiful Cigar Girl: Mary Rogers, Edgar Allan Poe, and the Invention of Murder* and *Teller of Tales: The Life of Arthur Conan Doyle,* taped phone interview, October 2, 2020.

VELELLA: Rob Velella, independent scholar and literary historian, taped phone interview, November 24, 2020.

Quotations from Poe's stories, poems, criticism, journalistic articles, essays, and letters are from these standard editions, as well as texts available at eapoe.org (Edgar Allan Poe Society of Baltimore):

The Complete Works of Edgar Allan Poe, ed. James A. Harrison, 17 vols. (New York: T. Crowell, 1902; reprinted in 1965 by AMS Press).

The Collected Works of Edgar Allan Poe, ed. Thomas A. Mabbott, 3 vols. (Cambridge, MA: Belknap Press of Harvard University, 1969–77; series continued at *The Collected Writings of Edgar Allan Poe,* with five volumes edited by Burton R. Pollin).

The Collected Letters of Edgar Allan Poe, orig. ed. John Ward Ostrom; revised, corrected, and expanded by Burton R. Pollin and Jeffrey A. Savoye (New York: The Gordian Press, 2008).

A MATTER OF DEATH AND LIFE

2   *"congestion of the brain"* James M. Hutchisson, *Poe* (Jackson: University Press of Mississippi, 2005). The author summarizes terms cited at Poe's death, pp. 246–47.

2   *"Lord help my poor soul!"* John J. Moran letter to Maria Clemm, November 15, 1849, Enoch Pratt Library. Many of the details provided to Poe's aunt and mother-in-law in this 1849 letter differ from those in an October 28, 1875, account by Moran, published in the *New York Herald* under the headline "Official Memoranda of the Death of Edgar A. Poe," p. 4, cols. 1–3. Both documents can be viewed at eapoe.org, the website of the Edgar Allan Poe Society of Baltimore.

2   *"I would be a millionaire if I had"* MEDEIROS.

3   *"His biography doesn't really start where"* PEARL.

4   *"spectral and imaginary objects"* Moran letter to Maria Clemm, November 15, 1849.

4   *"It's almost as if a publicist stepped in"* MEDEIROS.

5   *"Edgar Allan Poe is dead. He died in Baltimore"* Rufus W. Griswold, "Death of Edgar A. Poe, *New-York Daily Tribune*, October 9, 1849, p. 2, cols. 3–4. The entire text can be viewed at eapoe.org, the website of the Edgar Allan Poe Society of Baltimore.

6   *"a pedagogic vampire."* Charles Baudelaire, *Edgar Allan Poe: His Life and Works* (1856): English translation in *The Unknown Poe,* ed. Raymond Foye (San Francisco: City Lights Books, 1980), p. 81.

6   *"The damage this article did to Poe's reputation was incalculable,"* Arthur Hobson Quinn, *Edgar Allan Poe: A Critical Biography* (Baltimore: The Johns Hopkins University Press, 1998 reprint of 1941 biography), p. 647.

7   *"Poe certainly drew on his life and experiences"* PEEPLES.

8   *"Students from the seventh grade on can intensely identify with Poe"* KENNEDY.

9   *"The Goth image of Poe can be limiting"* KENNEDY.

10   *"There's almost no relationship between the myth and the man"* POE.

10   *"The popular image of Poe is so far off the mark"* EDDINGS.

11   *"The madman howling at the Moon was Griswold's invention"* POE.

11   *"The image of Poe has been terribly exaggerated and distorted"* BLOCH.

12   *"Go to a horror convention"* JANG.

12   *"Poe also enjoys the moment when someone is in on the joke"* LEWIS.

12   *"One reason is that we work through our nightmares"* KING.

13   *"Poe's call was irresistible,"* BRADBURY.

13   *"I came along and read all those guys"* Pamela Staik, "Stephen King Makes an Impression at Big Read Kickoff," *Charlotte Sun*, March 25, 2010.

13   *"I heard his voice and was drawn to it"* RICE.

15   *"He was drawn to macabre and melancholy subjects"* PETTIT.

16   *There are eight known photographs of Poe* Michael J. Deas, *The Portraits and Daguerreotypes of Edgar Allan Poe* (Charlottesville: University of Virginia,

1989). Deas identifies all of the known portraits and photographic images of Poe, detailing the histories of each and derivative artwork made from them.

16 *"There is an otherworldly quality to the later daguerreotypes"* DEAS.

17 *"Poe was an incredibly prolific writer and hard worker"* PEARL.

17 *"The favorite image of Poe is pasty-faced and cackling"* McKENNA-UFF.

18 *"no part of that sentence was true"* SEMTNER.

19 *"Around his name has accumulated a mass of rumor"* Quinn, *Edgar Allan Poe: A Critical Biography,* p. xix.

19 *"That's true of his death in spades, but"* SAVOYE.

19 *"There is that arc of improvement with Poe"* PEEPLES.

20 *"There are so many instances where Poe is"* JEROME.

21 *"Do not fear for Eddy."* George Woodberry, *The Life of Edgar Allan Poe: Personal and Literary* (Boston: Houghton Mifflin Company, 1909), vol. 2, p. 309.

"PALE AND HAGGARD"

22 *"pale and haggard"* John Sartain, "Reminiscences of Edgar Allan Poe," *Lippincott's* 43, no. 3, (March 1889): p. 413. The entire text can be viewed at eapoe.org, the website of the Edgar Allan Poe Society of Baltimore.

23 *"I am about to bestir myself in the world of Letters"* Edgar Allan Poe, letter to John R. Thompson, January 13, 1849.

23 *"Literature is the most noble of professions"* Edgar Allan Poe, letter to Frederick W. Thomas, February 14, 1849.

24 *"I am full of dark forebodings"* Edgar Allan Poe, letter to Annie Richmond, dated after May 5, 1849.

24 *"He had rushed in on me in terror for his life"* Sartain, "Reminiscences of Edgar Allan Poe," p. 413.

24 *"I did not let him see that I noticed it"* Sartain, "Reminiscences of Edgar Allan Poe," p. 413.

25 *Could this be true? If so* John Evangelist Walsh, *Midnight Dreary: The Mysterious Death of Edgar Allan Poe* (New Brunswick, NJ: Rutgers University Press, 1998), pp. 76–85.

26 *"is the sudden bright glare of reality."* Walsh, *Midnight Dreary,* p. 114.

27 *The preponderance of likelihoods and logic place Poe in Philadelphia* Dwight Thomas and David K. Jackson, *The Poe Log: A Documentary Life of Edgar Allan Poe, 1809–1849.* (Boston: G. K. Hall & Company, 1987), pp. 812–13.

27 *"If this moustache of mine were removed"* Sartain, "Reminiscences of Edgar Allan Poe," p. 413.

28 *It was a popular recreation spot* Kenneth Silverman, *Edgar A. Poe: Mournful and Never-ending Remembrance* (New York: HarperCollins Publishers, 1991), p. 416.

28 *"At this place there was light enough, chiefly from"* Sartain, "Reminiscences of Edgar Allan Poe," p. 414.

29   *"I have been taken to prison once"* Edgar Allan Poe, letter to Maria Clemm,
      July 7, 1849.

29   *"what takes so many there for a few hours only"* Sartain, "Reminiscences of
      Edgar Allan Poe," p. 415.

30   *One theory that attempts to reconcile the timeline* Jeffrey Meyers, *Edgar Allan
      Poe: His Life and Legacy* (New York: Charles Scribner's Sons, 1992), p. 245.

"FROM CHILDHOOD'S HOUR"

33   *"Born January, 1811."* Edgar Allan Poe, "Memorandum [Autobiographical
      Note]," May 29, 1841 (reproduced in several collections, Poe's complete ver-
      sion can be viewed at eapoe.org).

34   *"one of the oldest and most respectable"* Edgar Allan Poe, "Memorandum
      [Autobiographical Note]," May 29, 1841.

35   *"out of his own very limited means supplied me"* Lafayette memories of David
      Poe Sr., quoted in Quinn, *Edgar Allan Poe: A Critical Biography*, p. 18.

35   *David made his stage debut on December 1, 1803*, Quinn, *Edgar Allan Poe: A
      Critical Biography*, pp. 19–20. Quinn's biography gives a rundown on David
      Poe's early theatrical career.

38   *"When you ponder where the writing came from"* SHAFFER-KOROS.

40   *"very pretty and lively and playful"* Susan Archer Weiss, "The Sister of
      Edgar A. Poe," *Continent* 3, no. 6 (June 27, 1883): recollections of the Poe chil-
      dren, pp. 816–17.

40   *A singular fashion prevails here this season* J. B. Hubbell, "Poe's Mother,"
      William and Mary Quarterly 21 (July 1941): pp. 250–54.

42   *"The writer of this article is himself the son"* Edgar Allan Poe, "The Drama,"
      Broadway Journal, July 19, 1845.

42   *"You look at his life and career, and you can see"* HUTCHISSON.

42   *"Richmond remained very dear to him"* HUTCHISSON.

44   *"In being John Allan's ward"* Kenneth Silverman, *Edgar A. Poe: Mournful and
      Never-ending Remembrance* (New York: HarperCollins Publishers, 1991), p. 11.

45   *"a lovely little fellow, with dark curls"* Eugene L. Didier, *Life of Edgar A. Poe*
      (New York: W. J. Widdleton, 1877), p. 28.

45   *"rosy-faced boy"* Didier, *Life of Edgar A. Poe*, p. 29.

46   *"the privileges of Fire to broil a slice of Bacon."* Quinn, *Edgar Allan Poe: A
      Critical Biography*, p. 65.

47   *"intelligent, wayward and willful."* William Elijah Hunter, "Poe and His En-
      glish Schoolmaster," *Athanaeum*, October 19, 1878, p. 497.

47   *"They're living near the British Museum."* KENNEDY.

49   *"a hot tempered and pedantic Irish bachelor."* Jeffrey Meyers, *Edgar Allan Poe:
      His Life and Legacy* (New York: Charles Scribner's Sons, 1992), p. 14.

49   *"wrote mere mechanical verses, Poe wrote genuine poetry"* Didier, *Life of Ed-
      gar A. Poe*, p. 30.

49   *As to Edgar's disposition and character as a boy* Quinn, *Edgar Allan Poe: A Critical Biography*, p. 83. Quinn's biography excerpts Clarke's letter.

50   *"the swiftest runner, the best boxer"* Didier, *Life of Edgar A. Poe*, p. 32.

50   *"At the time, Poe was slight in person"* Didier, *Life of Edgar A. Poe*, p. 34.

52   *At the time of which I speak, Richmond was one* John H. Ingram, *Edgar Allan Poe: Life, Letters, and Opinions* (London: John Hogg, 1880), p. 24.

55   *"This lady, on entering the room, took his hand"* Sarah Helen Whitman, *Edgar Poe and His Critics* (New York: Rudd & Carleton, 1860), p. 49.

57   *"a beautiful boy"* Quinn, *Edgar Allan Poe: A Critical Biography*, p. 91.

59   *Poe, as has been said, was fond* Quinn, *Edgar Allan Poe: A Critical Biography*, p. 108.

"I MUST DIE"

61   *"It sure looks like at some point he was treated for cholera"* MACKO.

64   *"I think the symptoms suggest some kind of"* PEEPLES.

65   *"He's rejuvenated as a poet at the end"* PEEPLES.

66   *"When he drank, the first drop maddened him"* George Lippard, "Edgar Allan Poe," *Quaker City* (Philadelphia) 2, no. 5, October 1849.

66   *"He came stealthily up stairs, as if conscious"* George Lippard, "Edgar A. Poe," *Dodge's Literary Museum* 9, no. 20 (October 21, 1854): pp. 315–16.

68   *"He held our hand for a long time"* Lippard, "Edgar Allan Poe," *Quaker City*.

68   *"They never saw him again."* Lippard, "Edgar A. Poe," *Dodge's Literary Museum*.

"SAVE ME FROM DESTRUCTION"

71   *"What most people don't understand is that Poe"* HANSMA.

72   *"encouraged independence but resented individuality."* Kenneth Silverman, *Edgar A. Poe: Mournful and Never-ending Remembrance* (New York: HarperCollins Publishers, 1991), p. 44.

77   *"Poe was easily fretted by any jest at his expense"* Thomas W. Gibson, "Poe at West Point," *Harper's New Monthly Magazine*, November 1867, p. 754.

81   *"was received with a general expression of disgust"* Gibson, "Poe at West Point," p. 755.

82   *"They were all very poor, but everything was wax neat"* Augustus Van Cleef, "Poe's Mary," *Harper's Monthly* 78 (March 1889): p. 635.

85   *"There are a lot of people writing this kind of stuff"* PEEPLES.

85   *"he had found his true vocation."* Peter Ackroyd, *Poe: A Life Cut Short* (New York: Nan A. Talese, The Doubleday Publishing Group, 2008), p. 57.

86   *"The idea of your chosen family is a more modern idea."* JANG.

89   *"were wholly unprepared"* Dwight Thomas and David K. Jackson, *The Poe Log: A Documentary Life of Edgar Allan Poe, 1809–1849* (Boston: G .K. Hall & Company, 1987), p. 132.

90   *His figure was remarkably good, and he carried himself* Arthur Hobson
      Quinn, *Edgar Allan Poe: A Critical Biography* (Baltimore: The Johns Hopkins
      University Press, 1998 reprint of 1941 biography), p. 204.
92   *"I think the dynamic with John Allan was doomed"* HUTCHISSON.
93   *"in a state of starvation."* Quinn, *Edgar Allan Poe: A Critical Biography,*
      p. 208.
95   *"Richmond always plays a key role"* PEEPLES.
99   *"that you have entirely conquered your late despondency."* Thomas and Jack-
      son, *The Poe Log,* p. 191.
99   *"I never shall forget my feelings"* Quinn, *Edgar Allan Poe: A Critical Biogra-
      phy,* p. 634.

"CONSIDERABLE FEVER"

101 *"attitude was easy and graceful."* Susan A. T. Weiss, "The Last Days of Edgar
      A. Poe," *Scribner's Magazine* (March 1878): p. 708.
102 *"He had trouble with booze"* EDDINGS.
102 *"There are years of sobriety for Poe"* JANG.
103 *"What drives me a little crazy is the treatment"* PEARL.
103 *"It's clear that Poe drank, but it's also clear"* STASHOWER.
104 *"How then did it happen, that during an intimate acquaintance"* Lambert A.
      Wilmer, "Recollections of Edgar A. Poe," *Baltimore Daily Commercial,* May
      23, 1866, p. 1.
105 *"The lecture of this talented gentleman"* Thomas and Jackson, *The Poe Log,*
      reviews of Poe's Richmond lecture excerpted, pp. 826–27.
106 *"I am fully prepared to love you"* Arthur Hobson Quinn, *Edgar Allan Poe:
      A Critical Biography* (Baltimore: The Johns Hopkins University Press, 1998
      reprint of 1941 biography), p. 634.
108 *"I noticed that Poe had no manuscript"* Susan Archer Weiss, *Home Life of Poe*
      (New York: Broadway Publishing Company, 1907), pp. 199–201.
109 *"He declared that the last few weeks"* Weiss, *Home Life of Poe,* pp. 713–14.
110 *"The evening before his departure from Richmond"* Quinn, *Edgar Allan Poe:
      A Critical Biography,* p. 636.
110 *"We were standing on the portico"* Weiss, *Home Life of Poe,* pp. 714.

"EXTREMITY OF TERROR"

111 *"He was unquestionably of an affectionate disposition"* Lambert A. Wilmer,
      "Recollections of Edgar A. Poe," *Baltimore Daily Commercial,* May 23, 1866,
      p. 1.
113 *"Do you want to know what made Poe such a master"* PRICE.
113 *"This isn't a different writer working in these different genres"* LEWIS.
114 *"The level of detail and specificity in some of those reviews"* HUTCHISSON.
115 *"Everybody wants Poe on their team."* PEEPLES.

115 *"He was the greatest journalistic critic of his time"* George Bernard Shaw, "Edgar Allan Poe," *The Nation*, January 16, 1909, p. 601.

117 *"He also had a lot of enemies because he was"* POE.

117 *"lashing dullness, as it always deserves to be lashed"* Thomas and Jackson, *The Poe Log*, p. 185.

118 *"Poe was a great critic of American nationalism."* KENNEDY.

119 *"Highly as I really think of Mr. Poe's talents"* Thomas and Jackson, *The Poe Log*, p. 236.

120 *"He always had the bearing of a Virginia gentleman"* SEMTNER.

120 *"You do need to consider Poe's Southernness"* HUTCHISSON.

121 *"I have sort of mixed feelings about the whole Southern identity"* PEEPLES.

122 *"Much is made of Poe thinking of himself as a Southern gentleman"* ARMIENTO.

122 *Poe dies right as we start the inevitable slide toward* KENNEDY.

124 *"Poe did not seem to understand what makes a great novel"* PETTIT.

124 *"He labored long and painfully to make himself"* Wilmer, "Recollections of Edgar A. Poe," p. 1.

125 *"With reason, of course."* PETTIT.

125 *"He's lost all of these women who meant so much to him"* ARMIENTO.

127 *"Mrs. Poe was a delicate gentlewoman"* Thomas Dunn English, "Reminiscences of Poe [Part 02]," *Independent* (New York), October 22, 1896, p. 1415 (text available at eapoe.org).

127 *"Poe was no saint, and he wasn't always easy to be around,"* PEARL.

127 *"If you could look through the peephole"* MEDEIROS.

128 *"And Poe didn't,"* KING.

129 *"Poe wasn't brilliant because he had the power"* CRAVEN.

129 *"Yes, he was writing for an audience and for a living,"* SAVOYE.

132 *"His enemies, and he had no shortage of them, were quick"* PETTIT.

134 *"Poe was more than just a horror writer,"* KENNEDY.

136 *"Poe always is trying to solve mysteries,"* LEWIS.

136 *"There was some criticism after 'The Murders in the Rue Morgue'"* STA-SHOWER.

137 *"our antecedents actually do go back to crime fiction"* DOUGLAS.

137 *"It really is a case of life imitating art,"* OLSHAKER.

138 *"If Poe had been a baseball player"* PETTIT.

139 *"They're in a row home, across the street from a sewage lot"* McKENNA-UFF.

"RATHER THE WORSE FOR WEAR"

140 *"Even a very small amount of alcohol had a terrible impact"* SAVOYE.

141 *"The only thing we're certain of is our uncertainty."* MEDEIROS.

141 *"They would riot at the drop of a hat,"* JEROME.

142 *"If he had been drinking and incapacitated himself"* JANG.

143 *When I entered the bar-room of the house* J. E. Snodgrass, "Death and Burial of Edgar A. Poe," *Life Illustrated,* May 17, 1856, p. 24.

144 *"The facts of the case are simply these: On Tuesday"* Joseph Evans Snodgrass, "The Facts of Poe's Death and Burial," *Beadle's Monthly* (May 1867): p. 283 (text posted at eapoe.org, the website of the Edgar Allan Poe Society of Baltimore).

145 *"Cooping is such a Baltimore explanation"* JANG.

145 *"No question, the cooping theory is compelling,"* ARMIENTO.

145 *"The detail that always fascinates me is that he was found"* STASHOWER.

145 *"Being cooped wouldn't have caused his death"* SEMTNER.

"BY HORROR HAUNTED"

148 *"the master of mystery deduced the identity of the murderer"* Norrie Epstein, *The Friendly Dickens* (New York: Viking, 1998), p. 139.

149 *"was characteristic of Poe that he could always find"* Hervey Allen, *Israfel: The Life and Times of Edgar Allan Poe* (New York: Farrar & Rinehart, 1934), p. 424.

151 *"the morbidity of the theme"* Una Pope-Hennessy, *Charles Dickens* (New York: Howell, Soskin, Publishers, 1946), p. 172.

151 *"The strain in Dickens that gave rise to the eerie delusions"* Edgar Johnson, *Charles Dickens: His Tragedy and Triumph* (New York: Simon & Schuster, 1952), pp. 396–97.

152 *"a novelist who delighted in creating mysteries within his fiction"* Peter Ackroyd, *Dickens* (New York: HarperCollins Publishers, 1990), p. 359.

152 *"the horrific, the sentimental and the detective."* Julian Symons, *The Tell-Tale Heart: The Life and Works of Edgar Allan Poe* (New York: Penguin Books, 1981). p. 184.

153 *"People have suggested that Poe's life was a sort of an ironic twist"* SAVOYE.

153 *I have read your occasional notices of my productions* Nathaniel Hawthorne letter, June 17, 1846, reproduced in George E. Woodberry, *The Life of Edgar Allan Poe: Personal and Literary* (Boston: Houghton Mifflin Company, 1909), pp. 211–12.

154 *"seemed to be to procure the comfort"* George Rex Graham, quoted in John H. Ingram, *Edgar Allan Poe: His Life, Letters, and Opinions* (London: John Hogg, Paternoster Row, 1880), p. 217.

155 *"Her manners were agreeable and graceful"* Frederick William Thomas, "Recollections of Edgar A. Poe" (manuscript notes at eapoe.org).

156 *"with whom I have influence"* Charles Dickens (letter, November 27, 1842, at eapoe.org).

159 *"His six years in Philadelphia"* Arthur Hobson Quinn, *Edgar Allan Poe: A Critical Biography* (Baltimore: Johns Hopkins University Press, 1998 reprint of 1941 biography), p. 403.

161 *"rather a step downward"* Nathaniel Parker Willis, "Letter About Edgar

Allan Poe," *Home Journal,* October 30, 1858, p. 2 (text posted at eapoe.org, the website of the Edgar Allan Poe Society of Baltimore).

161 *"a quiet, patient, industrious, and most gentlemanly"* Arthur Hobson Quinn, *Edgar Allan Poe: A Critical Biography* (Baltimore: The Johns Hopkins University Press, 1998 reprint of 1941 biography), p. 434.

161 *"It's these kinds of descriptions of Poe"* HUTCHISSON.

162 *"He certainly wrote the poem that broke all records"* LEWIS.

165 *"All that animosity toward Longfellow is at least partly"* HUTCHISSON.

165 *"No question, Longfellow is a prince of a guy,"* LEWIS.

166 *"He stupidly attacks Longfellow for plagiarism"* PETTIT.

167 *"Poe saw himself as an outcast,"* KENNEDY.

168 *"So it's very clear at that point that he doesn't hate"* LEWIS.

170 *"Everything seems to be going from bad to worse"* HUTCHISSON.

174 *I once went down to the City in the same train* Augustine O'Neil memory quoted in John H. Birss, "Poe in Fordham: A Reminiscence," *Notes and Queries,* December 18, 1937.

174 *"The cottage had an air of taste and gentility"* James A. Harrison, *Complete Works of E.A. Poe* (1902), vol. 1: *Biography,* chap. 12, p. 261.

177 *"a great blessing."* John H. Ingram, *Edgar Allan Poe: His Life, Letters, and Opinions* (London: John Hogg, 1880), vol. 2, p. 112.

177 *"he always loved you."* Augustus Van Cleef, "Poe's Mary," *Harper's Monthly* 78 (March 1889): p. 639.

"AS IF A CORPSE"

180 *"very abusive and ungrateful on former occasions"* J. E. Snodgrass, "E.A. Poe's Death and Burial," *Spiritual Telegraph* (New York) 4, no. 39 (January 26, 1856): p. 155 (text posted at eapoe.org, the website of the Edgar Allan Poe Society of Baltimore).

180 *"mere incoherent mutterings were all that were heard"* Snodgrass, "E.A. Poe's Death and Burial," p. 155.

182 *"When brought to the Hospital he was unconscious of his Condition."* J. J. Moran letter to Maria Clemm, November 15, 1849, printed in *Life and Letters of Edgar Allan Poe,* ed. James A. Harrison (1903), p. 335.

183 *We soon saw he was a gentleman; and as our family* Mary O. Moran's recollection printed in *Life and Letters of Edgar Allan Poe,* ed. James A. Harrison (1903), p. 337.

183 *"was immediately placed in a private room, carefully undressed"* John J. Moran, "Official Memoranda of the Death of Edgar A. Poe," *New York Herald,* October 28, 1875, p. 4.

186 *"Moran goes on the lecture circuit, redirecting himself . . ."* SHAFFER-KOROS.

187 *"One thing it almost certainly wasn't was rabies,"* SAVOYE.

187 *"There's no record of an animal bite,"* SHAFFER-KOROS.

187 *Donnay has noted that Poe suffered from many of the physical and mental*

symptoms "Edgar Allan Poe and the The Tell-Tale Face of Carbon Monoxide Poisoning," Multiple Chemical Sensitivity website, mcsrr.org.

188 *The Department of Environmental and Toxicologic Pathology researchers* "Test Results of Edgar Allan Poe's Hair," eapoe.org, updated September 3, 2020.

188 *"Edgar lived another two and a half years, and the testing"* SEMTNER.

189 *"Hair is the long-term record, so whatever killed him"* MACKO.

189 *"There was no evidence of organic pollutants that were significantly higher"* MACKO.

189 *"There are all of those romantic accounts of him surviving"* SEMTNER.

190 *"You can't solve it using these tests, but you can"* MACKO.

190 *"As soon as I heard that he was at the college, I went over,"* Neilson Poe, October 11, 1849. letter to Maria Clemm, printed in Arthur Hobson Quinn, *Edgar Allan Poe: A Critical Biography* (Baltimore: The Johns Hopkins University Press, 1998 reprint of 1941 biography), pp. 642–43.

191 *"When I returned, I found him in a violent delirium"* J. J. Moran letter to Maria Clemm, November 15, 1849.

191 *"He will die; he is dying now."* John J. Moran, *A Defense of Edgar Allan Poe* (Washington, DC: William F. Boogher, 1885), p. 71 (text posted at eapoe.org, the website of the Edgar Allan Poe Society of Baltimore).

"I SHALL HARDLY LAST A YEAR"

193 *"I write to say that the medicines arrived the next train"* John H. Ingram, *Edgar Allan Poe: His Life, Letters, and Opinions* (London: John Hogg, 1880), vol. 2, p. 111.

194 *I made my diagnosis, and went to the great Doctor* Ingram, *Edgar Allan Poe,* vol. 2, p. 115.

196 *[I]t was quite early in the forenoon when we reached the depot,* Mary Elizabeth LeDuc (née Bronson), "Recollections of Edgar A. Poe," *Home Journal,* July 21, 1860, p. 3 (text posted at eapoe.org, the website of the Edgar Allan Poe Society of Baltimore).

197 *"seemed quite inconsistent with the gloomy and grotesque character"* Ingram, *Edgar Allan Poe,* p. 123.

200 *"You can't dismiss 'Eureka' altogether, but the claims"* KENNEDY.

201 *"Poe gives us characters in the grip of the pursuit of some exciting knowledge"* KENNEDY.

201 *"Poe always wanted to find the rational, whether it was in the solution"* POE.

202 *"This is yet another way that the stereotype is wrong"* POE.

202 *During one of his visits to Shew's house* Arthur Hobson Quinn, *Edgar Allan Poe: A Critical Biography* (Baltimore: The Johns Hopkins University Press, 1998 reprint of 1941 biography), p. 563.

205 *"very abominable."* Anne Lynch letter to Helen Whitman, January 31, 1848, Sarah Helen Whitman Papers, John Hay Library, Brown University, Providence, Rhode Island.

205 *"admired exceedingly"* Anne Lynch letter to Helen Whitman, February 21, 1848, Sarah Helen Whitman Papers, Brown University.

206 *"he is in such bad odour with most persons"* Anne Lynch letter to Helen Whitman, February 21, 1848.

206 *"not because it is not beautiful in itself"* Anne Lynch letter to Helen Whitman, March 10, 1848, Sarah Helen Whitman Papers, Brown University.

206 *"I see by the Home Journal that your beautiful invocation has reached"* Frances S. Osgood letter to Helen Whitman, March 26, 1848, Sarah Helen Whitman Papers, Brown University.

208 *"His taste for drink was a simple disease"* John Moncure Daniel, "Characteristics of Edgar A. Poe," *Richmond Semi-Weekly Examiner,* October 19, 1849, p. 2 (text posted at eapoe.org, the website of the Edgar Allan Poe Society of Baltimore).

211 *"The excesses of Shelly, Byron, and Goethe that she defended"* Kenneth Silverman, *Edgar A. Poe: Mournful and Never-ending Remembrance* (New York: HarperCollins Publishers, 1991), p. 368.

213 *"Poe knew what he was doing, and he would have known"* JEROME.

214 *"He ages dramatically in the last three years of his life"* DEAS.

"DOUBLY DEAD"

220 *Perhaps to his dim and tortured brain, he seemed to be on the brink* Arthur Hobson Quinn, *Edgar Allan Poe: A Critical Biography* (Baltimore: The Johns Hopkins University Press, 1998 reprint of 1941 biography), p. 640.

221 *"the most likely candidate."* Julian Symons, *The Tell-Tale Heart: The Life and Works of Edgar Allan Poe* (New York: Penguin Books, 1981), p. 153.

221 *"in his 'Official Memoranda,' published in 1875, Moran"* William T. Bandy, "Dr. Moran and the Poe-Reynolds Myth," *Myths and Reality* (Baltimore: The Edgar Allan Poe Society, 1987), p. 32 (text posted at eapoe.org, the website of the Edgar Allan Poe Society of Baltimore).

221 *"Doctor, it's all over."* John J. Moran, *A Defense of Edgar Allan Poe* (Washington, DC: William Boogher, 1885), p. 72 (text posted at eapoe.org, the website of the Edgar Allan Poe Society of Baltimore).

222 *"a figment of Moran's imagination."* Bandy, "Dr. Moran and the Poe-Reynolds Myth," p. 31.

222 *"there seems no reason to question its general truth."* Symons, *The Tell-Tale Heart: The Life and Works of Edgar Allan Poe,* p. 153.

223 *After death he was washed and carefully laid out, dressed* John J. Moran, "Official Memoranda of the Death of Edgar A. Poe," *New York Herald,* October 28, 1875, p. 4.

224 *A grave had been dug among the crumbling mementos of mortality* Joseph Evans Snodgrass, "The Facts of Poe's Death and Burial," *Beadle's Monthly,* May 1867, pp. 285–86 (text posted at eapoe.org, the website of the Edgar Allan Poe Society of Baltimore).

225   *"cold-blooded and unchristianlike."* George P. Clark, "Two Unnoticed Recollections of Poe's Funeral," *Poe Newsletter* 8, no. 1 (June 1970) (text posted at eapoe.org, the website of the Edgar Allan Poe Society of Baltimore).

225   *"Even though he made so little money off of 'The Raven,' he"* ARMIENTO.

225   *"The end is very Poe-esque, from the missing days to the funeral,"* JANG.

225   *"Someone approached Thomas Dunn English and asked him"* JEROME.

226   *"We haven't changed,"* JEROME.

226   *"His biggest mistake was dying before his enemies."* POE.

226   *"It certainly was not Griswold's intention to do Poe a favor"* VELELLA.

227   *"Somebody else created Poe's persona, and it was somebody who"* VELELLA.

227   *"No one is the villain of his own story,"* VELELLA.

228   *"Poe didn't accept the pieties and the truisms of the culture"* LEWIS.

228   *"There's nothing Victorian, wholesome, convivial, or communal"* KENNEDY.

229   *"Poe really anticipated the feel of our own time, even more"* KENNEDY.

229   *"We recognize Poe's modern view of the dark side of humanity,"* SAVOYE.

229   *"Most scholars who write about and teach poetry are committed to thematic"* McGANN.

230   *"That attitude remains prevalent at the universities, where"* POE.

230   *"One of the academic charges against Poe is that he is a popular writer"* McGANN.

231   *"This poor woman has lost her daughter and a son-in-law"* JANG.

232   *"That was most likely a rock,"* HANSMA.

232   *"The brain tumor theory really came from research for the novel"* PEARL.

"PENETRATE THE MYSTERIES"

235   *"Everyone has an opinion, and that opinion is"* JEROME.

235   *"As dubious as the record is, the best evidence"* HANSMA.

236   *"An ice-cold case from the middle of the nineteenth century would be"* DOUGLAS.

237   *"Unless you dig up that body and find a hatchet sticking out"* SAVOYE.

237   *"He died when there was no real compelling need to document"* HANSMA.

237   *"It is unknowable because everything was carelessly handled"* HANSMA.

238   *"No question in my mind that tuberculosis is at the top"* HANSMA.

238   *The oldest known evidence for TB in humans was found* Robin Lloyd, "Bones Reveal Oldest Case of TB," October 14, 2008, livescience.com.

239   *"As a historian of medicine, retrospective diagnosis is very much"* PEITZMAN.

239   *"Given his family history and the time he lived, he"* BOOM.

239   *"We don't know what killed him, but there's no question"* KENNEDY.

239   *"It's entirely possible to have tuberculosis for much of your life"* PEITZMAN.

239   *"If you're exposed and infected and you're otherwise healthy"* BOOM.

240   *"And they told him he had lesions and an undiagnosed case"* McKENNA-UFF.

240 *"Poe's symptomatology at death fits the dying tubercular"* HANSMA.

240 *"There's a popular image of Poe, which isn't reality, but"* OLSHAKER.

241 *"I believe it was tuberculosis, and there are so many factors"* SHAFFER-KOROS.

241 *"makes the most sense,"* SEMTNER.

241 *"Cholera is an acute illness, but, as horrible as it is, it's"* BOOM.

242 *"It's certainly plausible,"* PEITZMAN.

242 *"TB meningitis is not something that develops overnight"* BOOM.

242 *"Tuberculosis meningitis was aggressive, catastrophic, and"* HANSMA.

243 *"Right now, the case for tuberculosis meningitis is highly probable"* SPUR-LOCK.

243 *"granular impressions (GIs) on the inner skull surface have been considered"* Olga Spekker, David R. Hunt, Laszlo Paja, Erika Molnar, Gyorgy Palfi, Michael Schultz, "Tracking Down the White Plague: The Skeletal Evidence of Tuberculosis Meningitis in the Robert J. Terry Anatomical Skeleton Collection," National Library of Medicine, National Center for Biotechnology Information, puremed.ncbi.nlm.nih.gov.

243 *"There is a part of me that doesn't want to know"* STASHOWER.

243 *"By leaving us so young and leaving so many mysteries behind"* ARMIENTO.

244 *"He was associated in the public's mind with Boris Karloff"* SEMTNER.

244 *"Poor Poe."* Peter J. Jarman, "The Latest Interview with the Living Legend," *Famous Monsters of Filmland,* no. 37 (February 1965): p. 28.

244 *"They caught the spirit of Poe, if not the specifics"* PRICE.

244 *"And we're all still reading Poe, in America and"* JEROME.

245 *"I think he knew,"* McKENNA-UFF.

245 *"There is a powerful universality in what Poe wrote about in those"* KENNEDY.

INDEX

Becky Dawidziak

MARK DAWIDZIAK is the author or editor of about twenty-five books, including three studies of landmark television series: *The Columbo Phile: A Casebook*; *The Night Stalker Companion*; and *Everything I Need to Know I Learned in the Twilight Zone,* his light-hearted 2017 tribute to Rod Serling's classic anthology series. He is also an internationally recognized Mark Twain scholar, and five of his books are about the iconic American writer. He spent forty-three years as a television, film, and theater critic at such newspapers as the *Akron Beacon Journal* and *The Plain Dealer*. His work on the horror side of the street also includes the novel *Grave Secrets*; *The Bedside, Bathtub & Armchair Companion to Dracula*; short stories; and comic book scripts. He lives in Ohio.